A Basic Course in Public International Law Research

Anthony S. Winer

Mary Ann E. Archer

University Press of America,® Inc.
Lanham · Boulder · New York · Toronto · Oxford

University Press of America,® Inc.
4501 Forbes Boulevard
Suite 200
Lanham, Maryland 20706
UPA Acquisitions Department (301) 459-3366

PO Box 317
Oxford
OX2 9RU, UK

Printed in the United States of America
British Library Cataloging in Publication Information Available

Library of Congress Control Number: 2005932926
ISBN 0-7618-3309-9 (paperback : alk. ppr.)
ISBN: 978-0-7618-3309-3

™ The paper used in this publication meets the minimum requirements of American National Standard for Information Sciences—Permanence of Paper for Printed Library Materials, ANSI Z39.48—1984

To the Memory of Manfred

- A.S.W.

To My Family

- M.A.E.A.

TABLE OF CONTENTS

UNIT A: BACKGROUND, GUIDANCE, EXERCISES AND PROBLEMS

UNIT B: BASIC DOCUMENTS FOR INVESTIGATION AND STUDY

PREFACE

This book provides the basis for a course in researching methods for Public International Law. In the usual law school curriculum, it is breaking new ground.

Many standard law school classes address public international law or particular areas within the subject. Similarly, of course, the standard course in legal writing covers researching methods. But most law school catalogs fail to offer courses specifically devoted to researching methods in International Law. We are redressing that failure with this book.

The course put forward in these pages is thoroughly interactive. The materials consist largely of reading exercises and research problems. The reading exercises deepen the student's understanding and appreciation of the primary sources of Public International Law. The research problems test the student's familiarity and facility with the research tools and resources available with respect to those sources. The primary activities of the course are thus student-centered. The course is principally focused on student learning through the completion of these exercises and problems.

The course includes instruction in basic substantive points of international law, as well as research methods. The substantive instruction is sufficiently detailed to provide a sound basis for the research work. But it is not so voluminous that it duplicates the standard survey course in Public International Law.

This makes the course suitable for at least two groups of students. First, the course is suitable for students who have not had the survey course in Public International Law, because it includes adequate substantive background to learn the research methods and complete the research problems. Secondly, the course is also suitable for students who are taking or have finished the standard survey course, because it complements the content of the survey course without excessively repeating it.

The course will also be useful for students in associated disciplines, in addition to students specifically studying law. These materials are appropriate for students in international political science courses, or courses in international relations or foreign affairs.

The Structure of this Book

Each Chapter introduces a distinct element of international law. The Chapters proceed from the most basic elements through to the more specialized. The Chapters themselves are bifurcated between segments that present substantive background and those that directly address the task of research.

The first half of each Chapter consists of two "Parts" that deal with the substantive legal background for the tasks the Chapter presents. Part One of each Chapter is an "Introduction and Overview" that describes the primary documents for a particular area in international law. Part Two then presents a set of "Reading Exercises" guiding students in the careful study of these documents. The documents themselves are reproduced in "Unit B" of the book.

The second half of each Chapter consists of two more "Parts" that address the actual task of research. Part Three of each Chapter provides "Guidance for Research," describing the basic tools available for researching in the area covered by that Chapter. Finally, Part Four of each Chapter contains a set of "Research Problems" designed not only to test the students' ability to apply the principles they've learned, but also to help them develop their knowledge and skills as they complete the Problems.

We believe, and have found from experience using these materials, that this dual approach is a most satisfactory means of providing students with a basic, but reasonably complete, understanding and facility for Public International Law Research.

Electronic Research Methods

In this area, as in all areas of research at the present time, significant issues are presented regarding the use of electronic resources. We believe that electronic resources offer great opportunities, because they make large amounts of information more readily available. Accordingly, we have designed our Research Problems, and composed our Discussion sections regarding the Problems, with the full expectation that students will use commercial and official electronic databases and the Internet. Indeed, we direct students in many cases to consult electronic sources.

At the same time, we also believe that the use of electronic sources should not completely displace the use of hard-copy material. Among other considerations, hard-copy sources still possess a degree of permanence and non-variability that is important for researchers working with official texts. Also, in legal fields, uniformity of reference and citation is often critical for effective communication. Accordingly, in our Research Guidance and Research Problems we also emphasize the necessity of being able to retrieve information from, and effectively use, hard-copy original sources.

Of chief importance in acknowledging this diarchy between electronic and hard-copy sources is the matter of authoritativeness. In creating the Research Problems, our goal was not only to familiarize the students with standard sources and sharpen their research skills but also to develop their ability to evaluate information in terms of authenticity, completeness and currency. This is a talent which will serve them well in practice.

The tendency of today's Post-Internet students is to find the quick answer by searching Google or Alta-Vista or some other full-text search engine. This is how they have often done their research in undergraduate school. While we want the students to become skillful users of reputable electronic databases, proprietary or "free" on the Internet, we hope to teach them that all Internet answers are not created equal. Throughout the Research Problems, we ask that they find the answers in "an authoritative source". We certainly do not intend to discourage them from using the excellent international law web sites developed by universities such as Pace, Harvard, Yale and the University of Chicago or the official sites of international organizations and governments. In particular, the recently developed EISEL site developed by the American Society of International Law is referenced at various points.

We do hope, however, and indeed insist, that students use these facilities on an informed basis and with a discriminating eye. We develop understanding of the need to arrive at authoritative sources and, where it is significant, dispassionately maintained resources. The mere availability of electronic sources and databases, even when they are of excellent quality, cannot substitute for the training and knowledge necessary to make responsible use of them.

Teaching Methodology

Our philosophy in preparing this book has been that the course should be practical, as well as furnishing a sound basis for relevant theory. We have structured the exercises and problems with this pragmatism in mind. These materials concentrate on fundamental doctrine and research sources and methods. The focus has not been on exposing students to the more abstruse corners of International Law information. Some material of a more arcane and specialized nature can be provided by individual instructors using this book, or in a more advanced course.

Similarly, we have employed some very practical pedagogical techniques in devising the exercises and problems. Some of the Reading Exercises, for example, require students to identify key elements of information in the readings and simply copy some of the information for purposes of their answers. While some might consider such techniques elementary, we view them as having distinct value. It is important that students internalize and become intimately familiar with the building blocks of International Law. A certain amount of mechanical repetition is the most effective way of achieving this internalization. Indeed, while this kind of instruction should not be overdone, we view it as part of the new approaches to legal education that are being advanced in more progressive classroom environments.

A separate "Teachers' Manual" is available for instructors that includes additional Parts "Five" and "Six" for each Chapter. Part Five contains a "Discussion of Reading Exercises" for each Chapter, while Part Six consists of a "Discussion of Research Problems" for each Chapter.

These can assist instructors in reviewing the Reading Exercises and Research Problems with students during class. However, we don't anticipate that class sessions will consist of instructors merely reciting the explanatory material included in the Teachers' Manual. Rather, we hope that instructors will use the explanatory material, as well as the questions themselves, as a "springboard" from which to engage in even more detailed discussions, of the type that would take place in a well-conducted doctrinal course on Public International Law.

The actual mechanics of how this book is used can, and probably must, vary from one teacher or set of teachers to the next. We find that a fairly straightforward pattern of assigning the Reading Exercises and Research Problems, followed by in-class review and discussion of answers and solutions, works extremely well. Also separately available is a CD-ROM that includes each of the exercise and problem sets. We anticipate that students and teachers will find this CD to be useful in the assignment and completion of the course material, whatever mechanical procedures are decided upon.

The teaching of International Law research, as a formally structured matter, is still a relatively new art. We hope that we can be helpful to teachers in various environments in providing instruction to students who will increasingly need to be proficient in this area.

Anthony S. Winer
Mary Ann E. Archer
St. Paul, Minnesota 2005

ACKNOWLEDGMENTS

We would like to thank the authors and copyright holders of the following works, who permitted their inclusion in this book:

International Chamber of Commerce, ICC Rules of Arbitration. Copyright © 1997, 2001 by International Chamber of Commerce. Published by the International Chamber of Commerce in ICC Publication 808, ISBN 92-842-1302-0, available from the ICC International Court of Arbitration, 38 cours Albert 1er, 75008 Paris, France, and at www.iccarbitration.org.

Ian Brownlie, Principles of Public International Law, 5th Edition. Chapter 1: Sources of the Law. Copyright © 1998 by Ian Brownlie and published by Oxford University Press. Reprinted by permission of Oxford University Press.

Malcolm N. Shaw, International Law, 5th Edition. Copyright © 2003 by M.N. Shaw and published by Cambridge University Press. Reprinted with the permission of Cambridge University Press.

Ivan A. Shearer, Starke's International Law, 11th Edition. Chapter 2: The Material "Sources" of International Law. Copyright © 1994 by Butterworth & Co. (Publishers) Ltd. Reprinted by permission of Oxford University Press.

We also express our deepest appreciation to all the students in all of our classes in recent years who, through their participation and forbearance, have aided us substantially with the development of these materials. We also express particular gratitude to our colleagues Ann Bateson and Meg Daniel, and to our assistants Deborah Hackerson and Jayme Ribaudo. The assistance of all was invaluable.

CHAPTER 1

UNITED NATIONS PRINCIPAL ORGANS

Part 1: Introduction and Overview

Modern international law is founded on the institutional structure of the United Nations. In the international political arena, officials and commentators in different countries can have varying views on the utility of the U.N. organization. Some politicians and public figures in some countries are skeptical of the U.N. They may say, for example, that the organization has insufficient credibility, or that it is wasteful, or that it acts as a barrier to meaningful action. However, regardless of such occasional expressions of dissatisfaction, the organization still serves as the foundation on which modern international law is based. Throughout our research endeavors we will continually experience this central influence of the U.N. organization.

The U.N. was established as one of the closing events of World War II. From the summer of 1944 through the summer of 1945, representatives of countries that would shortly emerge as among the victorious powers in the War engaged in negotiations for the structure of a new international organization. These negotiations occurred in various stages, but finally culminated in a conference in San Francisco attended by representatives of about 50 countries. The countries that were most influential at the San Francisco conference were the United States of America, France, Britain, China and the Soviet Union (now Russia). The treaty ultimately agreed to, the "Charter of the United Nations," was signed on June 26, 1945 and became effective on October 24 of that year.

It is this U.N. Charter that now serves as the structural foundation for much of international law. We will become very familiar with this Charter as our research in international law progresses. The U.N. Charter serves as a sort of Constitution for the U.N. organization, in that it describes its structure and the functioning of its principal elements. The Charter has also taken on something in the nature of constitutional significance internationally. This is because it tends to be viewed as a more foundational document than most other treaties. It serves as a repository of basic values on which many other international law rules and treaties rest. Amendments to it tend to be viewed as weightier and more momentous than would be the case with amendments to most other treaties.

According to the U.N. Charter, the central U.N. organization is composed of six distinct principal organs. These are: the General Assembly, the Security Council, the Secretariat, the Economic and Social Council, the Trusteeship Council and the International Court of Justice. Each of these organs, except the last, conducts many of its principal operations at the U.N. headquarters complex in New York City. The International Court of Justice is located in The Hague, which is a small city several miles southwest of Amsterdam that is also the seat of government for The Netherlands. In addition to these six principal organs, the U.N. has numerous ancillary organizations, headquartered at various locations throughout the world. We will be focusing on the six principal organs in this chapter; Chapter 2 will address the ancillary organizations.

The General Assembly

The General Assembly is the only one of the six principal U.N. organs in which each member of the U.N. is always represented. Accordingly, in terms of the number of persons constituting the body, it is the largest of the six principal organs. Every Member of the U.N., pursuant to the Charter, is a member of the General Assembly, and each member of the General Assembly has a representative voice equal to that of every other. At this writing, there are 191 Members of the General Assembly.

This characteristic of the General Assembly, that its membership is composed of delegations from every U.N. Member country, each with an equal voice, has several consequences. Smaller Member countries tend to attach substantial value to their participation in the General Assembly, since it is the only direct means through which they can consistently formally communicate their views. Similarly, smaller states (and often others as well) regard the General Assembly as a particularly legitimate body, since all countries of the U.N. are represented in it. However, in part resulting from this situation, votes in the General Assembly do not reflect any weighting for world population. A country such as China (2000 population of 1.2 billion) has the same voting strength in the General Assembly as Nauru (2000 population of 11,000). There is accordingly a distinct limitation on the extent to which General Assembly actions can be considered majoritarian in nature.

The General Assembly can be thought of as a "town meeting of the world," or a "world assembly." In this connection, however, it should be noted that the function of the General Assembly is primarily deliberative. The relevant provisions of the U.N. Charter make it quite clear that the business of the General Assembly is primarily the discussion, consideration and debate of the issues that come before it. There are relatively few respects in which the Charter permits the General Assembly to actually take, or direct others to take, concrete action in the physical world. This may indeed in part be a reflection of the non-majoritarian character of its composition and functioning.

For the most part, the General Assembly conducts its business by means of passing resolutions. The Charter prescribes the manner of voting, and of course each Member has an equal vote. For the most part, the Charter provides that resolutions can be passed by a majority of the members present and voting. However, for certain matters having structural or operational significance for the General Assembly as a body, the Charter requires a 2/3 majority of those Members present and voting. The Charter also contains a mechanism through which a Member that is in arrears, to a specified extent, in its payments to the U.N. can lose its vote in the General Assembly.

The Security Council

The Security Council consists of 15 Members of the United Nations. Five of the 15 Members have permanent seats on the Security Council, and the remaining 10 are filled through rotating 2-year terms. Among the 10 non-permanent Members, the 2-year terms are staggered, so that every year five Security Council seats are vacated and filled by new Members in rotation. Most voting on the Security Council is on the basis of a required super-majority vote; 9 votes are normally required to pass most General Assembly resolutions, while a bare majority would require only 8 votes. Furthermore, each of the five permanent members also is said to possess a "veto" on most Security Council actions.

The U.N. Charter provides that the Security Council has primary responsibility for the maintenance of international peace and security. Because the Security Council has this responsibility, the Charter grants to it more substantial powers than are accorded to the General Assembly. The most dramatic example of this is Chapter VII of the U.N. Charter, which gives the Security Council the authority to authorize economic and military action by Member States to maintain or restore international peace and security.

In this respect, the Security Council can be distinctly contrasted with the General Assembly. As noted above, U.N. Charter provisions make it clear that the General Assembly is to function primarily as a deliberative body that discusses issues and formulates recommendations or suggestions for Member States or other U.N. bodies. The Security Council, on the other had, through Chapter VII of the Charter, possesses power to direct actions in the physical world by Member States and many of the various organizations within the U.N. structure.

The Secretariat

The Secretariat is the administrative arm of the U.N. organization. It is headed by a Secretary-General, who is described by the Charter as "the chief administrative officer" of the U.N. The duties of the Secretary-General are described in Chapter XV of the Charter, but also in various other provisions, such as Article 20 (authorizing the Secretary-General to convoke special sessions of the General Assembly, upon the request of the Security Council or a majority of the members of the U.N.).

Although headquartered in New York City, the Secretariat operates out of U.N. offices all over the world. As of this writing, the staff of the Secretariat numbers approximately 9000 persons throughout virtually all the U.N. offices. Among the most prominent U.N. offices outside New York City are those in Geneva, Nairobi and Vienna.

The Charter provides that Secretaries-General are appointed by the General Assembly upon the recommendation of the Security Council, but does not by its terms prescribe a term of office for the Secretary-General. Each Secretary-General's term is decided upon by the Security Council and General Assembly in connection with the appointment itself. The current practice, however, is for each Secretary-General to serve renewable 5-year terms.

Including the current Secretary-General, Mr. Kofi Annan of Ghana, there have been a total of seven Secretaries-General since the founding of the U.N. Although nothing in the Charter prescribes the sex of the office's holder, all have been men.

The Charter provisions for the Secretary-General give other organs of the U.N. broad authority to direct his activities, but there is only a limited scope of actions the Secretary-General can take on his own initiative, without direction or authorization from other U.N. bodies, such as the Security Council or the General Assembly.

One of the Secretary-General's more substantial duties under the Charter is the submission of each budget for the organization (required every two years). Each submitted budget must then be approved by the General Assembly. Budgets are approved and executed every two years. The budget for 2000-2001 was U.S. $2,535 million.

The Economic and Social Council

Among the primary purposes of the U.N. Organization are the maintenance of international peace and security. The Security Council bears substantial responsibility in these endeavors, assisted by the General Assembly. However, the Charter also includes among the organization's purposes a set of duties that might be said to encompass a set of "softer" goals and purposes. A key example would be Chapter IX of the U.N. Charter, which requires that the U.N. organization promote higher standards of living, full employment and conditions of economic and social progress and development.

The U.N. Charter bestows the responsibility for these functions on the Economic and Social Council, established in Chapter X of the Charter. This Council is often referenced through the acronym, "ECOSOC".

ECOSOC consists of 54 Member States, as elected by the General Assembly, each serving a term of three years on the Council. The 54 Member States on the Council are divided into three equal groups of 18, with staggered terms, so that each year 18 ECOSOC members vacate their seats and are replaced by 18 new members. However, retiring members are eligible for re-election.

The Charter requires ECOSOC to set up commissions to advance the purposes it prescribes for ECOSOC. Some of the commissions that ECOSOC has established are founded upon particular subject-areas of concern (such as its Statistical Commission and its Commission on Population and Development). Other such commissions are organized on a regional basis (such as its Economic Commission for Africa and its Economic and Social Commission for Western Asia).

A principal function of ECOSOC is to co-ordinate the activities of the specialized agencies within the U.N. system. These specialized agencies will be discussed in greater detail in Chapter 2. Basically, these agencies are functionally independent international organizations established by separate treaties among their founding states. Examples would be The World Health Organization, the World Bank, and UNESCO (the United Nations Educational, Scientific and Cultural Organization). Although these agencies are substantially independent, the Charter envisions that ECOSOC will enter into contractual agreements with them defining the terms on which each will maintain a relationship with the larger U.N. organization. It would be too much to say that ECOSOC has oversight over these agencies, but it is charged with facilitating co-operation among them and with the U.N. organization.

The Trusteeship Council

The U.N. Charter, as adopted in 1945, set forth the terms of a "Trusteeship System." The Charter's framers designed this System to apply to certain territories that, at the end of World War II, they considered to be not in a position to exercise complete sovereignty and independence. The Charter established the Trusteeship Council to assist in the U.N.'s oversight of the management of the territories within this Trusteeship System.

In the ensuing decades, all territories subject to the Trusteeship System became either independent states or otherwise allied themselves with independent sovereign entities. Accordingly, the Trusteeship Council no longer functions on a regular basis. The five permanent members of the Security Council nevertheless retain authority, in accord with the Charter, to call Trusteeship Council meetings as the need arises.

The International Court of Justice

The International Court of Justice is the principal judicial organ of the United Nations. As noted earlier, it sits at The Hague in the Netherlands. It will be discussed in much greater detail in Chapter 3 of this book.

CHAPTER 1	Part 2: Reading Exercises

Student Name: ______________________________

Read and review the United Nations Charter. This appears in the "Documents" Unit of this Course Book ("Unit B"). Then answer the following questions based on your reading and review of Part 1 of this Chapter ("Introduction and Overview") and the United Nations Charter.

1. The United Nations Charter establishes six principal organs as constituting the structure of the United Nations organization. See if you can supply the name of each such organ without consulting the Charter or the descriptive discussion earlier in this chapter.

   ____

   ____

   ____

   ____

   ____

   ____

   Now turning to the text of the United Nations Charter, which of its provisions is the most direct and succinct authority for the proposition that the Charter creates these six principal organs? (For this and all other questions, give Article number and, where appropriate, paragraph number.)

   ____

2. How many countries currently are members of the General Assembly?

____

From which element of the materials supplied for this course did you obtain your answer for this question?

____

3. How many votes does each member of the General Assembly have in the Assembly?

____

Which provision(s) of the Charter provide(s) the authority for your answer?

____

4. Below are listed several actions the General Assembly might wish to take. Which ones are authorized by the relevant provisions of the Charter, and which ones are not?

(In the blank appearing after each such proposed action, indicate by "yes" that the action is authorized, or by "no" that it is not. Also indicate in the blank the provision(s) of the Charter on which your answer is based.)

(a) The General Assembly wishes to debate the advisability of supporting a proposed peace treaty between two warring states. ______________________________

(b) The General Assembly wishes to declare its support of a proposed peace treaty between two warring states, and to inform those states of its support for the treaty.

____

(c) The General Assembly wishes to pass a resolution requiring that two warring states accede to the provisions of a proposed peace treaty. ______________________________

(d) The General Assembly wishes to send a small force of armed United Nations peacekeeping personnel to help assure the maintenance of international peace and security in a politically sensitive area. ____________________

(e) The General Assembly wishes to study the advisability of each country in the world adopting the parliamentary form of democracy, as opposed to the presidential form of democracy, and wishes to make a recommendation to the countries of the world based on such study. ____________________

(f) The General Assembly wishes to order each member of the United Nations to adopt a parliamentary system of democracy.

____

(g) The General Assembly wishes to consider and approve a given year's budget for the United Nations organization. __________

____

(h) The General Assembly wishes to decide on the question of whether a new state that has applied to become a member of the United Nations, should in fact be admitted to membership in the United Nations. ____________________

5. Suppose that a member of the General Assembly falls three years behind in making its required payments to the United Nations. Does the Charter require that anything happen to that member's ability to participate in the activities of the General Assembly?

Circle one: Yes Maybe Not Necessarily No

Brief Explanation of above answer: ____________________

____

Charter provision on which your answer is based: ____________________

6. Which of the following matters can be decided upon by the General Assembly on the basis of a simple arithmetic majority of the members present and voting?

(a) The decision to expel a Member.
(b) The decision to suggest to the Security Council that it send peacekeeping forces to a particular region because of the General Assembly's view that there is a situation in that region that is likely to endanger international peace and security.
(c) The decision to suspend the rights and privileges of membership with respect to any Member.
(d) The passage of a resolution generally condemning human rights violations throughout the world.

On which provision(s) of the Charter do you base your answers to the above?

____

7. Regarding the basic structure and operations of the Security Council:

(First provide the answer in the first blank, then indicate the relevant provision of the Charter in the second blank after the semicolon.)

(a) How many Members of the United Nations sit at any given time on the Security Council?

________; ____

(b) How many votes does each member of the Security Council have?

________; ____

(c) In general terms, how many votes are required for a decision to pass in the Security Council?

_________; ____

(d) How are most members of the Security Council chosen to be on the Council?

_________; ____

(e) What is the length of the term that most members of the Security Council serve in that capacity?

_________; ____

(f) It is sometimes said that certain members of the Security Council have a "veto" on actions by the Security Council.

Which countries currently have this veto right?

____

____

____

Which provision of the Charter provides for this veto? ______

Does any provision of the Charter use the word "veto" in this connection? ________________________________

If so, which one? ______________________________

8. "True or False" Questions. For each of the following quoted statements, circle the word "True" above it if you believe it is true, and the word "False" above it if you believe it is false. In each case, in the blank above the statement and after the words, "True" and "False," indicate the provision of the Charter on which your selection is based.

(a) True False ________________________________

"Under the terms of the United Nations Charter, the members of the General Assembly are generally free to decide for themselves whether they will accept and carry out the decisions of the Security Council."

(b) True False ________________________________

"The Security Council may generally establish subsidiary organs as it deems necessary for the performance of its functions, but only with the consent of the General Assembly."

(c) True False ______________________________

"The terms of the United Nations Charter encourage parties to a dispute to seek a solution to the dispute by means of negotiation, enquiry, mediation, conciliation, arbitration, judicial settlement, resort to regional agencies or arrangements, or other peaceful means of their own choice; however, parties are merely encouraged to take these courses of action—they are not mandatory."

(d) True False ______________________________

"If parties to a dispute, the continuance of which is likely to endanger the maintenance of international peace and security, fail to settle it by means of negotiation, enquiry, mediation, conciliation, arbitration, judicial settlement, resort to regional agencies or arrangements, or other peaceful means of their own choice, the United Nations Charter requires them to refer the dispute to the Security Council."

(e) True False ______________________________

"The United Nations Charter generally requires all members of the United Nations to make available to the Security Council armed forces, assistance and facilities necessary for maintaining international peace and security."

9. Chapter VII of the United Nations charter is titled, "Action with Respect to Threats to the Peace, Breaches of the Peace, and Acts of Aggression." The first four Articles of this Chapter, Articles 39-42, are significant. It might be said that these four provisions describe a "progression of measures." Briefly indicate in the blanks below how these provisions might be viewed as stating a "progression" of possible measures.

Article 39: ______________________________

Article 40: ______________________________

Article 41: ______________________________

Article 42: ______________________________

10. It is generally believed that two provisions of the United Nations Charter state a centrally important "non-intervention principle."

(a) One of these, the one most frequently cited, prohibits Members of the United Nations from using violent means to interfere with the territorial integrity or political independence of any other state. This is the provision of the Charter most frequently used by those who wish to condemn military invasions by one state against another. Which provision is it?

____

(b) Another, related, provision of the Charter also protects Members of the United Nations against intervention into their domestic affairs, whether by military or other means. Which provision is this?

____

(c) Another provision of the Charter, which appears much later in its text, has been generally interpreted to provide an exception to the rule against violent intervention. This later provision refers to a certain "inherent right" of states and, in effect, allows Members to use force, whether "individual or collective," against other states under certain circumstances.

(1) Which provision is this? ____________________

(2) What is the inherent right referred to? __________

____

(3) Under this provision, when can this "inherent right" be exercised? (That is, what is the condition precedent before it may be exercised consistent with the Charter?) __________________________

____

(4) What requirements does this provision impose on Members using force in this way, with respect to the Security Council? _______________________

____

11. The chief administrative officer of the United Nations is given what title under the United Nations Charter? ____________

(a) What provision of the Charter indicates that this is this officer's title? ____________

(b) Under the Charter, how is this officer appointed? ____________

____

What is the Charter provision providing this information? ___

(c) By the way, from your general field of knowledge, can you provide the name of the person who is the current holder of this office? ____________

(d) What is the name of the organ (or branch) of the United Nations that this officer heads? ____________

12. Below are listed several actions that the officer discussed in Question 11 above might wish to take. Which ones are authorized by the relevant provisions of the Charter, and which ones are not?

(In the blank appearing after each such proposed action, indicate by "yes" that the action is authorized, or by "no" that it is not. Also provide in the blank the provision(s) of the Charter on which your answer is based.)

(a) The officer wishes to bring to the attention of the Security Council a situation that in the officer's opinion threatens the maintenance of international peace and security. ____________

(b) The officer wishes to order United Nations peacekeeping forces into a sensitive area in order to maintain international peace and security. ____________

(c) The officer wishes to make an annual report to the General Assembly on the work of the United Nations.

____

(d) The officer wishes to expel a member of the General Assembly. ____________

(e) The officer wishes to serve in his official capacity at a meeting of the Security Council. ____________________________

13. If the General Assembly entrusts to this officer the function of preparing a report on a particular subject, does the Charter require that this officer prepare such a report?

_____; What provision of the Charter furnishes the basis for your answer? ____

14. Under the United Nations Charter, every treaty and every international agreement entered into by any U.N. Member must be registered as soon as possible with a specified organ of the U.N.

(a) With which organ of the U.N. must this registration be made?

____

(b) What is the consequence of a Member's failure to make such registration?

____

____

(c) Which provision(s) of the Charter furnish(es) the basis for your answers above?

____

15. Suppose that, after becoming a Member of the United Nations, a state enters into a bilateral treaty with another state that contains provisions inconsistent with that state's obligations under the United Nations Charter.

(a) Under the Charter, which set of obligations prevails, those under the Charter, or those under the later treaty?

____

(b) Now suppose that a bilateral treaty was entered into first, before the state became a Member of the U.N. Which set of obligations prevails then; those under the Charter, or those under the earlier treaty?

____

(c) Same question as (a), above, except that the subsequent treaty is a multilateral convention, with 15 other signatories, all of whom are members of the U.N.

____

(d) Same question as (b) above, except that the earlier treaty is such a multilateral treaty.

____

(e) What provision(s) of the Charter serve(s) as the basis for your answers above?

____

16. "True or False" Question. Circle the word "True" above the following quoted statement if you believe the statement is true, and the word "False" above it if you believe it is false. In the blank above the statement and after the words, "True" and "False," indicate the provision of the Charter on which your selection is based.

True False ________________________________

"A proposed amendment to the United Nations Charter will always come into force once the terms of such amendment have been adopted by 2/3 of the members of the General Assembly and ratified in accordance with their respective constitutional processes by 2/3 of the Members of the U.N."

17. Assume that when the United Nations Charter came into force on October 24, 1945, 56 states, including all the permanent members of the Security Council, had signed the Charter. Under the terms of the Charter, how many of those 56 states would have needed to ratify it by October 24 for it to come into force?

____

Which provision of the Charter is the basis for your answer? ________

18. In how many different languages is the text of the United Nations Charter authentic?

____

What are these languages?

____

____

Which provision of the Charter is the basis for your answer? ________

CHAPTER 1

Part 3: Guidance for Research

Much valuable information for the student of public international law appears in the reports, resolutions, "parliamentary" proceedings and other documents produced by the six principal organs of the United Nations. Until 1996, these documents were also the most difficult to obtain unless a large academic library, preferably a U.N. Depository Library, was nearby. Progress in information technology, particularly the development of the Internet, has improved access, but problems still remain, especially if the document you seek is dated earlier than 1960.

The United Nations Charter, Article 15, mandates that the organs of the United Nations submit reports to the General Assembly, and Articles 64 (Economic and Social Council), and 73 (Trusteeship Council) also call for the preparation of reports. There is no requirement for registration or publication of these reports or other documents similar to that for U.N. treaties and "international agreements". (*Cf.* U.N. Charter Art. 102.)

Authorities report that the United Nations produces many thousands of documents per year. These include treaties, to be covered in a later chapter, "parliamentary documentation" such as reports of plenary sessions, resolutions, discussions, minutes of ad hoc meetings, and minutes and reports from standing committees and consultative bodies. There is also supporting documentation—preparatory papers and studies done on behalf of the principal organs by their staffs or the staff of the Secretariat.

There are also press releases (which can be useful because of their timeliness), correspondence and other miscellaneous documents submitted by Member States. (Some of these can be politically quite sensitive for some Member States—such as the CIA training manual for the Nicaraguan contras submitted to the Secretariat by the Sandinista government, then the official government of Nicaragua.) The majority of these documents are accessible to the public, although some Security Council reports can be confidential.

Historically, the United Nations has supported an extensive publication program, offering many documents for sale through its New York and Geneva offices. In addition, a world-wide program of depository libraries was established very early on. These depository libraries are listed at the U.N. web site.

(www.un.org) There are presently 405 depository libraries in 146 countries. As noted above, recent advances in information technology make access to primary U.N. documents much more feasible than before. It is no longer necessary to resort to U.N. depository libraries as often as may have earlier been the case.

One of these advances in information technology is *accessUN*, a very comprehensive electronic index to all types of U.N. documents. This is a proprietary product to which many universities have subscribed. The database is searchable by keyword, document type, date, and document number. It is also possible to designate search fields such as title, author, etc. One drawback to *accessUN* is that only a relatively small number of documents are available in full text. However, the user will retrieve the all important document identification numbers (see below) and can then locate the document at the nearest U.N. depository library or purchase the document from the U.N. Sales Office.

The U.N. also produces a large number of journals, bulletins, and brochures in the official languages of the body. Many of these are not widely known outside the rarified circles of diplomats and publicists. *The Journal of the United Nations* is available at no charge via the U.N. web site and is a basic and very under-used research tool. This publication is not only the "calendar" of the U.N. but also now provides links to major documents even before they have been officially released.

The traditional identification of U.N. documents is a Sales Code and/or an Official Records Designation. Both of these identifiers use a number of symbols to describe the document. In some cases, the document is only identified by a symbol in the several printed indices to UN documents (see below.)

A typical Sales Code identifier, found on the back of the title page, looks like this: E.69.II.C.1, denoting that this document is in the English language "E", that it was written in 1969, that it deals with the world economy—"II.C." (pursuant to the U.N.'s own subject classification scheme), and that it is publication number 1 in that series. If you are fortunate enough to know the Sales Code of the document you are seeking, using it is the most efficient method of retrieving the document from a U.N. Depository Library. In the real world, however it is really not useful—it is not a searchable term in either Westlaw or Lexis, or the U.N.'s web site.

Much more useful is what the U.N. calls the "Official Records Designation". This identifier also uses symbols and numeric codes. It is used, however, by only four organs: the General Assembly, the Security Council, the Economic and Social Council and the Trusteeship Council. Opinions of the International Court of Justice, which will be covered in a later chapter, have very different citations. The Secretariat also uses a different system of document identification.

A typical designation for records from these four organs would appear, for example, as: A/55/3 – where "A" designates that it is a General Assembly document, "55" denotes the 55th session of the General Assembly and "3" indicates that it was the third document produced at this session. These designations can get much more lengthy, with special codes designating committees, amendments, etc. A good explanation of these symbols (and the Sales Codes) is found at the U.N. web site.

Should you have the designation code for a document, you can use it as a search term in the Westlaw or LexisNexis *International Legal Materials (ILM)* database to retrieve the document. Your success is limited to the scope of the database on Westlaw or LexisNexis, i.e., the years covered. LexisNexis contains ILM from 1962, its first year of publication. At present time, Westlaw coverage is from 1980 (Volume 19-). It is possible also to use the code to search the UN web site.

International Legal Materials is a valuable print resource which predates the advent of electronic access to U.N. documents. It is published bi-monthly by the American Society of International Law (ASIL). Starting in 1962, it was/is often the first place to find recent treaties and other U.N. documents. Its pages are a strange combination of type styles and formats—rather like the slip opinions of courts or the slip laws of legislatures. Appearance has been sacrificed to timely publication of U.N. documents. This approach allows for the publication of current documents in ILM long before they could be found in more official sources.

An annual subject index to ILM is published in each November issue. There are also ten-year indices; 1962-1971, 1972-1981, 1982-1991. If you can at least identify the decade in which the document you are seeking might have been published, you can find it in the subject indices. Note, however, that the indexing is very broad. You may need to search a lengthy list of specific documents under a broad heading to find what you want. Now that ILM is available on Westlaw and LexisNexis, it has become much easier to use.

Another starting point for finding U.N. documents is the *Yearbook of the United Nations.* Most law school libraries will have this title. The volumes contain detailed accounts of the actions of the principal organs of the U.N. during the year, bibliographic citations to primary documents (the Official Record Designation), and the full text of major resolutions. Because the full text of only some documents is reprinted, the *Yearbook* can be frustrating to use. Now, however, the researcher can move from the *Yearbook* to the Index to Proceedings of the various organs and then, utilizing the U.N. web site, to the wanted document.

Finally, the several encylopediae of the U.N. can be most useful as a starting point for a researcher. The most commonly available one is the four-volume *Encyclopedia of the United Nations and International Organizations* by Osmanczyk and Mango (3rd edition). Like the *Yearbook*, it gives a quick overview of U.N. activities and organizations and can provide helpful citations for further research.

Research Strategies

In tackling any research problem, it is helpful to ask the following questions:

1) What type of document am I looking for? Is it a treaty? Resolution of the General Assembly or the Security Council? Report?

2) What is the time frame for the desired document? Can you even place it within a decade?

3) What are the keywords (and potential search terms) associated with this document?

CHAPTER 1	Part 4: Research Problems

Student Name: ______________________________

The following Research Problems are designed to help you use the information contained in Parts 1 and 3 of this Chapter, and experience gained from completing the Reading Exercises in part 2.

1. In 1975, the U.N. General Assembly adopted a resolution equating Zionism with racism. This is sometimes referred to in discussion as the "Zionism Is Racism" resolution.

   (a) Using the hard-copy searching techniques discussed in the "Guidance for Research" part of this Chapter, find the "Zionism Is Racism" resolution. What is a correct formal citation to it?

   ____

   (b) How did the Japanese delegation to the General Assembly vote on this resolution?

   ____

   (c) Now try answering these questions using at least one electronic method of research. Are your answers similar?

   ____

2. In 1992, the U.N. Security Council adopted a resolution establishing a United Nations Protection Force for the former Yugoslavia ("UNPROFOR"). In the vernacular, military forces such as UNPROFOR are often called "U.N. Peacekeeping Forces." The Security Council established

UNPROFOR in light of the threat it perceived to international peace and security presented by the situation in the former Yugoslavia.

(a) Using hard-copy research techniques, what is a correct formal citation to the Security Council Resolution that established UNPROFOR?

____

(b) Under this resolution, how often should the U.N. Secretary General report to the Security Council on progress towards peaceful political settlement?

____

3. In 1993, the U.N. World Conference on Human Rights in Vienna adopted a "Declaration and Programme of Action" that is viewed as significant among many international human rights activists. Among other things, this "Vienna Declaration" is known for stating that equal rights for women should be viewed as an international human rights issue. In popular discussion, this concept is sometimes expressed as "Women's Rights Are Human Rights." The actual language from the Vienna Declaration is somewhat different from the popular conception, and appears as part of the "General Principles and Areas of Concern" included as Sub-Part I of the Declaration.

(a) Using hard-copy research techniques, find the Vienna Declaration referenced above, and in particular the provision of the Declaration that is the basis for the assertion that "Women's Rights Are Human Rights." What is a correct citation to the Declaration and this provision?

____

(b) Write the sentence from the Declaration that serves as the basis for this assertion.

____

4. In each of his annual reports issued in 2000 and 2001, the U.N. Secretary-General has highlighted the subject of HIV/AIDS.

   (a) What is a complete citation for the provisions in each of the two Annual Reports for the primary discussion on HIV/AIDS?

   ____

   (b) What was the worldwide cumulative death toll from this disease reported in the Annual Reports for each of these two years?

   __________________ __________________

5. The status of Jerusalem has been a subject of intense agitation for many years. Upon the fall of the Ottoman Empire, the League of Nations issued to Great Britain a "Mandate for Palestine." Shortly before the termination of this Mandate, the U.N. General Assembly adopted a Resolution providing for the partition of Palestine into an Arab State and a Jewish State. This Resolution is sometimes called the "U.N. Partition Resolution."

   (a) Using hard-copy research techniques, determine the citation to the Partition Resolution.

   ____

   (b) Under the Partition Resolution, what was to be the status of Jerusalem? (That is, was it to be part of the Arab State or part of the Jewish State?)

   ____

(c) What is the Latin phrase that the Partition Resolution used to describe the anticipated status of Jerusalem?

____

(d) Was the Partition Resolution ever implemented?

____

6. Armed Iranian militants seized the U.S. embassy in Tehran on November 4, 1979, ultimately taking hostage 53 of the U.S. citizens inside. Many in the international community urged the U.N. Security Council to adopt a resolution condemning the seizure and the taking of hostages.

(a) How long did it take the U.N. Security Council to adopt a resolution addressing the seizure?

____

(b) What is a complete citation to this resolution?

____

(c) Did the resolution contain language condemning the seizure?

____

(d) How many members of the Security Council voted in favor of the resolution?

____

CHAPTER 2

OTHER UNITED NATIONS BODIES

Part 1: Introduction and Overview

The United Nations system is built principally around the six principal organs described in Chapter 1. However, many of the most significant activities of the U.N. are carried out by programs and agencies that are distinct from the principal organs. Indeed, many international lawyers, advocates and activists have more frequent contacts with U.N. program and agency offices than with the principal organs. This Chapter focuses on these programs, agencies and other bodies.

There are various categories of U.N. bodies distinct from the principal organs. Most commonly, these bodies can be broken down into five sub-groups: Programs, Funds, Commissions, Specialized Agencies, and Related Organizations.

United Nations Programs and Funds are creations of the General Assembly. They come into being through resolutions adopted by the General Assembly and depend on the General Assembly for their budgeting and oversight of their management. Accordingly, Programs and Funds report regularly, and are responsible, to the General Assembly.

Each Program or Fund tends to be devoted to a particular subject-matter area or areas, such as population management or environmental protection. As the name implies, each U.N. Fund has, as a significant element of its activity, the disbursement of money to assist Member Countries in achieving goals that that particular Fund is charged with pursuing. Examples of U.N. Funds are the United Nations Population Fund and the United Nations Children's Fund (widely known as "UNICEF").

United Nations Programs are generally functionally similar to Funds, in that they too are created by General Assembly resolution and are responsible to the General Assembly. Programs also tend to be devoted to specified subject-matter areas, and an important part of some U.N. Program activities can also involve the disbursement of money to Member Countries. Prominent examples of U.N. Programs are the United Nations Development Program and the United Nations Drug Control Program.

Specialized Agencies, on the other hand, are not created by General Assembly resolutions. Instead, they are created by formal treaties entered into directly by individual countries. The countries thus creating any particular Specialized Agency are generally regarded as "members" of the Agency thus created. Specialized Agencies are responsible for their own budgets. They do furnish regular reports to the General Assembly, but they are not generally responsible to the General Assembly in the sense of receiving oversight or in the sense of being directly accountable. Well-known examples of Specialized Agencies are the International Labor Organization, the World Health Organization and WIPO (the World Intellectual Property Organization).

Although the U.N. Charter neither creates nor provides for any of the Specialized Agencies by name, the Charter clearly contemplates their establishment and operation. Also, although the Charter envisions that the Specialized Agencies are to be operationally independent, it also requires that they be brought into a relationship with the U.N. pursuant to the Charter's terms.

As noted earlier in Chapter 1, the U.N. Charter gives significant responsibility to the Economic and Social Council ("ECOSOC") in connection with the Specialized Agencies. Chapter X of the Charter envisions that ECOSOC will enter into agreements with the Specialized Agencies to define the terms on which each Specialized Agency will conduct its relationship with the U.N. organization. All such agreements are subject to approval by the General Assembly.

The U.N. Funds, Programs and Agencies are members of the U.N.'s Administrative Committee on Co-ordination ("ACC"), which manages the distribution and circulation of information generated by the various Funds, Programs and Agencies reporting to it. The ACC meets regularly to consider management issues facing the U.N. system and its various sub-organs. The Secretary-General is the Chair of the ACC.

Organizations related to the U.N. (often referred to from inside the U.N. as "Related Organizations") are also created by formal treaties among individual countries, but they have an even greater degree of independence from the rest of the U.N. system than Specialized Agencies. They do not generally co-ordinate their activities through the ACC, and can view their operations as being more functionally distinct from the U.N. organization than most of the Specialized Agencies. Leading examples of Related Organizations are the World Trade Organization ("WTO") and the International Atomic Energy Agency ("IAEA").

Finally, as noted earlier in Chapter 1, the Economic and Social Council also creates a variety of functional commissions and regional commissions as an element of its work under the Charter. These commissions are a functional part of ECOSOC.

CHAPTER 2	Part 2: Reading Exercises

Student Name: ______________________________

Unit B of this book contains the constitutive documents for the following U.N. bodies:

United Nations Conference on Trade and Development ("UNCTAD")
United Nations Educational, Scientific and Cultural Organization ("UNESCO")
Organization for the Prohibition of Chemical Weapons

Review these documents in Unit B, and then answer the following questions regarding them:

REGARDING THE UNCTAD DOCUMENT:

1. Which of the following phrases most accurately describes the nature of this Document? Is it a treaty, a court opinion, a regulation, or some other kind of Document?

   (a) An International Treaty
   (b) A Court Opinion
   (c) A Regulation
   (d) A Resolution
   (e) A Statute

On which provision(s) of the Document is your response based? Why does the text you cite support your answer?

____

____

____

2. Upon reviewing this Document, under which of the following categories would UNCTAD most appropriately be classified?

(a) Principal Organ of the U.N.
(b) U.N. Fund or Program
(c) U.N. Specialized Agency
(d) U.N. Related Organization
(e) An Agency of the United States Government

On which provision(s) of the Document is your response based? Why does the text you cite support your answer?

____

____

____

3. When was UNCTAD established? ____________________

Which provision of this Document is your source for this answer?

____

4. This Document establishes a permanent organ of UNCTAD to carry out the functions that fall within UNCTAD's competence. What is the name of this organ?

____

(a) What is the citation to the provision of the Document that establishes this organ? ____________________________

(b) Does the document prescribe a specific number of members for this organ? Yes No

(c) On which provision(s) of the Document is your answer based, and why?

____

____

(d) How is the membership in this organ determined? On which provision of the Document is your answer based?

____

______________________________; ____________

5. Does the Document require the permanent organ of UNCTAD to establish any subsidiary organs? If so, how many, and what are they? Which provision(s) of the Document most specifically serve(s) as the basis for your answer?

____

____

____

6. Does the Document prescribe voting requirements for UNCTAD and for the permanent organ established by the Document? If so, how do the voting requirements differ for the two entities? On which provision of the Document do you base your answer?

____

____

____

____

7. The Document describes in some detail a particular kind of negotiated resolution of differences as a precursor to voting and as a basis for recommending actions to be taken by particular countries. What is the term of art used by the Document to describe this form of negotiated resolution? On which provision(s) of the Document do you base your answer?

______________________________; ____________

8. The Document directs that UNCTAD establish an administrative body for the "proper servicing" of UNCTAD and its subsidiary bodies. After answering each of the following questions, also supply the provision(s) of the Document on which you base your answer.

(a) What is the name of this body?

______________________________; ____________

(b) What is the name of the office of the person who heads this administrative body?

______________________________; ____________

9. What entity or organization is responsible for the expenses of UNCTAD and its subsidiary bodies? On which provision of the Document do you base your answer?

______________________________; ____________

REGARDING THE UNESCO DOCUMENT:

10. Which of the following descriptions most accurately describes the nature of this Document? Is it a treaty, a court opinion, a regulation, or some other kind of Document?

(a) An International Treaty
(b) A Court Opinion
(c) A Regulation
(d) A Resolution
(e) A Statute

On which provision(s) of the Document is your response based? Why does the text you cite support your answer?

11. Upon reviewing this document, under which of the following categories would UNESCO most appropriately be classified?

(a) Principal Organ of the U.N.
(b) U.N. Fund or Program
(c) U.N. Specialized Agency
(d) U.N. Related Organization
(e) An Agency of the United States Government

On which provision(s) of the Document is your response based? Why does the text you cite support your answer?

12. Among the "Purposes and Functions" of UNESCO described in the Document, almost all of the elements of the description are positive statements setting forth affirmative duties of UNESCO. Only one element of this description is negative, purporting to act as a restraint rather than an authorization for the scope of UNESCO's activities. State which provision of the Document sets for this restraining statement, and briefly describe the nature of the restraint.

_______________; _________________________________

____

13. How many organs of UNESCO does the Document establish? What are they? On which provision(s) of the Document is each of your answers based?

_______________; _______________

____

____

_________________________________; ___________

14. Which UNESCO organ would most correctly be classified, according to the text of this Document, as the "policy-making" body of the Organization? As a general matter, what type of majority within this organ is required for a decision? In each case, which provision serves as the basis of your answer?

_________________________________; ___________

_________________________________; ___________

15. What is the name of the executive organ of UNESCO? How many members does it have? What does the Document provide about the need to maintain the geographical diversity of the members of that organ? In each case, which provision of the document is the basis for your answer?

______________________________; ______________

__________; ______________

____

____

______________________________; ______________

16. This Document provides that questions or disputes concerning its interpretation must be referred either to a particular body or to an arbitral tribunal. What is the particular body specified, and on which provision(s) of the Document is your answer based?

______________________________; ______________

17. What is the nature of the relationship between the budget of UNESCO and the broader United Nations organization? On which provision(s) of the Document is your answer based?

____

______________________________; ______________

REGARDING THE DOCUMENT WITH RESPECT TO THE ORGANIZATION FOR THE PROHIBITION OF CHEMICAL WEAPONS:

The text included in Part B of this book is Chapter VIII of what is popularly called the "Chemical Weapons Convention". The full legal name of the Convention is the "Convention on the Prohibition of the Development, Production, Stockpiling and use of Chemical Weapons and on their Destruction." Only Chapter VIII of the Convention, dealing with the establishment of the Organization for the Prohibition of Chemical Weapons, constitutes the "Document" for the purposes of this Reading Exercise.

18. As noted above, the Document is a portion of a larger text. Which of the following descriptions most accurately describes the nature of this larger text? Is it a treaty, a court opinion, a regulation, or some other kind of text?

(a) An International Treaty
(b) A Court Opinion
(c) A Regulation
(d) A Resolution
(e) A Statute

On which provision(s) of the Document is your response based? Why does the text you cite support your answer?

____

____

____

19. Upon reviewing this Document, under which of the following categories would the Organization for the Prohibition of Chemical Weapons most appropriately be classified?

(a) Principal Organ of the U.N.
(b) U.N. Fund or Program
(c) U.N. Specialized Agency
(d) U.N. Related Organization
(e) An Agency of the United States Government

On which provision(s) of the Document is your response based? Why does the text you cite support your answer?

____

____

____

20. What are the three organs established by this Document?

____

____

____

On which provision of the Document is your answer based?

____

21. The Document identifies a "principal organ" of the Organization. Answer the following questions regarding this principal organ, in each case supplying the provision(s) on which your answer is based.

(a) What is the name of this principal organ?

______________________________________; __________

(b) The Document provides three different voting thresholds for determining when decisions are passed within this principal organ. In which provision of the Document are these three thresholds prescribed, and in which types of cases would each threshold apply?

____

____

____

____

22. How many members does the Document prescribe for the Organization's Executive Council? On which provision of the Document is your answer based?

_____________________________; _________________

The Document prescribes a fixed geographic allocation for members of the Organization's Executive Council. Indicate the number of members allocated to each of the following regions, and the provision of the Document on which the answers in each case are based.

________	Africa	____________
________	Asia	____________
________	Eastern Europe	____________
________	Latin America & the Caribbean	____________
________	Western Europe & Other States	____________
________	One other party	____________

23. How many provisions of the Document make explicit reference to the United Nations or any of its organs? Supply a reference to all such provisions, including a brief description of the nature of the reference to these organs.

____

____

____

____

24. What are the constituent elements of the Technical Secretariat, as described in the Document, and on which of its provisions is your answer based?

____

____

____

________________________________; ____________

QUESTIONS IN COMPARISON OF ALL 3 DOCUMENTS:

25. How would you rank the 3 agencies we've reviewed in terms of their independence from the primary organs of the United Nations? [Provide ranking from most independent ("1") to least independent ("3").]

    [1] ________________________________

    [2] ________________________________

    [3] ________________________________

26. On the basis of these documents, how would you rank the 3 agencies in terms of the degree to which the officials pursuing their work are required to be from geographically diverse areas? [Provide ranking from most stringent geographic diversity requirement ("1") to least stringent ("3").]

    [1] ________________________________

    [2] ________________________________

    [3] ________________________________

CHAPTER 2	Part 3: Guidance for Research

While, as noted above, the development of the Internet has had a profound effect on access to United Nations documents generally, nowhere is it demonstrated more clearly than with the various reports, statements and other documents produced by the numerous additional bodies of the international organization. As you learned in your reading exercises, these bodies are variously constituted and funded. Their documentation policies also vary; making it very difficult in the pre-Internet days to obtain their work product unless you had access to a U.N. Depository Library. With very few exceptions, neither Westlaw nor LexisNexis offers access.

Today, each body generally has its own web site, making document access much easier despite variations in coverage and in navigating the site. The Internet addresses and content of these sites are also comparatively stable—since they are official sites of the agencies, they are less likely to change without notice. The gateway to these sites can be Google, but a more fail-safe method is to access the United Nations web site and then navigate to the U.N. Organization Chart. Here you will find the names of the principal organs and their related agencies. Clicking on the name takes you to the body's web site.

Despite the development of electronic resources for tracking down agency information and documents, the printed encyclopedias and yearbooks continue to be a quick, efficient source for much good information. The standard reference works cited in Chapter One such as Osmanczyk's Encyclopedia of the United Nations are widely available, well indexed and often the fastest route to information about a program or agency and its activities.

Research Strategies

Many of the "thinking points" listed for Chapter One are operative here:

1. What exactly does answering the Research Problem require? Is it information about the agency? Is it information possibly contained in an agency publication?

2. What are the time parameters for the problem? Does this fit within the scope of the print or electronic resource one might use?

3. What constitutes an "authoritative source"? And why?

CHAPTER 2	Part 4: Research Problems

Student Name: ______________________________

The following Research Problems are designed to help you implement the information contained in Parts 1 and 3 of this Chapter, and experience gained from completing the Reading Exercises in part 2.

1. The Russian MIR space station (initially launched by the Soviet Union) is near disintegration and pieces are expected to begin falling to Earth in the near future. As early as 1967, the U.N. Committee on the Peaceful Uses of Outer Space was addressing the question of man-made objects launched into space falling back to Earth. In that year, the Committee's Legal Subcommittee issued a report summarizing the Subcommittee's work until that point. This Report was issued at the Sixth Session of the Subcommittee's work.

   (a) Using both electronic and hard copy research techniques, find this Report issued by the Subcommittee. Give the correct formal citations to it.

   ____

   (b) The Report, in its discussion of "Liability for Damage Caused by the Launching of Objects into Outer Space", states that members have come to agreement on particular issues. Assume that the various points on which the Subcommittee members agreed have become legally effective. Assume that your car is hit by a piece of MIR (a pun if you understand Russian), and that the U.S. elects to espouse your claim against Russia. What is the latest date, after the occurrence of the accident or the identification of the party that is liable, on which a claim may be presented? Give the exact citation for your answer.

____

2. Each Halloween in the United States, internationally-minded children collect "trick or treat" contributions for UNICEF. Also, during the December holiday season throughout the world, many firms and individuals send holiday cards produced on behalf of, and promoting, UNICEF. Using both hard-copy or electronic research techniques, answer the following questions.

(a) What did the acronym "UNICEF" originally stand for?

____

(b) Where is its headquarters?

____

(c) When did UNICEF adopt its most recent mission statement?

____

(d) Many of UNICEF's resources come from private sources, such as the sale of greeting cards. What percentage of its revenue is attributable to non-governmental and private payments and contributions, including U.N. specialized agencies and other special sources?

____

3. As a junior attorney employed by a corporate law firm, you have been assigned to work with a client that manufactures and sells lawn furniture. The client has previously only sold its products inside the United States, but is contemplating pursuing sales to buyers in Western Europe. You have been told that a U.N. body called "UNCITRAL" has adopted an international convention governing "contracts for the international sale of goods". You wonder whether this convention could have legal applicability to your client's planned sales.

(a) What does "UNCITRAL" stand for?

___

(b) What is the institutional objective for UNCITRAL?

___

(c) UNCITRAL was established by a resolution of the U.N. General Assembly. What is a complete citation to the resolution?

___

(d) What is the formal name for the convention regarding international sales of goods promulgated by UNCITRAL? Where and when was it ultimately executed?

___

___

4. The International Law Commission is an expert group involved in the development and codification of international law rules. Its members are elected for 5-year terms by the U.N. General Assembly. It creates draft documents intended to express suggested rules of international law that would be optimal if broadly adopted. The ILC is accordingly analogous to an international version of the U.S. American Law Institute, which drafts the "Restatements" of various areas of U.S. law.

(a) How many members does the ILC have?

___

(b) Below are 3 international treaties that were originally based on ILC drafts. Through investigating the ILC using hard copy or electronic sources, determine in which city and in what year each treaty was executed.

(i) Convention on the Law of Treaties

___ ___

(ii) Convention on Diplomatic Relations

___________ ______________

(iii) Convention on Succession of States in Respect of Treaties

___________ ______________

5. An organization chart of the "United Nations System" appears as an element of one of the websites maintained by the U.N. in connection with the activities of its organizations. Referring to this chart, which of the following entities are "Specialized Agencies" of the U.N., and which are not? What do the acronyms stand for?

(a) UNHCR SA?____________ ________________________

(b) IMF SA?____________ ________________________

6. Now that you have located the organizations listed above on the U.N. Organization Chart, find and correctly cite the following documents or data by visiting their web sites:

(a) The recent wars in Afghanistan and Iraq have endangered historical and archaeological sites. In May of 1954, a formal convention was signed under UNESCO auspices that would address the danger to cultural property in the event of armed conflict. Find this convention at the UNESCO website, and provide the formal name of the convention and the precise date of signature.

____

____

Is the US a "High Contracting Party" that has ratified the convention? ___________

(b) You are the corporate counsel for Kentucky Fried Chicken (now owned by Pepsico, Inc.) and you wish to find the International Patent Classification for the fryers like the one patented by Col. Sanders. Find this information at the WIPO site.

____

____

(c) Locate and cite the 2002 UNCTAD report on the Least Developed Countries. How many countries have that classification according to UNCTAD?

____

(d) According to the UNHCR, how many Afghans were repatriated in 2002? Cite to the appropriate document.

____

(e) In 1996 the IMF developed an initiative to assist "Heavily Indebted Poor Countries". Find the report describing this program and list three African countries that will be offered this debt reduction help.

____

____

____

(f) When and where was World Trade Organization established?

__________; ______________________________

Cite to the most authoritative electronic source of your answer.

____

____

7. Prior to the U.S. invasion of Iraq on March 20, 2003, the International Atomic Energy Agency (IAEA) conducted inspections in Iraq to determine the status of Iraq's nuclear program. The results of their inspection were reported to the Security Council in a series of documents, the most significant of which were the update report for the Security Council pursuant to Resolution 1441 dated January 27, 2003 and the "Work Programme of the International Atomic Energy Agency in Iraq pursuant to Security Council Resolution 1284" that was given to the Security Council on the day of the U.S. invasion. The Director General of the IAEA also orally reported to the Security Council on December 19, 2002 and January 9 and 27, 2003, February 14, 2003 and on March 7, 2003.

(a) Find the update report of January 27, 2003. What is a correct citation to this report?

____

(b) What is the name of the current Director General of the IAEA?

____

(c) Find a transcript of his remarks on March 7, 2003 and give a correct citation.

____

(d) What was the conclusion made by the Director General on this date concerning Iraq's nuclear capability? Quote and cite the pertinent language.

____

____

____

CHAPTER 3

INTERNATIONAL COURT OF JUSTICE

Part 1: Introduction and Overview

The International Court of Justice is sometimes called the "World Court", and international lawyers most frequently refer to it by its acronym, "the ICJ". As indicated in Chapter 1, it is one of the six principal organs of the U.N.

When the U.N. was established in 1945, the organization's founders believed in the importance of a judicial body that would have the authority to resolve legal disputes between states. The ICJ was designed to fulfill this function. Accordingly, the U.N. Charter states that the ICJ is the "principal judicial organ" of the U.N. When states that are Members of the U.N. (or potentially, even states that are not Members) have legal disputes with one another, they can agree to submit the disputes for resolution before the ICJ.

The workings of the ICJ are set forth in a separate treaty called the "Statute of the International Court of Justice". This Statute was appended as an annex to the U.N. Charter. The Statute is a very significant document in modern International Law for a variety of reasons, some of which will also be emphasized in Chapter 4. The ICJ Statute is included in the Documents Unit for this Course Book, and will serve as the basis for the Reading Exercises in the immediately following Part 2 of this Chapter.

The ICJ is the successor to a nearly identical court established under the earlier regime of the League of Nations. The judicial body established by the League of Nations was called the "Permanent Court of International Justice", or "PCIJ". The PCIJ was also constituted according to a written statute, and indeed the ICJ Statute was directly patterned in 1945 after the Statute of the PCIJ. Cases decided by the PCIJ are considered today to have the same weight and dignitary force as cases decided by the ICJ, even though the League of Nations no longer functions.

Fifteen members sit at any one time on the ICJ. Although no two can be from the same state, they are nevertheless expected to act as independent jurists rather than official representatives of their home countries. Sometimes the extent of the actual independence of the ICJ members has been questioned, but empirical studies do not seem to have uncovered blatant biases.

The selection of members for the ICJ is somewhat complicated, but bears a brief description. As a formal matter, members of the ICJ are elected by the General Assembly and the Security Council, each chamber proceeding independently from one another. An absolute majority is required in both chambers in order for any candidate to be elected a member of the ICJ. The ICJ Statute sets forth fairly elaborate procedures, in Articles 10 through 12, to address situations in which vacancies remain open and no candidate can command a majority of both the General Assembly and the Security Council.

More interesting from the perspective of the structural history of international law is the manner in which candidates are initially nominated for consideration. The nomination process depends on the Permanent Court of Arbitration, which was established under the 1899 and 1907 Hague Conventions on the Pacific Settlement of International Disputes. These Conventions, entered into in the aftermath of the Franco-Prussian War, were an early attempt at comprehensive international organization to foreclose violent international conflict. Given that both World Wars of the twentieth century later ensued, one cannot help but note their lack of success. They are, however, important from the standpoint of the incremental development of modern international law.

Each state party to the Hague Conventions was to nominate 4 persons "of known competency in questions of international law, of the highest moral reputation, and disposed to accept the duties of arbitrator". The accumulated roster of all persons so nominated by each signatory state was then inscribed as the list of members of the Permanent Court of Arbitration (or "PCA").

In reality, the PCA was not a perennially sitting court, but rather simply a facility by which the list of PCA members would be made available to states desiring to have their differences resolved through arbitration. When two or more states decided to have their differences arbitrated under the auspices of the PCA, they would choose their arbitrators from the list composed of all these persons nominated by the signatory states.

The ICJ statute refers to the 4 persons nominated by each state signatory to the Hague Convention(s) as the "national group" for that state. In short, when vacancies arise in the ICJ, each national group within the PCA in turn nominates as many as four candidates to fill each ICJ position. It is the aggregate of these nominations from the national groups on which the General Assembly and Security Council then vote.

By the way, the PCA still exists, and indeed maintains its headquarters in the same building out of which the ICJ operates. However, in the years since 1899, other developments have eclipsed the PCA. Of course, the U.N. framework now tends to be a more prominent means, rather than formal arbitration, of addressing sovereign resort to violent conflict.

Moreover, when states do decide to engage in arbitration in the modern arena, the arbitration is often arranged on an ad hoc basis. A dramatic example was the arbitration of the U.S. and Iranian claims resulting from the Iranian hostage situation in 1980. That arbitration was managed using the good offices of the government of Algeria, rather than any formal permanently constituted body such as the PCA. The International Chamber of Commerce, based in Paris, is another prominent arbitral body: however, it is used primarily for private international disputes. In spite of these more recent developments, the PCA remains as one additional option for states and other international actors desiring to pursue arbitration.

These observations raise another issue; the current utility of the ICJ itself. Perhaps unfortunately, the ICJ has never served as the prominent international judicial organ that the 1945 U.N. framers probably hoped for. In the years since its inception, the ICJ has only decided (so far) about 100 contentious cases or so. Questions of dire international import have tended to evade resolution by the ICJ. The Court seems to have been more frequently used to resolve more deliberative matters, such as border disputes, maritime jurisdictional questions, and aerial transportation incidents. This function, of course, is not without its importance, but it is probably more limited than that which was originally intended.

Nevertheless, those involved in international legal issues need to have a sound understanding of the basic structure and operation of the ICJ. It has served as a model in certain respects for later bodies, such as the Court of Justice of the European Communities. Also, in studying significant aspects of the ICJ's structure and operation, one tends to increase one's familiarity with fundamental issues of international law and international dispute resolution in general. For example, as suggested by comments earlier in this Chapter and as described more fully in the next, the ICJ Statute itself performs an important role in defining the sources of international law.

CHAPTER 3	Part 2: Reading Exercises

Student Name: ______________________________

Read and review the Statute of the International Court of Justice and the relevant provisions of the U.N. Charter. The ICJ Statute is included in Unit B of this book, as was the U.N. Charter. Then answer the questions below based on your reading and review of the document. (Some questions may also require that you visit an internet website, as indicated.)

1. Which of the following statements is most correct? (circle one)

   (a) All countries that are Members of the United Nations are automatically parties to the ICJ Statute, and all countries that are parties to the ICJ Statute are Members of the United Nations.

   (b) All countries that are Members of the United Nations are automatically parties to the ICJ Statute, but not all countries that are parties to the ICJ Statute are necessarily Members of the United Nations.

   (c) All countries that are parties to the ICJ Statute are automatically Members of the United Nations, but not all Members of the United Nations are parties to the ICJ Statute.

   (d) There is no automatic relationship of any kind between status as a Member of the United Nations and status as a party to the ICJ Statute.

   Which provision(s) of the United Nations Charter and/or the ICJ Statute is/are the basis for your answer?

   ____

   (For this and all other questions, give the name of the document, the Article number and, where appropriate, the paragraph number.)

2. In what city and country does the International Court of Justice usually sit?

____

What textual provision(s) support(s) your answer? ______________

3. Upon a visit, if necessary, to the U.N. website, which of the following are not parties to the ICJ Statute? (circle those that are not parties)

(a) Switzerland
(b) Nauru
(c) North Korea
(d) Taiwan

On which textual provision(s) do you base your answer? __________

4. "True" or "False" Question. Circle the word "True" above the following quoted statement if you believe the statement is true, and the word "False" above it if you believe it is false. In the blank above the statement and after the words, "True" and "False," indicate the textual provision(s) on which your selection is based.

True False ______________________________________

"The International Court of Justice is the principal judicial organ of the United Nations."

5. How many members (i.e., judicial officials) sit on the ICJ? _________

Which of the following honorific terms is used to describe the office of each member of the ICJ?

(a) Justice
(b) Judge
(c) Magistrate
(d) Lord

Which textual provision(s) is/are the basis for your answers? ________

6. In general, what is the length of the term of years for which each member of the ICJ serves in that capacity? ______________________

   How often are members of the ICJ elected? ______________________

   How many are elected at a time? ______________________________

   Which provision(s) of the ICJ Statute serve(s) as the basis for your answers? ____

7. Which of the following bodies or officers does not have a role in choosing the members of the International Court of Justice?

   (Circle those that do not have such a role. If you believe the particular body or officer does have such a role, indicate in the line following that selection which textual provision(s) support(s) that view.)

   (a) The General Assembly ______________
   (b) The Secretary-General ______________
   (c) The Security Council ______________
   (d) The Permanent Court of Arbitration ______________
   (e) The International Law Commission ______________

8. The presiding member of the International Court of Justice is referred to in the ICJ Statute as:

   (a) The Chief Justice
   (b) The Chief Judge
   (c) The President
   (d) Chief Lord Justice

   Which textual provision supports your answer? ___________________

9. "True" or "False" Questions. For each quoted statement below, circle the word "True" above the statement if you believe the statement is true, and the word "False" above it if you believe it is false. In the blank above each statement and after the words, "True" and "False," indicate the textual provision(s) on which your selection is based.

(a) True False ____

"Under the provisions of the ICJ Statute, all members of the ICJ must sit for all matters before the Court, unless they are on leave or are prevented from attending by illness or other serious reasons."

(b) True False ____

"Only states and international organizations may be parties in cases before the International Court of Justice."

10. Which of the following statements is a correct reflection of the provisions of the ICJ Statute?

(a) The International Court of Justice may not give advisory opinions; it may only decide cases and controversies brought before it between adverse parties.

(b) The International Court of Justice may on occasion give an advisory opinion, but never upon the request of any person or entity other than the General Assembly or the Security Council on matters within their scope of activities.

(c) The International Court of Justice may give an advisory opinion at any time on any subject, upon the simple request of any organ or specialized agency of the United Nations.

(d) None of the statements (a) through (c) above is correct.

Which textual provision(s) serve(s) as a basis for your response?

____

11. "True" or "False" Questions. For each quoted statement below, circle the word "True" above the statement if you believe the statement is true, and the word "False" above it if you believe it is false. In the blank above each statement and after the words, "True" and "False," indicate the textual provision(s) on which your selection is based.

(a) True False ____

"The Statute of the International Court of Justice absolutely prohibits any state that is not a party to the Statute from being a party to any case before the Court."

(b) True False ____

"States that are parties to the Statute of the International Court of Justice have, by signing the Statute, indicated that they will bring all their disputes with other states before the Court; they may not choose to resolve their differences before other tribunals."

12. Which of the following statements is most correct?

(a) Each Member of the United Nations has the choice, within its discretion as a sovereign state, as to whether it will comply with any decision of the International Court of Justice in any case to which that Member is a party.

(b) If any party to a case before the ICJ fails to perform the obligations incumbent upon such party under the Court's judgment, the Court may directly order an appropriate punishment against that party.

(c) If any party to a case before the ICJ fails to perform the obligations incumbent upon such party under the Court's judgment, the Secretary-General may directly order an appropriate punishment against that party.

(d) If any party to a case before the ICJ fails to perform the obligations incumbent upon such party under the Court's judgment, the General Assembly may directly order an appropriate punishment against that party.

(e) The United Nations Charter does not require that any decision of the International Court of Justice be complied with by any state other than any United Nations Member states that are parties to the relevant dispute before the Court.

On what textual provision(s) is your answer based? ________________

13. What are the official languages of the International Court of Justice?

____

On what textual provision(s) is your answer based? ________________

14. "True" or "False" Questions. For each quoted statement below, circle the word "True" above the statement if you believe the statement is true, and the word "False" above it if you believe it is false. In the blank above each statement and after the words, "True" and "False," indicate the textual provision(s) on which your selection is based.

(a) True False ________________________________

"The Statute of the International Court of Justice requires that the parties before it be represented by agents."

(b) True False ________________________________

"The Statute of the International Court of Justice requires that the deliberations of the Court shall be secret, and indicates that a member of the Court whose opinion differs from the opinion reflected in a judgment of the Court is not required to deliver a separate opinion."

(c) True False ________________________________

"All questions before the Court shall be decided by a majority of the number of the members of the Court who shall have been elected to the Court at the time of decision."

15. A key precept of Anglo-American common-law jurisprudence is stare decisis; the principle that once a particular matter has been resolved between two parties by a court opinion in a particular jurisdiction, any issues of law decided in such opinion serve as precedent for future court disputes in that jurisdiction between any future parties.

Does the Statute of the International Court of Justice adopt the principle of stare decisis?

Circle one: Yes No Uncertain

On what textual provision(s) is your answer based? ______________

16. Are decisions of the International Court of Justice subject to appeal?

____

Is there any way that a party that loses in an action before the Court can request further consideration?

____

____

On what textual provision(s) are your answers based? ____________

17. Under what circumstances may a state that is not a party to an action before the Court be permitted to intervene in the action?

____

____

____

On what textual provision(s) is your answer based? ______________

Being issued by the principal judicial organ of the United Nations, International Court of Justice opinions tend to have substantial weight in Public International Law. Accordingly, some students might be tempted to view the ICJ as a sort of "Supreme Court" of international law. This would, of course, be a great exaggeration, since (as noted in Chapter 4 below) the ICJ's jurisdiction is so limited. Nevertheless, within its sphere of authority ICJ opinions exert significant influence. The ensuing Research Problems are therefore designed to increase familiarity with, and build a facility for research regarding, opinions of the ICJ.

Broadly speaking, there are currently three sources to consult in order to obtain the texts of ICJ opinions: the official hard-copy reported published decisions, the ICJ website, and Westlaw. At press time for this book, ICJ opinions were not available as a distinct database on Lexis.

Reported Published Decisions in Hard-Copy Reporter Volumes

Since its inception, the ICJ has published a hard-copy reporter series officially including the definitive texts of most of its orders, judgments and other rulings. The Title of the series is "International Court of Justice: Reports of Judgments, Advisory Opinions and Orders," and Rule 21.5 of the current Bluebook specifies that this title be abbreviated in case citations as "I.C.J." In our normal discourse, we refer to this series as the "ICJ Reports". Reprinted editions of the earliest volumes of the ICJ Reports have been made available through the offices of William S. Hein & Co., and some U.S. law libraries have taken advantage of this service.

The concept evidently used in compiling the volumes of these reports is similar to that used in compiling decisions in U.S. reporters, such as United States Reports ("U.S.") and the federal and regional reporters. The decisions in each case are reported, followed by any concurring or dissenting opinions. Cases are presented in roughly chronological order, and are captioned by party names and dates. The volumes serve solely as reporters and contain no additional secondary substantive material. Accordingly, U.S. law students, at least at a basic level, should feel fairly comfortable using the ICJ Reports.

However, there are several points of difference between standard U.S. reporters and the ICJ Reports that would often limit the usefulness of the ICJ Reports for U.S. law students and lawyers. Most noticeably, the ICJ Reports are bilingual, with the English text of each decision on the left-hand pages and the corresponding French text on the opposite right-hand pages. This, of course, is in keeping with the specifications in Article 39 of the ICJ Statute. Although this may take some getting used to, it should not present a problem for most researchers.

Of more significance is the limited indexing available for the ICJ Reports. Unfortunately, there are no digests or head note numbering systems that might facilitate searching the internal portions of the reported decisions. Therefore, material in the ICJ Reports can only be searched or scanned by date, title, or other summary features of each decision.

In addition, the mechanisms for locating opinions even by date and title are limited. The only finding aids included in the ICJ Reports are indexes and tables of contents at the end of each yearly compendium. A further difficulty is that the indexes and tables of contents appear only in this annual format; there is no cumulative indexing or listing of contents.

Accordingly, if one wishes to find a case exclusively using the ICJ Reports, it is generally best to have a fairly good idea of its title (or general subject matter) and date. One then needs to consult the index and table of contents at the end of each annual compendium to see if the case is included within that year. Although one will generally find the desired material, the effort can be cumbersome.

An additional reason for this is that the ICJ tends to publish numerous decisions concerning the same case. In the first place, the ICJ often will publish a separate judgment or order on key procedural matters, such as jurisdiction or requests for filing extensions. Then, a judgment on the "merits" will appear separately, and be so denominated. Finally, on occasion there is also a separate judgment regarding the award of damages or other adjectival matters. Accordingly, each case can involve as many as a dozen or more reported orders, judgments and other rulings, appearing in various different volumes. This is a key difference between the ICJ Reports and most U.S. reporters, for example, and naturally adds to the complexity of searching the annual indexes and tables of contents.

It might also be noted that, although the indexes and tables of contents are generally provided in a bilingual format, for some years the bilingualism apparently failed, and either the index or the table of contents is given only in French, or the English entries are incomplete. A willingness to parse French text, at least at a superficial level, is thus often a useful trait in searching the ICJ Reports.

ICJ Website

If a researcher is inclined to use electronic methods to access ICJ decisions, the most authoritative source would be the ICJ website. As of the press time for this book, the URL for the ICJ is www.icj-cij.org. Under the menu item "Decisions", listed on the menu of the ICJ home page, one can access some of the reported ICJ decisions.

The primary disadvantage of accessing decisions in this manner is that the availability is incomplete. The "Contentious Cases" list provided at this point of the website does not necessarily include all decisions issued in a given year. Furthermore, not all of the decisions that are listed are provided in the form of electronic links.

Additionally, some of the earlier ICJ decisions that are made available through electronic linkages from this list are themselves not searchable for particular language. This, of course, somewhat limits their utility for researching.

Westlaw

Opinions issued by the ICJ are available on Westlaw. All the Westlaw documents are in searchable form. Accordingly, this medium may be more useful for most researchers than the ICJ website, although Westlaw (unlike the website) would be a commercial rather than an official source. Westlaw versions of decisions do, however, generally indicate page alignment from the ICJ Reports, so page references from the official ICJ Reports can be determined.

Although Westlaw can thus present an attractive means for accessing ICJ decisions, some of the inconveniences described above regarding the hard-copy ICJ Reports necessarily carry through to the Westlaw format. For example, searching on the basis of a mere case name will still yield search results encompassing all decisions issued for that case, including procedural and adjectival decisions. The researcher may still need to determine which of several, perhaps many, decisions of the same name listed in the search results will be most useful.

CHAPTER 3	Part 4: Research Problems

Student Name: ______________________________

The following Research Problems are designed to help you use the information contained in Parts 1 and 3 of this Chapter, and experience gained from completing the Reading Exercises in Part 2.

Perform the necessary investigation and research to answer these questions. In the course of your investigation, you may use whatever combination of electronic and hard-copy research activities that you find to be most suitable for you. However, your final answer for those questions requiring citations to "the most definitive source" must include citations to the definitive hard-copy texts.

1. For a period of time during the mid-1940's a condition of war existed between Albania and Greece. One of the causes of belligerency was conflicting claims over the North Corfu Channel, which adjoins the Western coast of both countries. As part of these hostilities, the Albanian government planted anti-navigation mines in the Channel. On October 22, 1946, a contingent of four British war vessels entered the North Corfu Channel and suffered substantial loss of life and property damage as a result of the detonating mines. The Albanian government claimed that the portion of the Channel in question was entirely within Albanian national waters, and that the British government knew that the Albanian government would repel any foreign incursion into the Channel with military force. Accordingly, Albania asserted that it could not be held responsible for Britain's intentional and knowing decision to send its war ships through the Channel.

   (a) The resolution of this dispute was the first contested case heard by the ICJ after its establishment in 1945. The ICJ ultimately rendered a judgment in which it finally resolved the *merits* of the controversy in April of 1949. This judgment is one of the most frequently cited decisions ever issued by the ICJ. Find the text of this judgment. Supply a complete citation to it at its most authoritative source, including the name of the case as it appears there.

____

____

____

(b) As part of its judgment, the ICJ held that "the North Corfu Channel should be considered as belonging to the class of international highways through which passage cannot be prohibited by a coastal State in time of peace" (that is, in time of peace vis-à-vis the flag state of the entering vessels). Find the page on which this holding appears at the source noted above.

____

____

____

2. The International Court of Justice has had cause on several occasions to examine a state's responsibility to foreign shareholders of a corporation operating within the state's borders. One of the earliest such cases, and probably the most important of the ICJ's rulings in this area, involved Barcelona Traction, Light & Power Company. This company had been incorporated in Canada in 1911, but many of its shareholders were Belgian nationals and most of its primary business concerned the delivery of electric power to consumers in northeastern Spain. Shortly after the Second World War, the Spanish government took certain actions arguably resulting in the bankruptcy of Barcelona Traction. Belgium then espoused the claims of the Belgian shareholders against the Spanish government before the ICJ.

(a) Belgium began the proceedings by submitting an application to the ICJ on September 23, 1958. The matter was finally resolved in a judgment issued by the ICJ in 1970. In the 12 years between the initial application and final resolution, the ICJ issued at least one order, judgment or ruling in the Barcelona Traction matter each year, except for one year. During which of those intervening years did the ICJ *not* issue an order, judgment or ruling of some kind?

(b) Supply a complete citation to the ICJ's final ruling in the Barcelona Traction matter at its most authoritative source, including the name of the case.

(c) One of the questions at issue in the case was which state had the authority to represent the Belgian shareholders before the ICJ. Belgium took the position that it could do so; Spain took the position that Canada was the more appropriate proponent for the shareholders. The ICJ, in resolving this particular point, examined the factual record and determined that "a close and permanent connection" had been established between the company and one of the states involved. Accordingly, the shareholders would need to seek the assistance of that state before the ICJ. Which state, in the Court's view, had this "close and permanent connection"?

(d) What is the page on which this determination appears in the Court's decision at its most authoritative source?

---

3. In February of 1979 an armed group of young Islamic "revolutionaries" stormed the American Embassy in Tehran, taking 70 employees prisoner including the Ambassador, killing two staff and ravaging the Embassy including the Ambassador's residence. The Iranian authorities did eventually disperse them, albeit somewhat reluctantly. However, on November 4, 1979, when Ayatollah Ruhollah Khomeini's government learned that former Shah would be allowed to come to the United States (actually to the Mayo Clinic) for medical treatment, a huge demonstration occurred outside the Embassy and militants again overran it. The Iranian security forces were nowhere to be seen. Embassy staff were again prisoners and the "Muslim Students Followers" also seized other American citizens throughout the city and

brought them to the Embassy compound. This hostage situation lasted until January 1981 and is believed to have been a factor in Jimmy Carter's defeat in the 1980 presidential election. The United States filed an application with the ICJ concerning this situation on November 29, 1979, and after issuing two orders on preliminary matters, the Court delivered its judgment a short while later.

Find the judgment issued by the ICJ in this case (this question is asking for the judgment itself, rather than the two orders issued prior to the judgment).

(a) What is the citation to the judgment?

____

____

(b) According to the ICJ's judgment in the case, the United States claimed in its Memorial that Iran had violated its international legal obligations to the U.S. under four international conventions or treaties. What were the names of these conventions or treaties?

____

____

____

____

(c) Did both parties appear at the hearing? ____________________

(d) Did the U.S. seek monetary damages in this proceeding? If so, how would such damages have been calculated?

____

____

(e) According to the judgment, the Iranian government conveyed two communications to the Court. On the basis of the second of these communications, can you briefly state why Iran felt that the Court could/should not give judgment on the case?

(f) The Court delivered its ultimate decisions on the merits in paragraph 95 of the judgment. Of the 6 numbered decision clauses, which were joined by the largest number of judges? Briefly, what did these clauses provide?

4. In 1984 Nicaragua filed an application with the ICJ alleging that military and para-military activities against Nicaragua were being supported by the United States government. Many in the region referred to the para-military forces as the "Contras," to indicate that these forces were opposed to the Sandinista regime then in control of Nicaragua. The operations of these Contra forces had gathered a substantial degree of repute (or disrepute, depending on one's point of view). Nicaragua argued that the assistance by the U.S. of the Contra forces was a violation of international law. After a preliminary judgment on jurisdiction in 1984, the Court rendered its judgment on the merits in June, 1986.

(a) Find the judgment of the ICJ *on the merits* in this case at an authoritative source, and provide a complete citation to the judgment at that source.

(b) According to the judgment, how many requests for relief against the United States did Nicaragua assert in its memorial to the Court? In which paragraph of the judgment are these requests from the memorial enumerated?

____

(c) According to the judgment, did the U.S. assert any requests for relief against Nicaragua at the merits stage of the case? If so, how many? From which paragraph of the judgment do you derive your answer?

____

____

____

(d) In paragraphs 26 through 31 of the judgment, the Court deals with a preliminary procedural issue, and discusses the relevance of Article 53 of the ICJ Statute to this issue. What is the procedural issue involved, and why does the Court cite Article 53?

____

____

____

____

____

____

____

____

(e) Under paragraph 206 of the judgment, the ICJ considers the possibility that there might be a general right of states to intervene in support of internal opposition in other states when the cause of such opposition appears particularly worthy. What is the ICJ's ultimate view of such a general right, as expressed in this paragraph?

CHAPTER 4

ICJ JURISDICTION, INTERNATIONAL LAW SOURCES, & ARBITRATION AMONG STATES

Part 1: Introduction and Overview

In the preceding Chapter, we looked in some detail at the International Court of Justice, which is one of the most formal arenas of dispute resolution in the international community. We saw that the ICJ is the judicial body of the United Nations organization, and offers one of the most prominent and visible means for states to resolve differences among one another. We also reviewed the Statute of the ICJ, which was initially adopted as part of the original United Nations documentation in 1945.

In this Chapter, we continue our study of international dispute resolution among states, and begin by emphasizing two particularly important aspects of the ICJ Statute. First, we focus on Article 36 of the ICJ Statute, which specifies the extent of ICJ jurisdiction. A casual observer might assume that any state that signs and ratifies the ICJ Statute would thereby be automatically assenting to ICJ jurisdiction over it in any case brought by or against it before the Court. This, however is not the case.

As we've seen in earlier Chapters, all U.N. Member States are automatically parties to the ICJ Statute. By ratifying the U.N. Charter, they functionally ratified the ICJ Statute. So, by in effect signing and ratifying the ICJ Statute through the U.N. membership process, the Member States merely agreed to the establishment of the ICJ and agreed to its generally functional role as part of the U.N. framework. Whether the ICJ has jurisdiction to decide any particular case, even when it involves only states that are parties to the ICJ Statute, is an entirely separate matter.

Article 36 of the ICJ Statute describes the ways in which the ICJ can have jurisdiction over particular disputes between states. It is accordingly a very significant provision of the ICJ Statute. In reviewing this provision, and completing the Reading Exercises based on it, you will gain an appreciation of how jurisdiction is determined and the issues that can be involved in any particular case.

Another important provision of the ICJ Statute is even more central than Article 36 to International Law as a whole. This is Article 38 of the Statute. This provision has fundamental significance to all of International Law, extending well beyond the context of the ICJ or even the U.N. as a whole. Article 38 states the most foundational concepts that are probably the most important fundamental ideas in the study and practice of International Law.

Article 38 states the sources of international law. Lay persons, and even lawyers who have not studied International Law, will often wonder where it is that International Law can come from. After all, there is as yet no real "world legislature" that has the authority to bind all states with any laws that it might adopt. (As we have seen, the U.N. General Assembly falls far short of this description.) Similarly, there is no "world President" or "world executive" that could enforce such laws or promulgate regulations implementing them. (Again, the powers of the U.N. Secretary-General do not rise to this level.)

So where does "International Law" come from, if not from a world legislature or world executive? Article 38 of the ICJ Statute answers this question. You will see in studying this provision and in completing the Reading Exercises based on it, that it enunciates 4 basic sources of International Law. All rules of International Law, properly so called, come from one of these 4 sources specified in Article 38.

This means that, among other things, states generally do not feel bound by a purported rule of International Law unless, at a minimum, such a rule can trace its lineage (directly or indirectly) to one of these four sources. It is this aspect of Article 38 that has such wide-ranging significance. Whether or not one is arguing before the ICJ, and whether or not one is operating within the U.N. framework specifically, it is still the case that, as a matter of general international law and practice, a rule must derive from a source that fits into one of these 4 categories in order to be binding. Article 38 thus has quite transcendent scope, and warrants our detailed attention.

Finally, in this Chapter, we consider a commonly used form of dispute resolution among states that is somewhat less formal and less prominent than ICJ adjudication. This is International Arbitration among states. The process of inter-state arbitration is less standardized than ICJ jurisdiction, but still is useful and critical to our knowledge International Law. Much of the formal arbitration that currently takes place between states occurs under the auspices of the Permanent Court of Arbitration, first discussed in Part 1 of the preceding Chapter 3.

The Permanent Court of Arbitration was established well before the creation of the U.N. Nevertheless, as noted in Chapter 3, it still operates out of the same building in the Hague in which the ICJ is situated. States can, and do, use the mechanisms it offers to resolve differences among them, when for one reason or another, the facilities of the ICJ are not desired. Also as noted earlier, the PCA operates pursuant to two Conventions for the Pacific Settlement of International Disputes, one from 1899 and the other from 1907. The 1907 Convention is reproduced in Unit "B" of this Course Book, and is the subject of the remaining portion of the Reading Exercises for this Chapter.

CHAPTER 4	Part 2: Reading Exercises

Student Name: ______________________________

Read and review Articles 36 and 38 of the Statute of the International Court of Justice, included in Unit B of this Course Book in connection with the preceding Chapter 3. Also review the 1907 Convention for the Pacific Settlement of International Disputes, included in Unit B for this Chapter 4. Then answer the following questions based on your reading and review of these provisions.

QUESTIONS ON ICJ JURISDICTION UNDER ARTICLE 36 OF THE STATUTE

1. Concerning Article 36 of the Statute of the International Court of Justice, which of the following statements is most likely to be *incorrect*?

   (Circle the answer you believe most likely to be incorrect. In the blank after each answer, indicate any particular provision of Article 36 that may lead you to believe that such answer is correct, or incorrect, as the case may be.)

   (a) In general terms, the International Court of Justice only has jurisdiction over those cases in which all the parties, in one form or another, have expressed consent to such jurisdiction.

   ____

   (b) The mere fact that a state party bringing an action before the ICJ is referring the case to the Court, does not automatically mean that the Court will have jurisdiction in the matter; the party or parties *against* whom the action is brought must also express consent to the Court's jurisdiction. ______________

(c) Compulsory jurisdiction by the International Court of Justice may be imposed on a state if such jurisdiction is provided for by the terms of a treaty or convention to which that state is a party. ____________________

(d) Within the specifications of Article 36, states may make voluntary advance declarations that they recognize the jurisdiction of the ICJ as compulsory. ____________

(e) The jurisdiction of the ICJ only extends to legal questions; the Court is without jurisdiction to decide any disputed questions of fact. ____________________

2. Suppose a state issues a declaration of compulsory jurisdiction, purportedly pursuant to Article 36 of the Statute of the International Court of Justice. The declaration, however, contains various exceptions and reservations. Which of the following exceptions and reservations is *least* consistent with the terms of Article 36?

(a) A reservation stating that the declaration is made on condition of reciprocity on the part of all states desiring to avail themselves of the declaration.

(b) An exception stating that the declaration will only be valid for 10 years.

(c) An exception stating that the declaration does not apply to matters which are essentially within the domestic jurisdiction of the declaring state.

3. A state issuing a declaration of compulsory jurisdiction is required to file the original declaration with:

(a) The International Court of Justice
(b) The Security Council
(c) The Secretary-General
(d) The General Assembly

4. In the event of a dispute as to whether the Court has jurisdiction, the matter shall be settled by:

(a) The International Court of Justice
(b) The Security Council
(c) The Secretary-General
(d) The General Assembly

QUESTIONS ON ARTICLE 38 OF THE STATUTE

5. Pursuant to Article 38 of the Statute of the International Court of Justice, the Court is required to apply legal rules from various named sources. Indicate what these sources are, in the *exact* language and in the *exact* order, stated in the Statute:

(a) ____________________

____

____

(b) ____________________

____

(c) ____________________

____

(d) ____________________

____

____

____

6. Under Article 38, may the parties to a dispute properly before the Court agree for the Court to decide the case without reference to international law at all, but rather out of generalized notions of justice and equity (*ex aequo et bono*)? ______________________________

7. Paragraph (c) of Article 38 refers to "civilized nations". Are there any nations that, for purposes of argument before the ICJ at the present time, you would care to consider not to be "civilized nations"? If so, which ones?

____

____

____

____

8. Does Article 38 provide any indication in its terms as to whether some of the sources listed in paragraph 1 of the Article are more important, or more significant (or less important, or less significant) than others? Which portion(s) of Article 38, if any, might contain such an indication?

____

____

____

____

9. Which of the following authorities is the ICJ apt to consider relatively more significant, and which is it likely to consider relatively less significant, as a potential source of international law?

(On a scale of 1 to 10, with "1" being the least important and "10" being the most important, provide a ranking for each of the following potential sources of international law under Article 38. You may assume that each potential source is equally relevant, in point of substance, to the question at issue. Assume also that the dispute before the Court involves only two states as parties.)

	Source of Law		Ranking
(a)	A multilateral treaty among 48 states, to which both states in the dispute before the Court are parties		______
(b)	A bilateral treaty between the two states in the dispute before the Court		______
(c)	A multilateral treaty among 48 states, to which one of the states in the dispute before the Court is a party, but to which the other state is not a party		______
(d)	The legal maxim that "the volunteer suffers no harm."		______
(e)	An international practice of long standing, not commemorated in any international agreement, that the families of ambassadors, as well as ambassadors themselves, enjoy diplomatic immunity.		______
(f)	The Constitution of the United States of America		______
(g)	A prior decision of the ICJ		______
(h)	A treatise on International Law written by a law professor on a prominent law faculty in a leading Western European country		______

	Source of Law		Ranking
(i)	A decision of the U.S. Supreme Court		______
(j)	A decision of the highest court of the Republic of Guinea-Bissau		______
(k)	A resolution passed by the United Nations General Assembly, by a vote of 105 to 63 (all other states not present or abstaining)		______
(l)	A resolution passed unanimously by the United Nations General Assembly		______
(m)	The generalized idea that a party should not profit from such party's own criminal acts		______
(n)	An arbitral award delivered by an arbitral tribunal, not affiliated with the U.N. or the ICJ, that was convened at the request of two states having a dispute with one another		______
(o)	A decision of the Court of Appeals of the State of New York		______
(p)	A decision of the Supreme Court of the State of Wyoming		______
(q)	The doctrine of international sovereign immunity, long recognized by the courts of most countries, providing that a state may generally not be sued in the courts of another state without the first state's consent		______

	Source of Law		Ranking
(r)	A document called "The Restatement (Third) of the Foreign Relations Law of the United States", prepared by a group of U.S. academics and judges called the American Law Institute (the "ALI"), that summarizes much of the body of international law, as recognized and interpreted by authorities in the U.S.		_____
(s)	A model treaty, not signed by any state, prepared by the International Law Commission (the "ILC"), a body within the U.N. organization that prepares model international law documents at the request of the General Assembly and other U.N. organs		_____
(t)	A multilateral treaty between 48 states, to which neither state in the dispute before the Court is a party		_____

QUESTIONS ON THE 1907 HAGUE CONVENTION

10. The 1907 Hague Convention is structurally organized around 3 distinct types of "pacific settlement of international disputes". Each of these 3 types is the subject of its own roman-numeral "Part" heading within the Convention. What are these 3 types of settlement mechanisms, and in which portion of the Convention is each described?

______________________________ __________________

______________________________ __________________

______________________________ __________________

11. "True or False" Questions. For each quoted statement below, circle the word "True" above the statement if you believe the statement is true, and the word "False" above it if you believe it is false. In the blank above the statement and after the words, "True" and "False," indicate

the provision of the New York Convention on which your selection is based.

(a) True False ________________________________

"Under the Convention's framework for Good Offices and Mediation, Contracting Powers make use of the services of individual natural persons who are certified as professional experts on the particular subjects under dispute."

(b) True False ________________________________

"The Convention provides that Contracting Powers that have disputes with one another can take advantage of Commissions of Inquiry, but indicates that such Commissions are for disputes that involve neither honor nor vital interests, arising from a difference of opinion on points of facts."

(c) True False ________________________________

"Under the terms of Part IV of the Convention, the Permanent Court of Arbitration is established, and all Contracting Powers are obligated to submit all disputes between them to the Permanent Court; there is no provision made for the submission of disputes to any other special Tribunals."

(d) True False ________________________________

"Under the Convention, when Contracting Powers decide to use the Permanent Court of Arbitration, they must initially try to agree among them which Members of the Court will serve as arbitrators. Failing such a direct agreement of the parties on the Arbitration Tribunal, each party appoints two Arbitrators, and these Arbitrators together choose an Umpire."

(e) True False ________________________________

"Arbitral Tribunals operating under the Convention may consider their decisions in private, but must conduct their proceedings in public."

12. One of the chief differences between the Convention's system for "International Commissions of Inquiry" and its system for "International Arbitration" is the extent to which the final result of the process is binding on the disputing states. For one of these types of proceedings, an award is issued that is binding on the parties. For the other, no such binding award is issued.

(a) Which system involves a binding award, and which provision of the Convention provides for this without any appeal?

____; ____________

(b) Another provision of the Convention explicitly provides that the other system does not contemplate the issuance of awards at all. Which provision is this, and what final document is contemplated, rather than an award?

__________________; __________________________________

(c) With respect to the document described in the immediately preceding point (b), what degree of freedom do the disputing states have in determining what effect to give the document?

____

CHAPTER 4	Part 3: Guidance for Research

In Chapter Three, you retrieved and reviewed cases brought before the International Court of Justice in which judicial opinion was sought on disputes between states. In addition to these judicial proceedings, states use the alternative dispute resolution technique of arbitration. Arbitration is not a new technique in international law. It has been used in all manner of disputes from national boundaries to environmental issues. In a later chapter, we will cover its use in commercial disputes between private parties.

Historical Collections

Very early arbitral opinions were compiled by legal scholar John Bassett Moore in two works with very long titles: *International adjudications: ancient and modern history and documents together with mediatorial reports, advisory opinions, and the decisions of domestic commissions, in international claims: ancient series* edited by John Bassett Moore: Buffalo, NY W.S. Hein, 1996. Originally to be published by Oxford University Press in 1936 in two volumes, only volume two was actually published. This volume contains "adjudications" from 1491-1504.

Moore's second work, *International adjudications: ancient and modern history and documents together with mediatorial reports, advisory opinions, and the decisions of domestic commissions, on international claims: modern series* edited by John Bassett Moore: Buffalo, NY: W.S. Hein, 1996 was published in six volumes. These volumes contain reports of arbitrations from 1794 to 1814.

In 1896, the US Government Printing Office published a six volume work edited by Moore: *International Arbitrations—History and Digest of the International Arbitrations to Which the United States Has Been a Party.* This work, like the two above, was reprinted by W.S. Hein in 1995. These volumes contain not only the arbitral decisions, but also extensive commentary on the history and process of international arbitration.

Moore's works remain the primary source in English for early arbitrations. Since many of these concerned boundary lines, both the hard-copy volumes and the microfiche versions contain maps and interesting topographical data on early North America.

Current Materials

As you learned in your Reading Exercises, the Permanent Court of Arbitration was first established at the Hague pursuant to treaty law initiated in 1899, and the PCA continues to hear cases. Decisions issued through the PCA process are published in a multi-volume work, from 1920 forward, issued by the United Nations. These volumes contain not only reports from the PCA but also from certain other arbitrations brought before other United Nations entities. *Reports of international arbitral awards* (French Title: *Recueil des sentences arbitrales*) New York: United Nations. 1948-. The reports are published in either French or English, but unfortunately generally not both. There are headnotes and each volume has an index. There is considerable delay in publishing the reports—at this writing a volume covering 2000 decisions is the latest one published. The series is often referenced by the acronym for its English title, RIAA.

An invaluable finding aid for arbitral awards appearing in the RIAA is a one-volume index work, The Permanent Court of Arbitration: International Arbitration and Dispute Resolution, edited by P. Hamilton, H.C. Requena, L. van Schletinga and B. Shifman. The Hague: Kluwer Law International, 1999. This volume lists, summarizes and digests many of the most significant award and decisions published in RIAA. It also contains references to sources other than RIAA in which original awards (or reports of them) can also be found.

Citations to these reports can be found in the electronic UN database, AccessUN, which provides the UN document number, etc. but not the full text. AccessUN is searchable by keywords, document type, date, and document number. A source for the full text, which is usually the UN's Document Sales Department, is given.

Although LexisNexis and Westlaw services provide access to commercial arbitral disputes, the Mealey International Arbitration Report, a subset of the Mealey Litigation Report, is available on LexisNexis and covers arbitration cases in which a state is a party. The full texts of cases from 1993 are included and searchable.

International Law Reports, published since 1919, contains reports of arbitrations as well as judicial opinions.

CHAPTER 4	Part 4: Research Problems

Student Name: ______________________________

The following Research Problems involve awards or other final determinations made in connection with arbitration proceedings between sovereign states.

Perform the necessary investigation and research to answer these questions. In the course of your investigation, you may use whatever combination of electronic and hard-copy research activities that you find to be most suitable for you. However, your final answer should in each case requiring citations be to the most definitive hard-copy source available.

1. The governments of the United States and the United Kingdom had a substantial disagreement from the late 1970's through the early 1990's concerning user charges imposed by the latter on U.S.-flag airlines at Heathrow Airport. The United States, espousing the claims of its air carriers, asserted that the authorities operating Heathrow were charging the U.S. carriers for more than their fair share of expenses. Ultimately an arbitral tribunal was established to resolve the dispute. One of the attorneys at the U.S. Department of State, a Mr. Samuel M. Witten, published a 1995 commentary on this arbitration.

   What is a citation to this commentary at its original source?

   ____

   ____

   ____

   ____

For each of the questions below, in addition to answering the question, provide a page citation to the provision of this report that supports your answer.

(a) The arbitration was begun pursuant to the terms of a bilateral treaty between the two states that had originally been signed in 1977. What was the name of this treaty, and which of its provisions provided for the arbitration of disputes?

____

____

____

(b) How many arbitrators were on the tribunal that heard the claims in this case?

____

____

(c) Was a sum of money ultimately paid in settlement of the dispute? If so, how much was paid, when, by whom and to whom?

____

____

____

2. One of the earliest arbitrations effectuated by the Permanent Court of Arbitration concerned a claim by France against Peru. The dispute under the so-called "French Claims Against Peru" arbitration resulted from the nullification by the Peruvian government of certain of its obligations arising out of contracts with foreign nationals.

The official version of the award in this arbitration was issued in French. Provide a complete citation to a report, in English (unofficial but authoritative) of this arbitration proceeding at a prominent hard-copy published reporter series.

In addition to supplying the answers for the following questions, also provide a citation to the provision(s) of this report that support your answers.

(a) What was the commercial commodity that was the subject of the nullified obligations?

(b) On what date did the Permanent Court of Arbitration render judgment?

(c) Did the tribunal find in favor of the French claim? If so, what was the quantity of monetary liability?

3. On July 10, 1985, a vessel named the *Rainbow Warrior* sank in the harbor of Auckland, New Zealand. It was ultimately determined that two agents of the French government had been responsible for the sinking, and that they had been acting under orders from the French government. Upon confirming its responsibility for the episode, the French government offered to provide an official apology and pay reparations. However, the New Zealand government considered that the offered reparations were inadequate, and also asserted that other types of relief were needed. Prominent among these was the claim that the

two French agents who rigged the explosive devices on the *Rainbow Warrior* should be compelled to serve meaningful prison sentences, a claim strongly resisted by France. In 1986, the two countries referred the resolution of their differences to the Secretary-General of the U.N. He ruled, *inter alia*, that the two French agents should be held in isolation under the custody of the French military authorities on the island of Hao in French Polynesia for three years.

The two agents were transferred to Hao on July 23, 1986, but thereafter their detention was the subject of controversy and recrimination between the two states. New Zealand felt that France was being too permissive in its administration of their detention. New Zealand argued that France had breached its obligations under the agreements finalized in connection with the Secretary-General's ruling, and France denied any such breach. The two states referred this dispute as to the proper terms for the agents' detention to arbitration in 1989, and an award was issued concluding the arbitration on April 30, 1990.

Find a copy, at an authoritative source, of this 1990 arbitral award in the "Case Concerning the Difference Between New Zealand and France Concerning the Interpretation or Application of two Agreements . . . Arising from the *Rainbow Warrior* Affair." Provide a complete citation to this award at an authoritative source.

____

____

____

____

In answering each of the following questions, please also indicate the provision(s) of the award that serve as the basis for your answer.

(a) What were the names of the two French agents?

____

____

(b) The main cause for the disagreement as to the terms of the agents' detention were medical conditions they developed while on Hao. France took the position that the medical condition of each agent required their removal to the French mainland, and summarily transferred them to Paris. What were these medical conditions?

(c) Did the Arbitral Tribunal's Decision require the two agents to return to Hao to continue their detention? Why or why not?

4. On June 30, 1965, India and Pakistan entered into a cease-fire Agreement that ended armed hostilities between them over their joint border separating what is now the Indian State of Gujarat from Southern Pakistan. The Agreement allowed for the two states to engage in arbitration proceedings to help define this border. That arbitration took place, and the Arbitral Tribunal issued its award on February 19, 1968.

Find the text, at an authoritative source, of the award in this case, the so-called "Rann of Kutch Arbitration", or more formally called "The Indo-Pakistan Western Boundary Case Tribunal." What is a complete citation to this award, at this source?

Please answer the following questions, in each case also indicating the provision of the award that serves as the basis for your answer.

(a) What were the names and nationalities of the three members of the Arbitral Tribunal?

(b) The map on the final page of the Award shows the line of the border as fixed by the Tribunal. This line begins with a point designated "WT" and ends at a point designated "ET." What did these initials stand for in the negotiations between the parties?

____

____

5. Conflicts between the United States and its ally, France, are nothing new. In 1803, France ceded the Louisiana territory to the United States. On April 30 of that year, a Convention between the two countries also provided that the U.S. would indemnify France for certain claims made against it by U.S. citizens. In general, these claims involved the boarding, seizure and looting of certain U.S. merchant ships by French "ships of war" and privateers during the chaotic period following the French Revolution; 1791-1795. The Convention provided for the arbitration of such claims pursuant to its terms. Although this arbitration had helped to prevent a war with France, and obtained some justice for American merchant ship owners, five years later in 1812, the U.S. would go to war with England over similar actions against U.S. shipping.

Find a report of the French Indemnity arbitration of 1803 in an authoritative source. Give the citation to this source.

____

____

____

(a) This report contains a detailed historical summary of the background events concerning this arbitration. One of the key elements of the arbitral process was the establishment of an "American Commission" to help resolve outstanding disputes. Find the portion of this report dealing with this American Commission. Who were its members? List them and give the cite for your answer.

____

____

____

(b) Who appointed them?

____

____

(c) At the end of this report appear charts outlining the awards and rejections as issued by the "American Board" pursuant to the arbitration. One of the ships whose claim was "admitted" was the good ship *Betsey*. Indeed, it appears that the *Betsey* may have been the claimant on more than one admitted award. On the claim filed under the voyage for which Captain Moody was master, what was the total amount awarded, in French *livres*?

____

CHAPTER 5

TREATIES TO WHICH THE U.S. IS A PARTY

Part 1: Introduction and Overview

In investigating questions of treaty law, most researchers in the United States undertake different methods, depending on whether the U.S. is a party to the relevant treaty or not. Accordingly, the Research Problems in this Course Book are divided into two groups: those involving treaties to which the U.S. is a party (covered in this Chapter 5), and those involving treaties to which the U.S. is not a party (covered in Chapter 6). The other elements of Chapters 5 and 6 (that is, the "Introduction and Overview", or Part 1, of each Chapter, and the Reading Exercises for each Chapter) are not divided in this way. Parts 1 and 2 of these two Chapters simply address different aspects of treaty law more generally.

Most of the rules of public international law are either contained in treaties or developed through the process of customary international law. Among those rules that have been reduced to writing, the more voluminous source is the treaty mechanism, rather than custom. The activity of treaty-making generally results in explicit written statements of rules, and in many cases can be accomplished with relative dispatch. Customary rules, however, generally take longer periods of time to develop, may never be reduced to writing, and can be characterized by a higher degree of ambiguity and dispute. Accordingly, of the binding rules of international law enforceable at any given time, the most readily discernible tend to be the result of treaties.

It is accordingly imperative, in understanding the mechanisms of international law, to understand the mechanisms of treaties. By far the most useful tool in doing so is the study and review of the treaty that sets forth the standards by which treaties are created and interpreted. This is the Vienna Convention on the Law of Treaties, which came into force in 1980. Because this treaty contains the elemental rules on the creation and administration of treaties, it is of central importance in public international law.

In spite of this importance, the Vienna Convention has encountered resistance from a relatively large number of significant states around the world. Among these is the United States, which although a signatory has never ratified.

In spite of this failure of ratification, the U.S. Department of State has taken the position, and most authorities agree, that at least many major parts of the Vienna Convention state customary international law.

Review of the Vienna Convention's text clarifies certain important distinctions. First, of course, is the distinction between a bilateral and a multilateral treaty. Quite simply, a bilateral treaty is one that has only two parties, while a multilateral treaty has more than two parties. A more involved concept is the idea of a "convention."

Generally speaking, a convention is a kind of treaty (usually multilateral) that is negotiated in the course of a series of one or more meetings among representatives of interested states. During these meetings, the representatives discuss and dispute issues regarding how the text of the relevant document should ultimately read. This series of meetings is itself sometimes termed a "convention," in much the same sense in which the word is used when professional groups (such as attorneys or physicians) meet to discuss matters of common interest.

However, once the series of meetings has been completed, and the convening representatives have agreed on a final text, the document itself is also called a "convention." The convening representatives, or at least those of them who agree with the final written product, will then sign the convention. By their signature, though, they don't usually mean to commit the states they represent to be bound by the convention's terms. They simply mean to affirm that the document in the form signed truly represents the ultimate output of the negotiations just completed. There may also be an implicit affirmation that it is the best document that could be negotiated under the circumstances.

It is then a political decision of the various governments involved in the negotiations (and other governments as well), as to whether to then ratify the convention. That is, they need to decide whether to formally accede to the terms of the convention to make it legally binding.

The distinctive feature of a treaty that is a "convention" that it is concluded in these two distinct steps: (a) negotiation and finalization during a real-time "convention" meeting or series of meetings, and then (b) subsequent ratification by states which decide, as a distinct matter, whether to be bound. Not all multilateral treaties are necessarily conventions. Sometimes groups of states can get together and negotiate the terms of a multilateral treaty with the idea that the signatures affixed at the end of the negotiations will be binding. The result will be a simple multilateral treaty that is effective upon execution by all the negotiating parties, and therefore not a "convention" in the normal sense. But for the most significant and "high-profile" multilateral treaties, the convention procedure is usually more common.

It can be important to keep these distinctions in mind when following the course of a particular treaty as it is being negotiated and developed. In the popular press, and in popular discourse, people can sometimes say that a treaty or convention has been "signed" without realizing that this may or may not mean that the signature results in an act that legally binds the government whose representatives sign.

However, whether a treaty is bilateral or multilateral, a convention or otherwise, nevertheless has no legally significant difference in terms of its enforceability. A treaty is equally enforceable, in accordance with its terms, regardless of the category into which it falls. Similarly, which characterization applies does not affect a treaty's governance by the Vienna Convention. The Vienna Convention applies to all treaties within its scope of coverage, as defined in its introductory provisions, whether they are bilateral or multilateral, and whether they are in the form of a convention or not.

One additional aspect of multilateral treaties and conventions is worth noting in this context. A state that signs or ratifies a multilateral treaty or convention generally can, if it so chooses, ratify with a "reservation." This means that the state consents to be bound by the treaty's terms, but makes an exception as to the matters explicitly stated in the reservation. A reserving state is generally declaring that it will not be legally bound by the provisions of the treaty covered in its reservation, or that it will only so bound to the extent specified in the reservation. Articles 19-23 of the Vienna Convention deal with the formulation, treatment, and effects of these kinds of reservations.

CHAPTER 5 | **Part 2: Reading Exercises**

Student Name: ______________________________

Read and review the Vienna Convention on the Law of Treaties. This is included in the "Documents" Unit of this Course Book. Then answer the following questions based on your reading and review of Part 1 of this chapter ("Introduction and Overview") and the Vienna Convention.

1. Retrieve a current list of the States Parties to the Vienna Convention. (An electronic list can be found by clicking on "International Law" at the U.N. home page, and selecting the "Treaties" option that then appears. By then selecting, first in "English," an option for "Access to Databases," it should be relatively clear how to obtain such a list.) Provide the names of three (3) countries that in your opinion are among the most politically and economically significant countries that are *not* parties to the Vienna Convention:

   ____

   ____

   ____

2. One of the most important features of the Vienna Convention is that it contains a definition of the word "treaty."

(a) Which provision of the Vienna Convention contains this definition?

(For this and all other questions, give the Article number and, where appropriate, paragraph and/or clause number or letter.)

____

(b) This definition of the word "treaty" could be broken down into four distinct elements, for analytical purposes. These elements are stated as the first part of a prose sentence immediately prior to the Convention's statement that a treaty may be embodied in a single instrument or in two or more related instruments. See if you can state the Convention's definition of the word "treaty," using the *exact* language employed in the Convention, as a series of distinct elements:

"treaty" means:

(i) ____

(ii) ____

(iii) ____

(iv) ____

3. Under the Vienna Convention, what is the difference between a "negotiating State" and a "contracting State"?

____

____

____

____

____

On which provision of the Convention is your answer based?

____

4. Which one of the following statements is most likely to be *incorrect*?

(a) Every convention is a treaty, but not every treaty is a convention.
(b) Every convention is a multilateral treaty, but not every multilateral treaty is a convention.
(c) Every bilateral treaty is a treaty, and every convention is a treaty.
(d) Every convention is a treaty, and every treaty is a convention.

5. "True or False" Questions. For each of the following quoted statements, circle the word "True" above the statement if you believe the statement is true, and the word "False" above it if you believe it is false. In each case, in the blank above the statement and after the words, "True" and "False," indicate the provision of the Vienna Convention on which your selection is based.

(a) True False ______________________________

"If an international agreement does not conform to the definition of a 'treaty' in the Vienna Convention, the agreement has no legal force at international law."

(b) True False ______________________________

"The Vienna Convention applies to any treaty which is the constituent instrument of an international organization."

(c) True False ______________________________

"A State has the capacity to conclude treaties under the Vienna Convention, only if such State demonstrates basic characteristics of independence."

(d) True False ______________________________

"The adoption of the text of a treaty at an international conference takes place by the vote of a majority of the states present and voting."

(e) True False ____________________________

"The consent of a state to be bound by only a part of a treaty is generally effective only if the treaty so permits or the other contracting states so agree."

6. Which of the following mechanisms, assuming there are no special agreements on the point in the text of the relevant treaty, is *not* an acceptable means for a state to declare its consent to be bound by the treaty under the Vienna Convention?

(a) signature
(b) exchange of instruments constituting the treaty
(c) ratification
(d) oral confirmation of the binding effect of the treaty
(e) accession
(f) approval
(g) acceptance

On which provision of the Vienna Convention is your answer based?

____

7. Suppose that representatives of Patria attend a convention of 72 states that meets in Iowa City, Iowa to arrive at the terms of a proposed convention on international electronic data privacy. After 6 weeks of discussions and negotiations, the representatives of all 72 states agree on the text of this convention. What comes to be called "The Iowa City Convention on International Electronic Data Privacy" provides for a new international agency called the IDPC (the "International Data Protection Commission"), and states become members of this IDPC by agreeing to become parties to the Convention. The Iowa City Convention indicates that the Convention will become effective, and the IDPC will come into existence, when ten (10) states agree to become parties to the Convention by ratifying or acceding to its terms. Although Patria is one of the 72 signatories to the Convention, it has not yet ratified or acceded to the Convention. Assuming that the Vienna Convention applies, which of the following statements is more correct?

(a) Until Patria ratifies or accedes to the Iowa City Convention, its actions in the area of electronic data privacy are completely unrestricted by the Iowa City Convention.

(b) There is usually some degree of restraint on Patria's actions in this area, even before it ratifies or accedes to the Iowa City Convention.

Provision of the Vienna Convention on which your answer is based: ________________

8. Which of the following examples are more likely, and which are less likely, to be a "treaty" within the meaning of the Vienna Convention? Using a scale of 1 to 10, with "1" being least likely, and "10" being most likely, rank each of the following examples in the blanks provided.

Agreement	Ranking
(a) A document defining the borders between two states, signed by both states	________
(b) An agreement between a developing country and a multinational corporation, pursuant to which the developing country agrees not to expropriate any of the corporation's property if the corporation establishes a branch operation in the developing country	________
(c) A capitalist country declares in several press releases that if a particular communist country ceases violations of patents held by the capitalist country's nationals, the capitalist country would look favorably on the communist country when setting import tariffs; six months later the communist country issues a 10-page declaration enforcing patent protections and the capitalist country promulgates regulations reducing its average tariff rate on goods from the communist country by 50%	________
(d) The Secretary of State of the U.S., in a telephone conversation with the ruler of a "rogue state," promises to end U.S sanctions against it if the state turns over a suspected terrorist to U.S. authorities, and state turns over the suspect	________
(e) The United Nations General Assembly passes a resolution (by a vote of 97 to 68, with the other states not present or abstaining) declaring that the Members of the U.N. solemnly condemn child labor, and proclaim that child labor violates basic human rights	________
(f) Six states sign a document in which each state declares its undying respect and admiration for the others, together with its	

concern for their safety, and each state promises to take very seriously any threat to the peace and security of any of the others

(g) Six states sign a document in which each state declares itself to be the permanent military ally of the others, also explicitly guaranteeing the safety of the others with its own military resources, and each state promises to send troops to the defense of any of the others immediately upon the occurrence of an armed attack, or upon the request of any of the others

(h) The World Bank enters into a 120-page loan agreement with a particular state, pursuant to which the Bank agrees to lend the state $75 million, and the state agrees to use the loan proceeds to build new irrigation projects, profits from which will be employed to repay the loan

(i) 73 states sign a document pursuant to which each state promises that it will refrain from allowing its nationals to transport toxic waste into the territory of any of the others; the prohibited levels of toxicity are explicitly defined in detail, and required punishments for nationals of each state attempting to violate the restrictions are prescribed

(j) The United Nations organization signs an agreement with a state, pursuant to which the state agrees to lease several parcels of land to the United Nations for the purpose of building a new headquarters and testing areas for a special agricultural development project

9. "True or False" Questions. For each of the following quoted statements, circle the word "True" above the statement if you believe the statement is true, and the word "False" above it if you believe it is false. In each case, in the blank above the statement and after the words, "True" and "False," indicate the provision of the Vienna Convention on which your selection is based.

(a) True False ______________________________

"Generally, states becoming signatories or parties to a treaty may not make reservations regarding the treaty unless the terms of the treaty specifically allow for reservations."

(b) True False ______________________________

"A reserving state may generally withdraw its reservation at any time, with or without the consent of any states that may have accepted its reservation, unless the relevant treaty otherwise provides."

10. Suppose that Patria is considering entering into a treaty with all the states of South America requiring each party to the treaty to extend Most-Favored-Nation treatment to all other parties. Patria would like to enter into the treaty in order to get the favorable "MFN" treatment from the other parties to the treaty. However, due to a history of bitter political rivalries, Patria does not want to extend MFN treatment to Brazil. Assume that the text of the treaty makes no mention of reservations or exceptions, and that the Vienna Convention applies. If Patria enters into the treaty, and makes a reservation to the effect that the obligations of the treaty will not bind Patria with respect to Brazil, which of the following statements is most likely to be correct?

(a) Patria is not permitted to make the reservation if it is incompatible with the object and purpose of the treaty.

(b) In order for Patria's reservation to be valid, Brazil must provide its written consent.

(c) If Brazil does not accept Patria's reservation, Patria can still make the reservation, but any other party to the treaty that has not previously made such a reservation for Brazil can refuse to apply the treaty's terms as between itself and Brazil.

Citation of authority for your answer:

____

CHAPTER 5	Part 3: Guidance for Research

Treaty research is not easy; but the finding tools and resources used are far more consistent and better organized than those for the other types of international law documents with which you have been dealing. In doing treaty research, the first strategy must be to determine whether the U.S. is a party, since the tools and techniques will differ substantially if this is not the case. Below is a list of standard resources, both hard-copy and electronic, which will be available to you in most academic libraries. Please note that many of the hard-copy resources are United States government documents and are classified with very different-looking call numbers (e.g., S9.10) than other materials. Additionally, several of these resources are generally maintained in microform. The most significant development in treaty research as in other international law documentation is the expansion of electronic sources, both proprietary and on the Internet. By no means, however, can one ignore the hard-copy sources.

Official Sources

The first official United States government publication of a treaty or other international agreement is in the form of a TIAS (*Treaties and Other International Acts Series)* print or slip copy. They are then published in the UST volumes, as described below. TIAS is acceptable in courts as evidence of the treaty or agreement in accordance with 1 U.S.C. Section 113. TIAS texts are thus primarily available in two official forms:

> *Treaties and Other International Acts Series.* (TIAS) Washington D.C.: Dept. of State, GPO, 1946-. Published first as pamphlets. First *official* source of U.S. treaties; however, there is a nine to ten year delay in publication after ratification by the Senate.
>
> *United States Treaties and Other International Agreements* (UST). v. 1-, 1950-. Official source 8 to 10 years out of date; indexes up to 15 yrs. out of date. This publication starts (1950) where Bevans (see below) stops.

Electronic Versions

"Treaties on LEXIS," is a single database combining TIAS, UST, and Bevans in one file, i.e., coverage of treaties from 1776 to date.

Westlaw describes its comparable database as: [Derived from] "Print publications United States Statutes at Large and United States Treaties and Other International Agreements as well as Slip Copy obtained directly from the federal government for Westlaw."

> The Oceana online database describes its content as:
> Treaties and International Agreements Online is a full text database containing over 10,000 treaties and agreements to which the U.S. is a party. The collection spans 220 years of U.S. international relations, beginning with the 1783 Treaty of Paris. Major topics include defense, trade, scientific and economic cooperation, finance, investment and aviation. New materials are added on a monthly basis. Documents are retained in the database as they go out of force; unratified treaties are also included. Nongovernmental relations with Taiwan are addressed with the inclusion of 160 agreements between the American Institute in Taiwan and the Taipei Economic and Cultural Representative Office in the United States. Editorial notes are provided by Erwin Surrency, Professor of Law and Director of Law Library, Emeritus at the University of Georgia.
> Treaties and International Agreements Online also contains over 1800 bilateral tax treaties between 280 countries and international organizations. Among the main topic areas covered are taxation of income, capital, estates and gifts and shipping and aircraft. Most documents contain concise annotations. Coverage includes treaties to which the U.S. is not a party. Annotations are provided under special arrangement with Walter and Dorothy Diamond.

Treaties and agreements are searchable by number, date, parties and full text keyword searches. Links to full text of the documents retrieved in the search are provided.

HeinOnline is the newest entry in the proprietary online treaty services. Subscribers to the online journals service can subscribe separately to the "Treaties and Agreements Library." It is very comprehensive; covering UST, TIAS, Bevans, *Treaties in Force 1955-2003* (see below), the *Guide to Treaties in Force 1982-2003* and *International Legal Materials 1962-2002,* Miller and Malloy. (See below.) An electronic version of the KAV indices is also available. Hein can be expected to keep the electronic files very current.

The search engine for HeinOnline Treaties and Agreements Library is very similar to that for the Oceana online database. One may search by treaty number, date, parties and full text Boolean keyword searching. Links are given to retrieve the full text of the documents. (PDF files.)

Acceptance by the courts of the electronic versions, even though taken from an official source, would still be at the discretion of the court.

Historical Collections

United States Statutes at Large. Washington D.C.: GPO, 1789-1845-. Note: Official source of U.S. treaties up to 1950. Beginning in 1950 treaties and international agreements were issued by the GPO as *United States Treaties and Other International Agreements. (UST)*

Bevans, Charles T., *Treaties and Other International Agreements of the United States of America, 1776-1949.*

Consolidated Treaties & International Agreements: Current Document Service. Edwin C. Surrency (ed.) Dobbs Ferry, N.Y.,: Oceana Pubs., Inc., 1990-97. Attempted to publish within 90 days of release or ratification, both executive agreements and formal treaties; accompanied by index binders.

Note: See description of the Oceana online database above which covers this material and expands on it.

Treaties and Other International Acts of the United States of America. Hunter Miller (ed.) Washington D.C.: GPO, *1931*.

Treaty Finding Tools (Hard Copy)

Treaties in Force: A List of Treaties and Other International Agreements of the United States in Force on January 1. Washington D.C.: US GPO, 1968-. Does not include treaties no longer in force; provides information as to parties, acceptance with reservations and termination of acceptance.: Gov Docs

A Guide to the United States Treaties in Force. Buffalo, N.Y.: W.S. Hein Co., 1983-. This is a helpful companion to the government publication described above.

United States Treaty Index: 1776-1990 Consolidation: Master Guide. Igor I. Kavass (ed. & comp.) Buffalo, N.Y.: W. S. Hein, 1991-. (updated by Current Treaty Index)

Current (Unofficial)

International Legal Materials (ILM) also available on-line through Lexis,Westlaw and HeinOnline. It is a frequently cited *unofficial* source of treaties.

Finding Tools (Electronic)

As noted above, several electronic versions of the US treaties are available which give access to the full text of treaties via comprehensive search engines.

Internet Sites:

Guide to Researching U.S. Treaties and Agreements (LLRX)
http://www.llrx.com/features/ustreaty.htm
Librarian Marci Hoffman provides a thorough guide, with links, to finding U.S. Treaties.

Treaties in Force
http://www.state.gov/s/l/c8455.htm
Most recent edition of the U.S. State Department's compilation of Treaties in Force.

Treaties in Force Jan 1, 2000
http://www.state.gov/www/global/legal_affairs/tifindex.html
This is the most current version available on the Web. The Bush Administration removed the January, 2001 version from the Web.

U.S. Senate Treaties Page
http://www.senate.gov/pagelayout/legislative/d_three_sections_with_teasers/treaties.htm
Status of treaties under consideration during the current legislative session.

Citation Rules:

Blue Book rules 21.1 et seq. cover treaties and international agreements. See also Rule 18 for citing to electronic sources.

The ALWD Citation Manual 2nd edition also covers treaties in its Chapter 21, and electronic sources in Chapters 38, 39, and 40.

CHAPTER 5	Part 4: Research Problems

The following Research Problems involve treaties or conventions to which the United States is a party.

Perform the necessary investigation and research to answer these questions. In the course of your investigation, you may use whatever combination of electronic and hard-copy research you find to be most suitable for you. However, your final answer should in each case requiring citations be to the most authoritative hard-copy source available.

1. There is no general obligation to extradite at customary international law. Accordingly, most legal obligations requiring states to extradite criminals or suspected criminals are contained in bilateral extradition treaties. The United States has currently effective extradition treaties with most major countries of the world, including (for example) Israel.

   (a) Find the text of the extradition treaty between the United States and Israel in an authoritative source.

   (b) Research Questions:

      (i) When did this treaty enter into force?

      ____

      (ii) Under the terms of this treaty, can a person be extradited solely for a crime related to traffic in illegal firearms? Which provision of the treaty provides the answer?

      ____

      ____

      ____

(c) Supply a correct "Bluebook" citation to this treaty in an authoritative source.

2. Does the United States currently have an extradition treaty with Singapore?

(a) If not, what source indicates the absence of such a treaty?

(b) If so, provide a correct "Bluebook" citation to the treaty in an authoritative source and indicate the date it came into force.

3. The North Atlantic Treaty Organization, or "NATO", is the most influential collective defense alliance of the modern world. Initiated in the context of the end of World War II, the organization assures the mutual defense of the United States, Canada, and most of the countries of Europe. During the Cold War, members of NATO were generally thought of as "the West," and sometimes the "First World," while members of the Soviet-led "Warsaw Pact" were generally thought of as "the East," and sometimes the "Second World." With the disintegration of the Soviet Union and the devolution of power in Eastern Europe, the Warsaw Pact has become defunct. NATO is still very much alive, however, and is still governed according to the provisions of the 1949 treaty that was its founding instrument.

(a) Find the text of the North Atlantic Treaty in an authoritative source.

(b) Research Questions:

(i) The key feature of NATO is that each of the members agrees to consider an armed attack against one member in Europe or North America as an armed attack against all. Which provision of the treaty states this principle? (Also provide a page cite to this provision.)

____

(ii) Twelve countries initially signed the treaty in 1949. How many additional countries have become fully-vested members since them? What are they?

____

____

____

____

(c) Provide a correct "Bluebook" citation to the North Atlantic Treaty in an authoritative source.

____

____

____

4. Which treaty has been assigned TIAS Number 7542?

____

____

(a) Research Questions:

(i) In how many languages is the treaty authentic? What are they?

(ii) How many parties signed the treaty? Who are/were they?

(b) Supply a correct "Bluebook" citation to the treaty in an authoritative source.

5. The International Covenant for Civil and Political Rights was adopted by the U.N. General Assembly on December 16, 1966. Since then 125 states have ratified, or otherwise become parties to, the Covenant. Many commentators regard it as one of the most significant documents in international human rights law.

(a) Find the text of the Covenant in its most authoritative source.

(b) Research Questions:

(i) In which languages is the Covenant's text authentic?

____

____

____

(ii) On what date was the Covenant "registered"?

____

(c) Supply a correct "Bluebook" citation to the Covenant in its most authoritative source.

____

____

____

CHAPTER 6

TREATIES TO WHICH THE U.S. IS NOT A PARTY

Part 1: Introduction and Overview

The United States is one of the most influential actors on the world stage, but not all international obligations necessarily involve the U.S. In particular, numerous treaties, both bilateral and multilateral, are signed and ratified each year to which the U.S. is not a party. Although this is a common occurrence, authoritative texts of such treaties can be more difficult for researchers in the U.S. to locate. The research portions of this Chapter 6 (Parts 3 and 4) address the means of doing this, and provide exercises to supply experience in doing so.

For purposes of this "Introduction and Overview" in this Part 1, however, we will continue our general review of the Vienna Convention on the Law of Treaties. The Vienna Convention is significant in its own right as an international law text, but also as a background document for the general framework of international law. Accordingly, the next part of this Chapter, the "Reading Exercises," also continues our general examination of the Vienna Convention.

Many of the Reading Exercises in Part 2 focus specifically on the relationship between U.S. federal law and the Vienna Convention. A fundamental set of issues concerns the procedures through which the U.S. signs and ratifies treaties. Pursuant to Article II, Section 2 of the U.S. Constitution, international treaties are to be negotiated and signed by the President, and then ratified by the Senate. This provision is often called the "Advice and Consent Clause."

In reality, of course, it is generally not the President (that is, the individual man or woman occupying the White House) who negotiates the treaties. Rather, employees and officers of the U.S., usually within the State Department, represent the President in the negotiations. However, since all such officers and employees are ultimately responsible to the President (or to people who are), as a conceptual matter it is usually said that the President both negotiates and signs treaties on behalf of the U.S.

Pursuant to the Advice and Consent Clause, when ratifying a treaty, the Senate must vote to approve the treaty by a 2/3 majority. A treaty negotiated by the President and ratified by the Senate by this 2/3 majority vote is often called an "Article II Treaty," a reference to the location of the Advice and Consent Clause in Article II of the Constitution. It is worth pointing out that the framers specified that only the Senate, as the "upper house" of the national legislature, would have this Advice and Consent authority, and not the House of Representatives or the Congress acting as a whole.

The Advice and Consent Clause also requires the Senate to confirm the President's appointment of ambassadors, ministers and consuls (as well as judges of the federal courts and other officers of the U.S.). However, when the Senate confirms these appointments of individuals to federal positions, only a simple majority vote is required. The 2/3 "super-majority" requirement only pertains to the ratification of a treaty.

Reference might be made at this point to the two different senses of the word, "ratification." In the preceding Chapter 5, we saw that (under international law) multilateral conventions rely on a system of "ratification" to establish which states are legally bound to the conventions. In this sense, only multilateral conventions are subject to this kind of "ratification" requirement. Bilateral treaties, for example, generally do not necessarily need to be ratified in this sense; their mere signature by the two parties indicates an intent to be bound.

However, as a matter of U.S. domestic law, all Article II Treaties must be ratified by the Senate. So, even if the President concludes a mere bilateral treaty with another state, that treaty needs to be ratified by the Senate under the Advice and Consent Clause if it is to be an Article II Treaty. Thus, the term "ratification" has two different and somewhat distinct senses: one in the context of the international enforceability of multilateral conventions, and the other in the context of the domestic enforceability of all Article II Treaties, whether bilateral or multilateral.

Another issue involving the relationship between U.S. constitutional law and international law is of significant interest, at least theoretically. This is the question of whether the President, with advice and consent of the Senate, can enter into an international treaty that would not be consistent with the U.S. Constitution if enacted as a mere federal statute. The question presents itself because the wording of Article VI, clause 2 of the Constitution, the so-called "Supremacy Clause", can be read to be ambiguous on the point.

Indeed, the U.S. Supreme Court has never squarely and clearly held, in a majority opinion, that treaties must, as a matter of U.S. domestic law, be consistent with the terms of the Federal Constitution. Nevertheless, many authorities on the U.S. Constitution have taken the position that, at least as a matter of domestic law, treaties entered into by the U.S. must be subject to the terms of the Constitution.

The result of this discussion as a matter of U.S. domestic constitutional law need not determine the position of the U.S. in such a case for purposes of international law. In other words, if it is indeed determined that a treaty that violated the U.S. Constitution was invalid within the borders of the U.S., that would not necessarily prevent the U.S. from being considered in violation of its international-law obligations under the treaty. The obligations imposed on the U.S. by international law and by its Federal Constitution are separate and distinct, and there is no conceptual guarantee that in any given case the legal position of the U.S. would be the same under both. The Vienna Convention does have something to say about this part of the issue, and particular questions in the Reading Exercises explore this matter further.

CHAPTER 6	Part 2: Reading Exercises

Student Name: ______________________________

Like the Reading Exercises for Chapter 5, these Exercises pertain to the Vienna Convention on the Law of Treaties, included in Part B, the "Documents" section, of this Course Book.

1. Article 26 of the Vienna Convention contains perhaps the most significant rule stated in the entire Convention. This is often referred to by a Latin phrase; the rule of *pacta sunt servanda*. In the blank provided, state the rule of *pacta sunt servanda* using the precise language given in Article 26 of the Vienna Convention.

   ____
   ____
   ____

2. Suppose President Herbert Shrub is in the final months of the term of his presidency of the United States. He executes, and a compliant Senate ratifies, a treaty with Saudi Arabia pursuant to which each country agrees to impose severe criminal penalties on any of its nationals who publicly criticizes the government of the other. Shrub loses the next election to an opposition candidate and control of the Senate shifts to the party previously in opposition.

   (a) Suppose the new U.S. administration dislikes the recently adopted "non-criticism treaty;" the incoming administration believes that since it was the former administration that signed the agreement and procured its ratification, and there is now a new administration, the agreement should not be effective. The new Secretary of State would accordingly like to be able to inform her counterpart for the Saudi government that, in the eyes of the U.S. the treaty is no longer binding.

Assume that in that situation the Saudi government would make an argument against such a position of the U.S., using the rule of *pacta sunt servanda*. State briefly what that argument would be.

____
____
____
____

(b) The new Secretary of State would like to argue that the "non-criticism treaty" *cannot* be binding on the U.S., because its terms are inconsistent with internal U.S. law (the Free Speech clause of the First Amendment), and that therefore the treaty was invalid as against the U.S. from the treaty's inception. Under the Vienna Convention, would this be a strong argument? (Refer to any provisions of the Convention that might be relevant to your answer.)

____
____
____
____

(c) Suppose that according to the text of the "non-criticism treaty," it entered into force on November 25. Suppose also that on the immediately preceding September 15, a U.S. national published an opinion essay in *The New York Times* that the Saudi government considers to be a vile and outrageous libel of its officers. This author's statements fall well within the definition of "criticism of government" contained within the treaty. The Saudis insist that this person be punished in accordance with the treaty notwithstanding the fact that the treaty entered into force after the offending statements were published. Assume that the non-criticism treaty does not address this issue by its terms, and that the questions raised in paragraphs (a) and (b) above are not at issue here. Are the Saudis likely to succeed with an argument to the effect that the Vienna Convention binds the U.S. to punish the offending author in this case? (Why or why not? Based on what provision(s) of the Vienna Convention?)

____
____
____
____

3. The meaning of a treaty is not always completely clear simply from its text; possible ambiguities can arise even from the simplest language in a treaty. Accordingly, the Vienna Convention sets forth certain rules to guide in the interpretation of treaties. Which of the following techniques of interpretation does the Vienna Convention treat as "general" rules of interpretation, and which does the Convention state to be "supplementary" rules of interpretation? (In the blank following each selection, indicate "general" or "supplementary," and the provision of the Convention on which your answer is based.)

   (a) interpretation in accordance with any agreement relating to the treaty which was made between all the parties in connection with the conclusion of the treaty;

   ____

   ____

   (b) interpretation in accordance with a good faith reading of the ordinary meaning of the terms of the treaty in their context;

   ____

   ____

   (c) interpretation in accordance with the preparatory work of the treaty;

   ____

   ____

   (d) interpretation in accordance with any subsequent agreement between the parties regarding the application of the provisions of the treaty;

   ____

   ____

4. Armenia and Azerbaijan are two neighboring countries located on the slopes of the Caucusus mountains between the Black Sea and the Caspian Sea. Within the Western part of Azerbaijan (near the Armenian border) is an enclave, completely surrounded by the rest of Azerbaijan, called "Nagorno-Karabakh." For many years, Nagorno-Karabakh, although within Azerbaijan, was populated largely by ethnic Armenians. Armenian troops crossed over into Western Azerbaijan during the early 1990's, and took military control of Nagorno-Karabakh and much of Western Azerbaijan. Now Armenia treats Nagorno-Karabakh as no longer part of Azerbaijan. Suppose Armenia

and Azerbaijan enter into a bilateral written agreement, in which they each recognize Nagorno-Karabakh as an independent state and Armenia promises to withdraw from all Azerbaijan territory. However, under the treaty, the recognition and withdrawal obligation are conditional on the new state including in a new written constitution, the complete renunciation of all claims to unification either with Armenia or Azerbaijan. This is the only provision of the treaty that refers to any actions whatever to be taken by the new state. Which of the following statements is most likely to be correct?

(a) The Armenia-Azerbaijan treaty cannot be effective to any extent unless and until the new state of Nagorno-Karabakh gives its express consent thereto in writing.

(b) The consent of Nagorno-Karabakh to the Armenia-Azerbaijan treaty would in all cases be presumed.

(c) The extent to which Nagorno-Karabakh can claim rights under the Armenia-Azerbaijan treaty may depend on whether Nagorno-Karabakh makes the referenced renunciation.

(d) Whether Nagorno-Karabakh makes the referenced renunciation is irrelevant to the question of whether it can claim rights under the Armenia-Azerbaijan treaty.

On which provision(s) of the Vienna Convention is your answer based?

____

____

5. Regarding the amendment of a multilateral treaty, and with special regard to Article 40 of the Vienna Convention, which of the following statements is least correct?

(a) If a multilateral treaty is amended, all parties to the original treaty must be parties to the treaty as amended in order for the amendment to be effective as between any of them.

(b) If a multilateral treaty is amended, any two or more parties to the original treaty can join in the amendment, and the amendment will in all cases be effective as between them; it simply will not be effective with respect to any parties to the original treaty that choose not to enter into the amended version.

(c) If a multilateral treaty is amended, any third state not previously party to the original treaty that becomes a party to the amended treaty is viewed as a party to the amended treaty, but may have rights or obligations with respect to states parties to the original treaty that do not join the amended treaty.

(d) If a multilateral treaty is amended, the effectiveness of the amended treaty might be affected by the extent to which all the states parties to the original treaty had been informed of the proposed amendment, and whether all states entitled to join in the amendment had been given the opportunity to do so.

6. Article 46 of the Vienna Convention sets forth the circumstances under which non-compliance with provisions of the internal law of a particular state regarding competence to conclude treaties can serve as a basis for invalidating that state's consent to a treaty. In the following cases regarding the purported ratification of a multilateral treaty by the United States, and assuming that the U.S. were a party to the Vienna Convention, would Article 46 furnish a basis for invalidating U.S. consent to the treaty?

(a) The President signs the treaty, but the Senate never votes on it. Instead, the House of Representatives votes on the treaty and approves it. These events become generally known in the international community. The then-current U.S. Secretary of State declares that the U.S. has effectively consented to the treaty. At a later point in time, after a change in U.S. Presidential Administrations, other signatories to the treaty demand that the U.S. comply with its terms. The new Secretary of State argues that U.S. consent was invalid.

(b) The President signs the treaty, and the Senate votes to ratify by a 51% majority. These events become generally known to the international community. The then-current U.S. Secretary of State declares that the U.S. has effectively consented to the treaty. At a later point in time, after a change in U.S. Presidential Administrations, other signatories to the treaty demand that the U.S. comply with its terms. The new Secretary of State argues that U.S. consent was invalid.

(c) The President signs the treaty, and the Senate votes to ratify by a 67% majority. However, the committee that had reported on the treaty was the Senate Committee on Finance, rather than the Senate Committee on Foreign Affairs. Assume that a U.S. federal statute required this action by the latter committee. The then-current U.S. Secretary of State declares that the U.S. has effectively consented to the treaty. At a later point in time, after a change in U.S. Presidential Administrations, other signatories to the treaty demand that the U.S. comply with its terms. The new Secretary of State argues that U.S. consent was invalid.

7. Article 53 of the Vienna Convention refers to "peremptory norms of general international law" (the so-called "*jus cogens*"). Which of the following treaties might be most vulnerable to the assertion that it conflicts with a peremptory norm of general international law?

(a) A treaty between two states requiring that the diplomatic personnel of each state who are accredited to the other state must reside in special segregated areas in the capital city of the receiving state, in which only diplomatic personnel from foreign countries are permitted to reside.

(b) A multilateral convention setting forth a list of circumstances, meticulously delineated but broad in scope, in which it would be permissible for each party to the convention to engage in torture of prisoners to obtain information vital to state security.

(c) A treaty between two states declaring that any persons holding dual nationality of the two states shall be subject simultaneously to annual income tax liability in both states, without credit in either state for payments made to the other.

(d) A multilateral treaty between five states, in which each agrees that it will not accept any immigrants from any of the others for a period of 10 years.

8. Questions 6 and 7 above have dealt with two bases on which treaties can be considered invalid under the Vienna Convention: (a) non-compliance with internal law regarding competence to conclude treaties and (b) violation of *jus cogens*. The Vienna Convention explicitly sets forth other bases on which treaties may be considered invalid, in provisions of the Convention placed between these two in the Convention's text. What are some of the other bases under the Vienna Convention on which treaties can be considered invalid?

____
____
____
____
____
____

9. "True or False" Questions. For each of the following quoted statements, circle the word "True" above the statement if you believe the statement is true, and the word "False" above it if you believe it is false. In each case, in the blank above the statement and after the words, "True" and "False," indicate the provision of the Vienna Convention on which your selection is based.

(a) True False ________________________________

"In the case of a multilateral treaty that required a minimum number of states to be parties for its effectiveness, if a large enough number of states withdraws from the treaty so that the number of parties falls below the number initially required for its effectiveness, the result is always that the treaty becomes null and void."

(b) True False ________________________________

"A treaty is considered terminated if all parties to it enter into a subsequent treaty covering the same issues whose text is so inconsistent with the original treaty that the two agreements cannot be honored at the same time."

(c) True False ________________________________

> "A material violation of a multilateral treaty by one of the parties to the treaty allows the remaining states in some cases to suspend or terminate the operation of the treaty with regard to the offending state, but never allows the remaining states to otherwise suspend or terminate the treaty with respect to any other parties."

10. The international law of treaties contains a doctrine sometimes known by the Latin name, "*rebus sic stantibus*." Under this doctrine, states can be excused from the performance of their obligations under treaties when the underlying factual circumstances have changed in particular ways. Under Part V, Section 3 of the Vienna Convention, which of the following changes in circumstances is least likely to allow a party to a treaty to escape its obligations under the treaty?

    (a) Performance of the obligations has become impossible because of the permanent disappearance or destruction of an object indispensable for the execution of the treaty.

    (b) A fundamental change of circumstances has occurred that was not foreseen by the parties, the existence of the prior circumstances constituted an essential basis of the parties' consent to the treaty, and the effect of the change is materially to transform the extent of the obligations still to be performed under the treaty.

    (c) Diplomatic relations between the parties to the treaty have been severed, and the existence of such diplomatic relations is indispensable for the application of the treaty.

    (d) A new peremptory norm of general international law has emerged that is in conflict with the treaty.

CHAPTER 6

Part 3: Guidance for Research

In today's increasingly smaller world, access to state papers such as treaties and international agreements to which the United States is not a party has never been more critical. Unfortunately, these documents have never been organized and indexed to the same level as U.S. materials. Nor have they been comprehensively collected by any but the largest libraries. Retrieving them has been an ongoing challenge for international law librarians until very recently.

Since 1945, the situation has much improved due to the efforts of the United Nations Secretariat. As noted in Chapter1, Article 102(1) of the United Nations Charter mandates that "Every treaty and every international agreement entered into by any Member of the United Nations . . . shall as soon as possible be registered with the Secretariat and published by it." Further, Paragraph Two states that if registration is not completed, "no party may invoke that treaty or agreement before any organ of the United Nations."

Today, treaties and agreements registered with the United Nations are available in both hard-copy and microform in the U.N. Depository Libraries and many academic libraries. Indices are available in hard copy, microform and CD-ROM.

But by far the most helpful development in this type of treaty research has been the creation and improvement of the online U.N. Treaty Collection. This electronic file contains over 40,000 documents incrementing each day. Once free, it is now available only by subscription and licensing terms restrict its use to the subscriber's site, e.g. on-campus use at a law school or university.

The current search engine, while it does not rise to the effectiveness of Google or LexisNexis and Westlaw, permits you to search by keyword, date, type of agreement, parties and U.N. Registration Number. Among the several databases offered by the U.N. electronic product are the cumulative indices, the League of Nations Treaties 1920-1945, and several "status files" which list treaties deposited with the Secretariat, along with some indication of signatories and thus the progress of the treaty toward effectiveness.

Although the U.N. online product is a tremendously valuable resource, it suffers from a lack of timeliness. For very current treaty developments, researchers need to use other sources such as International Legal Materials (available on Westlaw and LexisNexis). ILM contains the text of many non-U.S. treaties which have been signed and also drafts of treaties. Neither ILM nor the U.N. claims that their files are totally comprehensive.

The timeliest sources of treaties are the government gazettes such as Germany's *Bundesgesetzblatt.* These are published in hard-copy by many countries. These publications contain texts of treaties and descriptions of their implementation. They are often very difficult to obtain since only the largest libraries subscribe to them. However, an increasing number of countries are publishing an electronic version of their gazette on the Internet. The University of Michigan compiles a list of these with their URL's at a special web site:

http://www.lib.umich.edu/govdocs/gazettes/index.htm.

Another problem for researchers is the fact that these gazettes are published in the language of the issuing government. Unlike the U.N. documents, there are no English translations at this early stage. Like many electronic sources, these do not go back in time much farther than 2000. This is not a serious disadvantage since earlier treaties hopefully will appear at the U.N. site.

Hard-Copy/Microform Resources

With the exception of the League of Nations treaties contained within the U.N. online Treaty Collection, almost none of the electronic treaty databases contain materials earlier than 1945-46. Exceptions to this are the digitized collections of important treaties which are being published on the Internet by several universities. One valuable site is Yale's Avalon Collection http://www.yale.edu/lawweb/avalon/avalon/htm. Here you will find treaties promulgated outside the League of Nations during the period between World War I and II. There are a number of others, often covering treaties in one subject area such as economics or the environment. There is a strong movement towards digitizing early material and one can expect to find more of it appearing on the Internet.

The primary sources for earlier treaties are collections such as Clive Parry's *Consolidated Treaty Series*, Clive Parry, ed., Dobbs Ferry, NY, Oceana Pubs, Inc. 1969-81. This very large set (over 200 volumes) contains the text of treaties from 1648 to the establishment of the League of Nations (1920). The text is offered in the original language with one or more translations—usually French and English. There is a five volume index available which may be searched by country, title and date.

Treaties, as noted above, which concern a specific area of the law are often reprinted in treatises on that substantive area. An example is *Basic Documents of International Economic Law,* Stephen Zamora & Ronald A. Brand (eds), Chicago: CCH International, 1990. A more general collection of basic treaties can be found in Ian Brownlie's *Basic Documents in International Law*, published by Oxford University Press from 1989-2002.

In addition, many countries publish collections of treaties to which they are a party. An example is the *United Kingdom Treaty Series* (1892-). International organizations such as the Organization of American States (OAS) also publish collections of the most important treaties. Some of these are beginning to appear on the Internet e.g. www.oas.org/juridico/english/treaties.html. Certainly the Internet is a good place to start searching.

Finding Tools

There are many of these, pre-dating the advent of electronic searching. These publications do not contain the text of treaties but give sources for them ranging from state paper collections to microform series. Locating the text of a treaty may involve searching in one of these tools and then locating a library which holds the source via university catalogs or World-Cat. At this point, the Inter-Library Loan Librarian becomes a vital partner in your research.

One of the most prominent of these finding tools is the multi-volume *Index to Multilateral Treaties: A chronological list of multi-party international agreements from the sixteenth century through 1963 with citations to their texts.* V. Mostecky, (ed). Cambridge, Mass: Harvard Law School Library Publications, 1965. Distributed by Oceana Pubs, Inc. There are supplements for 1966-1968. The order of entries is strictly chronological, but subject and regional indexes are also provided. This is considered one of the very best sources for locating obscure treaties. The first treaty listed is dated 1596.

Although published by another publisher, *World Treaty Index,* Peter H. Rohn, 2nd ed, Santa Barbara, CA: ABC-Clio Information Services, carries on the indexing and locating of treaties 1900-1980. The main volumes list treaties in chronological order, but there are also party and subject indices as well as other useful features such as a table of abbreviations for the sources listed. This volume is particularly helpful in finding the citations for the UNTS and LNTS series.

Another useful and recently developed resource is the Electronic Information System for International Law (or "EISIL"), prepared and maintained by the ASIL. Its URL is http://www.eisil.org. It covers treaty collections and other databases, and includes many links to other sites, at which primary and secondary documents can be found.

CHAPTER 6	Part 4: Research Problems

Student Name: ______________________________

The following Research Problems involve treaties or conventions to which the United States is not a party.

Perform the necessary investigation and research to answer these questions. In the course of your investigation, you may use whatever combination of electronic and hard-copy research that you find to be most suitable for you. However, your final answer should in each case requiring citations be to the most authoritative hard-copy source available.

1. The Congress of Vienna, meeting from 1814 through 1815, was called by the leading European powers upon the conclusion of the Napoleonic wars. One of the chief purposes of the Congress was to re-draw the political map of Europe after the trauma of Napoleon's ill-fated conquests. The Congress stated the results of its deliberations in various international agreements, but the most fundamental and wide-ranging was the general "Act of the Congress of Vienna." Although far from perfect, this document proved to be the most important international agreement of the 19th century, and helped lay the groundwork for peace in Europe for nearly 100 years.

   (a) Find the text of the Act of the Congress of Vienna at an authoritative source.

   (b) Research Questions:

      (i) In what language is the text provided at this source?

      ____

      (ii) Eight countries took part in the negotiations at the Congress of Vienna, but only seven of those countries actually signed the "Act." From your review of the text at this source, can you determine which one of the eight states taking part in the Conference did not sign the "Act"?

____

(c) Supply a correct Bluebook citation to the "Act" at this source.

____
____
____

2. During the Cold War, the political map of the world was roughly divided into two camps, "East" and "West." Broadly speaking, the western portion of the map consisted of the United States and its allies, while the eastern portion consisted of the Soviet Union and its allies. We have seen earlier in our work for this course that the western alliance was built on the North Atlantic Treaty, and we have had occasion to review the terms of this treaty. The eastern alliance was in turn founded on a treaty that was known as the "Warsaw Pact." Like the North Atlantic Treaty, the Warsaw Pact was a multilateral treaty providing for a defensive military and security alliance among the states signatories.

(a) Find the text of the Warsaw Pact at its most authoritative source.

(b) Research Questions:

(i) Which states were the original signatories to the Pact?

____
____
____

(ii) The Warsaw Pact was executed in Russian, Polish, Czech and German, all texts being equally authentic. At this most authoritative source, all four texts are reproduced, along with English and French translations. At which page of this source does each text begin?

Russian: ________	German: ________
Polish: ________	English: ________
Czech: ________	French: ________

(c) Supply a correct Bluebook citation to the Pact at this source:

____
____
____

3. The Franco-Prussian War began with a formal declaration of war by France against Prussia on July 18, 1870. The initiating events involved a disagreement over who should succeed to the vacant throne of Spain, but the conflict really concerned broader issues involving the balance of power on the European continent. The coalition of German states that fought on the Prussian side proved far more capable than the French forces, and ultimately France was forced to sign a humiliating Armistice Agreement. The Armistice was signed during negotiations from January 28 through February 16, 1871. The Armistice had the effect of dislodging the "Second Empire" in France, which was replaced by the "Third Republic." It also resulted in the transfer of Alsace and Lorraine to Germany. Accordingly, the seeds were sown for continuing enmity between the two powers, which came to such repeatedly violent consequences during the 20th century.

(a) Find the text of the Armistice Convention ending the Franco-Prussian War at an authoritative source.

(b) Research Questions:

At most sources, the most readily available text of the Armistice Agreement is in French, but key elements concerning it can be discernable even if one does not possess knowledge of French.

(i) What is the date of the Armistice Convention itself, and in what city was it signed?

____
____

(ii) The signatory for the German Confederation was Otto von Bismarck. Who was the signatory for France?

____

(c) Supply a correct Bluebook citation to the Armistice at this source:

____
____
____

4. On September 29, 1938, four nations—Germany, the United Kingdom, France and Italy—signed a treaty at Munich which some still consider a symbol of the futility of appeasing a dictator fixated on world dominance. Known as the Munich Pact, the agreement dismembered Czechoslovakia, encouraged Hitler's dreams of a "Greater Germany" and tragically did not achieve "peace in our time." The German invasion of Poland that effectively started World War II took place less than a year later.

(a) Find a text of the Munich Pact.

(b) Research Questions:

(i) Who were the individuals who signed the Pact, and what was the position of each at the time?

(A) ____________________________________
(B) ____________________________________
(C) ____________________________________
(D) ____________________________________

(ii) In Article 6 of the Pact, there is language that foreshadows the "ethnic cleansing" practiced by Serbia in the 1990's. What is this language?

____
____

(c) Supply a correct Bluebook citation to the Pact at this source:

5. Although recent events in the Middle East have diminished its luster, the signing of a peace treaty between Egypt and Israel in 1979 remains a triumph of statesmanship. Based on what became known as the Camp David Accords, these negotiations and other efforts would win the 2000 Nobel Peace Prize for Jimmy Carter.

(a) Find the text of the text of the 1979 treaty at an authoritative source.

(b) Research Questions:

(i) In this treaty, Israel agreed to withdraw all its armed forces and civilians from an important piece of real estate. Provide the name of this geographic region and a citation to the treaty provision concerned.

(ii) Concomitantly, both parties agreed to establish normal relationships between them, including "full recognition, diplomatic, economic and cultural relations [and] termination of economic boycotts and discriminatory barriers to the free movement of people and goods." Provide a citation to the treaty provision concerned.

(c) Supply a correct Bluebook citation to the treaty at this source.

CHAPTER 7

CUSTOMARY INTERNATIONAL LAW

Part 1: Introduction and Overview

After treaties, the most significant source of international law is probably international custom. Rules derived from this source are called "Customary International Law" rules. We have seen in earlier Chapters that "international custom" is one of the four sources of international law specified in Article 38(1) of the ICJ Statute. This source appears second in the Article 38(1) list of sources. This alone, in the view of some observers, warrants the consideration of custom as being second in importance only behind treaties.

However, it is not merely the formality of its placement in Article 38(1) that results in the significance of Customary International Law. Many important rules of International Law have existed for extended periods as fundamental norms of international behavior before states have been able to secure broad explicit agreement in treaties. A leading example is the case of torture. The Convention Against Torture did not enter into force until 1987, but for many years before that there was no doubt a Customary International Law rule against torture. Without the availability of the construct of Customary International Law, the international community would have been without a binding legal norm prohibiting torture until the treaty could have been finalized late in the twentieth century.

Despite its utility, the idea of custom as a legal construct, as opposed to explicitly enacted legislative codes, may seem strange to readers more acquainted with modern common-law and civil-law concepts. After all, most lawyers think of themselves as finding laws in statute books, regulatory codes and case reporters, or the like. The laws in such sources are based on written legislation, regulations or decisions, not something so amorphous as custom.

This apparent strangeness is further borne out if one compares treaties with Customary International Law. Treaties can be analogized to other instruments of domestic law. Since they represent agreements among parties that are presumed to be autonomous, they resemble contracts. Like contracts, they are most often negotiated, involve an exchange of responsibilities and benefits, and are finalized by a set of signatures. At the same time, treaties can also be analogized to domestic statutes. Like domestic statutes, treaties are also negotiated by the bodies that are responsible for drafting their terms, these negotiating bodies generally represent constituents who will usually be governed by the final documents, and the final documents often will have the force and effect of law.

Customary International Law, however, does not lend itself as readily to analogy to domestic-law methods and procedures. The readings included in "Unit B" for this Chapter 7 will describe these methods and procedures, and their uniqueness will probably be apparent to most readers.

The uniqueness of Customary International Law may be more apparent than real, however. Commentators have pointed out that even domestic legal systems, in early phases of their development, rely on the existence and cultivation of custom as a source of legal rules. Primitive cultures often have relied on what is customarily acceptable and unacceptable as a means of determining which behaviors will be officially permitted or punished. The idea of Customary International Law thus has a certain pedigree that establishes a link with, rather than a distinction from, domestic law-making tradition.

And lest one should too quickly conclude that this necessarily implies a certain primitiveness for the modern international law, we should recall that custom plays important roles in modern legal systems as well. In the United States, some doctrines of constitutional law (such as the limits of "substantive due process") are often said to be based in what is "traditional" in the country's legal development. What is "traditional" in this sense can well be analogized to what is considered "customary" in the international sense. Similarly, the "Constitutional" system of British government relies on an unwritten Constitution, the basis of which might be said to have parallels with legal constructs based on tradition or custom.

One distinct advantage of rules of Customary International Law is generally that, once established, they are universally applicable. This is a clear distinction with treaty law. Treaties only create binding obligations for the states that sign and ratify them. A rule of Customary International Law, however, most often binds all states regardless of whether in a given setting any particular state approves or disapproves of the rule.

In part for this reason, international activists and advocates can be vigorous proponents for the existence of particular rules of Customary International Law. Legal and advocacy journals and periodicals will often contain generous quantities of opinion on the part of commentators arguing for this or that newly discovered or newly generated rule of Customary International Law. These commentators are very much aware that if they can secure the acceptance of their view that such a new rule has been established, it will by its nature usually bind all states. This is a distinct advantage over the treaty process, usually involving detailed and laborious negotiation and compromise.

As indicated in some of the reading for this Chapter 7, there are a small handful of situations in which rules of Customary International Law may not be completely universal. However, these occur in a small minority of cases, and in general the topic is of justly substantial interest for reformers and legal contenders of all persuasions and backgrounds.

CHAPTER 7	Part 2: Reading Exercises

Student Name: ______________________________

In Unit B of this Course Book, review the reading selections by I.A. Shearer, Malcolm Shaw and Ian Brownlie on Customary International Law. Then complete the following Reading Exercises.

1. The idea of Customary International Law is often contrasted with the idea of mere international "usage." Both the Brownlie and Starke selections elaborate on the distinction between them.

   (a) Brownlie's discussion occurs early on in his discussion. How does he describe the difference between a usage and custom?

   ____
   ____
   ____

   (b) Starke's discussion of the distinction, also occurring near the beginning of his treatment of the subject, is somewhat more detailed. Of the several statements he makes in this regard, which of his descriptions of the distinction most closely parallels Brownlie's statement?

   ____
   ____
   ____

2. According to Shaw, there are "two basic elements in the make-up of a custom." Similarly, Starke maintains that "before a particular usage may be considered as amounting to a customary rule of international law, two tests may be satisfied." Thus each author believes that basically two elements must be present in order for a posited rule to indeed be viewed as a rule of customary international law. In each case, what are these two elements?

(a) Shaw's "two basic elements":

(i) ______________________
(ii) ______________________

(b) Starke's "two tests":

(i) ______________________
(ii) ______________________

3. Turning initially to the first of these elements, Shaw states that "there are a number of points to be considered concerning its nature." He lists four points as component characteristics of the nature of this first element.

(a) What are the four component points of the first element of Customary International Law, as noted here by Shaw?

____
____
____
____

(b) Brownlie, on the other hand, also isolates four "elements of custom". What are his four elements of custom?

____
____
____
____

(c) As between these two lists of four points, three could be said to be common between them. Which are these three?

____
____
____

(d) If asked to make a succinct comparison between these two analyses, how would you formulate such a brief comparison?

____

____

____

____

____

____

4. It was noted above that Shaw and Starke state two broad elements, or tests, to determine whether a particular practice or usage qualifies as a rule of Customary International Law. The second of these is usually stated in terms of a Latin phrase, although the exact text of the Latin phrase may vary from one authority to the next. Indeed, these three authors each transcribe the Latin phrase in a slightly different way. What are the three different Latin transcriptions?

(a) Starke: ______________________________________

(b) Shaw: ______________________________________

(c) Brownlie: ____________________________________

5. Starke includes a distinct discussion as to how national and international courts should respond to an assertion by a litigant that a rule of Customary International Law exists. Starke suggests that the court must "investigate whether or not the rule invoked is a validly established rule of international custom." He adds that the court should "examine all possible materials," and proceeds to list five types of materials that should be examined. What are the five types of items that he includes in this list of materials that courts should examine?

____

____

____

____

____

CHAPTER 7

Part 3: Guidance for Research

The sources from which customary law is derived are exceedingly diverse. Treaties, diplomatic correspondence, policy statements, national legislation, resolutions of multi-national bodies such as the U.N. General Assembly, decisions of national and international tribunals, even press releases can be examined for evidence of "state practice" and the norms of behavior that publicists describe as customary law. It is this very wealth of resources that can make research in this field difficult for the student and practitioner. Where to start? Where to stop?

A number of these resources have been examined in earlier chapters and the techniques for searching them apply to problems of customary law. However, there are some special resources which we have not discussed—both hard-copy and electronic, that will be useful in capturing what some have termed international common law. By no means is the list below intended to be comprehensive; rather it is a very limited guide for the beginning student.

Yearbooks and Digests

Yearbook of the International Law Comission, New York: United Nations, 1956-

"Annual Yearbook of International Law", published yearly in *American Journal of International Law*, American Society for International Law. Note: The AJIL regularly contains a section on state practice. This journal is available on LexisNexis and Westlaw.

There is a series of digests covering U.S. state practice in international law published by the U.S. Government Printing Office, beginning with *Digest of Published Opinions of the Attorneys-General and of the Leading Decisions of the Federal Courts, with Reference to International Law, Treaties, and Kindred Subjects.* Compiled by John L. Cadwalader, Washington, D.C.: USGPO, 1877. This work, found in most large academic and law school libraries, has an alphabetical topical index which is not particularly user-friendly.

Cadwalader's work was followed by a publication with an equally long title: *Digest of the International Law of the United States; Taken from Documents Issued by Presidents and Secretaries of State, and from Decisions of Federal Courts and Opinions of Attorneys-General.* Compiled by Francis Wharton. Washington, D.C.: USGPO, 1887. This work is arranged by very broad subject areas but does have a better index.

In 1906, John B. Moore compiled a treatise with the same title, but known to most law librarians as *Digest of International Law . . .* Washington, D.C.: USGPO, 1906. Moore's eight volume work superseded the two earlier compilations and contains a much more useable index. It contains material from circa 1776 to 1906. It is considered an invaluable source for early U.S. state practice and is much more widely available than the preceding works.

Three other compilations have been published; covering 1906 to 1986. Later material has been compiled in annual volumes entitled *Digest of United States Practice in International Law.* There is a cumulative index available.

Restatement of the Law (Third) of the Foreign Relations Law of the U.S. Washington, D.C.: American Law Institute, 1987—Available on LexisNexis and Westlaw.

Non-US decisions and other materials are published in two primary sources:

Repertory of the Practice of the United Nations Organs. New York: United Nations, 1955-

United Nations Juridical Yearbook. New York: United Nations, 1965-

Diplomatic Materials

Foreign Relations of the United States. U.S. Department of State. Washington, D.C.: USGPO, 1948. The official record of U.S. foreign affairs documents from both the State Department and the White House from 1932-, published somewhat irregularly but generally every four years. Some volumes are available via the Internet at the State Department's web site: www.state.gov. However, there is a statement at the site indicating that material can be and has been removed, apparently at the discretion of the administration.

Earlier documents were published in *Papers Related to the Foreign Relations of the United States.* These were sent to the Congress with the President's annual message and are available from 1861-1869 and 1870-1931. Most depository libraries will have these publications.

More difficult to find is the comparable compilations from the United Kingdom; *British and Foreign State Papers*, 1812-1968. This multi-volume work contains not only UK documents, but those from other governments as well, some of which are translated into English. As well as diplomatic correspondence, some hard-to-locate treaties can be found here which are not included in the League of Nations or United Nations Treaty Series. Again, some of these documents, as they are declassified, are available on the Internet.

Almost all developed nations publish similar works—unfortunately not all translated into English. Only the very largest libraries will hold these and they are generally beyond the scope of this course.

Decisions of National and International Tribunals

These sources have been covered in earlier chapters, but students should remember that the decisions of the national courts, the European Court of Justice and the ICJ are available on Westlaw and LexisNexis. An increasing number of jurisdictions including the ICJ post decisions on their websites. The primary hard copy source is *International Law Reports.*

National Legislation

Normative principles of customary law can be found in legislative and administrative law. For non-U.S. law sources, an invaluable resource is *Foreign Law: Current sources of codes and basic legislation in jurisdictions of the world.* Thomas Reynolds and Arturo Flores. Littleton, CO: F. B. Rothman, 1989-. This work, regularly updated, provides commentary and sources for foreign law. Since this work was first published, legislation has begun to be available on the Internet and many links are listed. Additionally, a Google search or accessing one of the many university websites can also be very helpful in locating this type of material. For administrative law, EUR-Lex, the official site of the European Union, can be useful.

Press Releases, Resolutions, Other Documents

Sources for these documents have been covered in the chapters on the United Nations and its ancillary bodies. For U.S. materials, *United States Code and Administrative News (USCANN)*, published by West is a very convenient and timely source for executive orders and some policy statements.

Publicists

The writings of learned scholars in the field are recognized as a source of international law by Article 38 of the ICJ Statute. There are many authors who could be listed. Some of the more authoritative ones include:

International Law, 5th ed. Malcolm Shaw. Cambridge, England: Cambridge University Press, 2003.

Principles of Public International Law, 6th ed. Ian Brownlie. Oxford; New York: Oxford University Press, 2003.

Oppenheim's International Law. 9th ed. L. Oppenheim, edited by Robert Jennings and Arthur Watts. London: Longman, 1992. Includes index and table of cases.

For an excellent overview, see the chapter on customary international law in Bernhardt's *Encyclopedia of Public International Law*, Amsterdam; New York: Elsevier North Holland, 2003.

CHAPTER 7 | **Part 4: Research Problems**

Student Name: ______________________________

The following Research Problems are designed to help you implement the information contained in Parts 1 and 3 of this Chapter, and experience gained from completing the Reading Exercises in Part 2.

1. The Spanish American War was of comparatively brief duration; it can be said to have begun in February of 1898 and to have ended in August of the same year. It involved the antagonism of the United States to the continued presence of declining Spanish power in the Western Hemisphere. On April 25, 1898, a U.S. naval gunboat captured a Cuban fishing sloop off the coast of that island, then still a colonial possession of Spain. The U.S. naval authorities commandeered the ship and took it to Key West, where they sold the ship and its contents, retaining the proceeds of sale as a prize of war. This act was affirmed by the Federal District Court in southern Florida, but the U.S. Supreme Court, in a famous opinion, reversed the District Court. In its decision on January 8, 1900, the Supreme Court discerned a rule of Customary International Law, as follows:

> By an ancient usage among civilized nations, beginning centuries ago, and gradually ripening into a rule of international law, coast fishing vessels, pursuing their vocation of catching and bringing in fresh fish, have been recognized as exempt, with their cargoes and crews, from capture as prize of war.

Since the Court viewed the Cuban vessel as satisfying the above description, the Court concluded that its capture violated international law, and ordered that the proceeds of the sale of the vessel and its cargo be restored to the complaining party.

(a) Find the official report of this U.S. Supreme Court case.

(b) Research Questions: Upon reviewing the Supreme Court decision you have retrieved, answer the following questions, in each case indicating the page number(s) on which you found your answer, using the numbering for the pages of the decision you used.

(i) The decision issued on this date involved in fact two different ships; the one described above and another one as well. What were the names of the two ships, and how long was each?

Name: ____________________; __________ feet
Name: ____________________; __________ feet
Page: ______________

(ii) The rule of Customary International Law transcribed in the narrative above appears on which page of the reported decision you have consulted?

Page: ______________

(iii) The broadest holding of this case is what it is most known for:

> "International law is part of our law, and must be ascertained and administered by the courts of justice of appropriate jurisdiction as often as questions of right depending upon it are duly presented for their determination."

On which page of the reported decision you have consulted does this holding appear?

Page: ______________

(c) Provide a correct Bluebook citation for this case:

____
____
____

2. Since the establishment of the United Nations, the extent to which states can legally use armed force against other states or external bodies in self-defense has been addressed by Article 51 of the U.N. Charter. Before that time, however, the general law of self-defense was largely a creature of Customary International Law. One of the leading precedents in this customary area involved the destruction of the *Caroline*, a U.S. steamship that was destroyed by marauding Canadian forces in upstate New York in 1837. At the time Canada was a British colony subject to a concentrated insurgency agitating for independence. This insurgency was being aided by groups of U.S. citizens, some of whom were using the *Caroline* to ferry militants and supplies from the New York shore of the Niagara River to various islands and other shoreline points in support of the insurgency. Finally, an antagonistic group of loyalist Canadian militants (who were later determined to be reporting to the British authorities) seized control of the ship while docked within U.S. waters, set fire to it, and sent it over Niagara Falls. One U.S. national was killed in the course of these events. A later exchange of notes between U.S. and British diplomatic personnel regarding the incident formed the basis of the customary law of self-defense for several generations thereafter, and may still have substantial importance.

(a) Various international law digests have included discussions and documentary collections regarding the *Caroline* affair. In general, the more complete treatments are found in those digests published in years closer to the time of the events. Retrieve a digest discussion that offers the most complete treatment of the *Caroline* affair.

(b) Research Questions: Upon reviewing the discussion you have retrieved, answer the following questions, in each case indicating the page number(s) on which you found your answer, using the numbering for the pages of the digest you used.

(i) In March 1841, New York State authorities took custody of one Alexander MacLeod, who claimed to have taken an active part in the destruction of the *Caroline*. They charged him with murder, although he was later acquitted. On what basis was he acquitted?

____

Page: _______________

(ii) The most famous language to emerge from the *Caroline* affair comes from an August 6, 1842 letter from U.S. Secretary of State Webster to Lord Ashburton, the British representative in the matter. The letter stated that the international-law allowance for self-defense "should be confined to cases in which the 'necessity of that self-defense is instant, overwhelming, and leaving no choice of means, and no moment for deliberation.'" What was Lord Ashburton's official title, as indicated in the digest's citation to this letter?

____

Page: _____________

(iii) Later in his letter to Lord Ashburton, Secretary Webster states that "the difference between the two governments is only whether the facts in the case of the *Caroline* make out a case" of a particular sort. What language does he use to describe the case that either is or is not made out by the facts of the *Caroline* incident?

____

____

Page: _____________

(c) Provide a correct Bluebook citation to the digest discussion that is the basis of your answers.

____

____

____

3. The famous "Asylum Case", decided by the International Court of Justice within the first few years of its existence, contains some important language regarding the criteria for a rule of Customary International Law. The case involved a Peruvian individual, Víctor Raúl Haya de la Torre, who was subject to criminal prosecution by the Peruvian authorities. Mr. Haya de la Torre sought and received diplomatic asylum in the Colombian embassy in Lima, the Peruvian capital. The Colombian government considered Haya de la Torre a

"political refugee." When the Colombian diplomatic authorities sought a safe conduct for Haya de la Torre to leave Peru, their request was denied. Before the ICJ, Colombia argued that conventions signed by both Peru and Colombia allowed each state to accord diplomatic asylum to political refugees. Colombia further argued that under these conventions Colombia, as the State granting asylum, could determine for itself which persons were political refugees. Colombia asserted that these conventions gave it the right to make this determination in its sole discretion, regardless of whether Peru concurred in the determination. Finally, Colombia asserted that even if the conventions involved didn't give Colombia this right to definitively determine Haya de la Torre's status, a rule of Customary International Law gave Colombia this right. Colombia also allowed that, even if such a rule were not general throughout the world, it was at least binding in Latin America.

(a) Find an English text of the Asylum Case at a definitive source.

(b) Research Questions:

(i) Probably the most important provision of the decision is the criteria for a rule of Customary International Law on these facts. The Court state that such a rule would need to be "in accordance with a constant and uniform usage practiced by the States in question, and that this usage is the expression of a right appertaining to the State granting asylum and a duty incumbent on the territorial State."

On which page of the decision at your source does this language appear?

____

(ii) To support its argument that a rule of Customary International Law existed, Colombia referred to the Montevideo Convention of 1933 as evidence of common practice and opinio juris. The Court did not consider this reference to the Montevideo Convention to be persuasive, in part because of the number of states that had ratified the Convention as of the date of the Court's decision. What is the number of states that had so ratified at that point, according to the

Court, and on which page of the opinion does this observation appear?

Number: ________________
Page: ________________

(iii) Near the beginning of its discussion of the customary law issue, the Court treats Colombia's argument based on the "Bolivarian Agreement of 1911." The Court says that this argument confuses two different kinds of asylum. What are these two kinds of asylum, according to the Court, and on which page does this statement appear?

____________________________ asylum and

____________________________ asylum;
Page: ______________

(c) Provide a correct Bluebook citation to a report of the decision at an authoritative source.

____
____
____

4. Although the United States has not ratified the Rome Statute of the International Criminal Court, it took an active part in negotiating the terms of the Statute. The Rome Statute contemplates a crime of "aggression," although the present text of the Statute does not attempt to define this crime. Delegates to the convention drafting the Statute were not able to agree on a definition, and instead reserved the issue for future amendatory conventions. During these initial negotiations for the Rome Statute, the U.S. Department of State took the position that the definition of the crime of aggression under the Statute should "rest on a strong foundation of customary law."

(a) In an appropriate digest of international law, retrieve the text of the December 6, 2000 presentation made on behalf of the State Department that included this argument.

(b) Research Questions: Upon reviewing the digest entry you have retrieved, answer the following questions, in each case indicating the page number(s) on which you found your answer, using the numbering for the pages of the digest you used.

(i) What was the name and title of the State Department official who delivered this presentation?

______________________; ______________________
Page: _____________

(ii) The State Department speaker referred to a General Assembly Resolution on the Crime of Aggression, but maintained that the Resolution did not state then-present Customary International Law. He acknowledged, on the other hand, that sometimes General Assembly resolutions could "become a focal point of a subsequent practice of states and harden into customary law." He called this possibility a certain kind of "effect." What kind of effect did he call this possibility?

The ______________________ effect of GA Resolutions.
Page: ___________________

(iii) In this presentation on the subject of customary international law, the State Department official also references a "controversy about" a specific General Assembly Resolution. What is the number that he gives for that resolution?

____
Page: ___________

(c) Provide a correct Bluebook citation for the digest entry covering this material.

____
____
____
____

5. The American Law Institute (or "ALI") has published many influential "Restatements" covering various areas of U.S. law. In 1987, it issued the third edition of the "Restatement of the Foreign Relations Law of the United States." This document, which practitioners in International Law sometimes call simply the "Third Restatement," is a concise source of international-law rules that is frequently consulted. It has proven useful not merely for academic commentators, but for professionals in many different countries dealing with areas of international law. The Third Restatement's coverage of Customary International Law has substantial significance. Each Section to the Third Restatement is also accompanied by official Comments and Reporters' Notes.

(a) Find a complete edition of the text of the Third Restatement at an authoritative source, which includes all Comments and Reporters' Notes for each Section.

(b) Research Questions:

(i) Two particular sections of the Third Restatement contain substantial material regarding the definition of Customary International Law. The first of these deals with the root materials that serve as the basis of international law, and the second immediately follows the first. Which are these two numerical sections?

____________ & ______________

(ii) According to one of the Comments for the first of these Sections, sometimes the practice of states in particular geographical sub-areas of the world may create sub-sets of customary law rules for these states as among themselves. What are 3 different phrases used in this Comment to describe these geographical sub-sets of customary international law? Which Comment for this Section contains this discussion?

____

____

____

Comment: ______________________

(iii) One of the Reporters' Notes for the first of these Sections discusses "Customary law" in particular. The Note describes a 1962 General Assembly Resolution as being an example of the way in which General Assembly resolutions can become rules of customary international law. What is name of this 1962 General Assembly Resolution?

____
____
____

(c) Provide a correct Bluebook citation for the section(s) of the Third Restatement described in Question 5(b)(i) above.

____
____
____

6. Some activists might argue that there is or should be a rule of Customary International Law requiring wealthier states to engage in foreign aid activities. A demonstration that governments believe that their conduct of foreign aid programs arises from purely political motives would tend to counter such an argument. In February of 1961 there was an exchange of memoranda involving U.S. State Department personnel that tended to indicate that U.S. foreign aid programs were undertaken for primarily political reasons. One such memorandum was dated February 8, and the other was dated February 23.

(a) Use the State Department's *Foreign Relations of the United States* series to find this exchange of diplomatic correspondence.

(b) Research Questions:

(i) What are the statements in each of these two memoranda that emphasize the expressly political character of the international aid effort there being discussed?

February 8 memorandum:

____
____
____

February 23 memorandum:

____
____
____

(ii) What is the name of the person making each of the referenced statements?

February 8 memorandum: ____________________

February 23 memorandum: ____________________

(iii) What are the subject-line titles of these two memoranda?

February 8 memorandum:

____
____

February 23 memorandum:

____
____

(c) Provide a correct Bluebook citation to these two memoranda at this source:

____

____

____

____

____

____

CHAPTER 8

ARBITRATION AMONG PRIVATE PARTIES

Part 1: Introduction and Overview

In Chapter 4, we looked at arbitration among sovereign states, chiefly in the context of the Hague Conventions of 1899 and 1907. In this Chapter 8 we turn to arbitration among private parties. Although the mechanisms of arbitration in the two contexts are similar, the legal environment is somewhat different.

Generally, when sovereign states resort to arbitration to settle disputes between them, they have concluded that all other options are less advantageous. The institutional and procedural inconveniences of the ICJ will often prevent states from choosing that forum. Similarly, less formal mechanisms of negotiation, conciliation and mediation may be viewed as unavailing, or may even have proven to be unavailing. Also, states usually enter into arbitration after the dispute among them has arisen.

When private parties resort to arbitration, however, the choice is almost always voluntary, and also pursuant to prior agreement. Private arbitrations occur almost always as a result of contractual agreements to arbitrate that have already been executed by the parties before the dispute arises. These arbitration agreements are usually clauses of larger contracts governing business arrangements or transactions. If, when the transaction or business relationship is underway, a dispute arises, the arbitration agreement in the underlying documents then "kicks in," and the arbitral process begins.

Parties are at liberty to negotiate their arbitration agreements, and in theory can provide for any combination of attributes for the arbitration that they wish. For example, parties can decide in advance on the number of arbitrators to be used, the language in which the arbitration will take place, how the arbitrators will be chosen, the maximum amount of time to be allowed to complete the arbitration, and so on.

Even though such terms of arbitration are, in theory, completely subject to the wishes of the parties, in reality most arbitration agreements do not specify the attributes for arbitration in such detail. Instead, most arbitration agreements incorporate by reference a "canned" set of rules already published by a particular arbitration institution.

There are several such institutions around the world. The most prominent is the International Chamber of Commerce (or "ICC"), headquartered in Paris. Others include the American Arbitration Association (or "AAA," headquartered in New York) and the London Court of International Arbitration. These are private associations that facilitate arbitrations among private parties by maintaining published sets of arbitration rules. The ICC, for example, publishes and maintains the Rules of Arbitration of the International Chamber of Commerce (or the "ICC Rules"), and the other arbitration institutions publish and maintain similar rules.

Accordingly, parties negotiating a business contract containing an arbitration agreement will often insert into the arbitration clauses a requirement that any arbitration arising out of the contract will be governed by a specified set of rules. For example, the contract might specify the ICC Rules, the AAA International Arbitration Rules, or London Court of International Arbitration Rules. In this way the parties can feel that details required for the management of an orderly arbitration will be adequately provided for in their contract, without actually having to negotiate the terms themselves.

The arbitration institutions also go a step further in facilitating arbitration, beyond merely publishing and maintaining rules. Most such institutions also maintain a permanent staff that assists arbitrating parties once arbitration proceedings have begun. For example, the ICC staff includes an "International Court of Arbitration," which is not really a court, but rather a staff of ICC-related personnel who are available to assist with the appointment of arbitrators (in certain cases), the replacement of arbitrators (should it become necessary) and other administrative matters. The precise roles and duties of these staff members for each institution are generally spelled out in that institution's rules.

An additional crucial factor regarding arbitration is that the awards issued by arbitral tribunals are generally binding. This means that the victorious party in an arbitration can take the award issued by the tribunal to a court in the home jurisdiction of the losing party, and procure a legal judgment against the losing party in that court. The judgment can then be legally enforced against the losing party pursuant to the domestic procedural law of the losing party's country.

This process is available because it is explicitly provided for under the 1959 Convention on the Recognition and Enforcement of Foreign Arbitral Awards, often called the "New York Convention." Under the New York Convention, the courts of each Contracting State are generally required to "enforce" arbitral awards issued by any arbitral body in other states. This means that the courts of each contracting state must issue a judgment on the basis of the foreign arbitral award, with only minimal opportunities for judicial review of the award.

The New York Convention also requires that courts in each Contracting State "recognize" arbitral awards issued by foreign arbitral bodies. This means that if two parties have previously arbitrated a given issue, and the arbitral tribunal decides it in a certain way, the losing party is precluded from trying to litigate that issue through standard adjudication in a national court.

Finally, the New York Convention additionally requires that courts in Contracting States "recognize" arbitration agreements themselves. This means that if a party requests a court in a Contracting State to adjudicate a particular issue, but that issue has been committed to arbitration in a valid arbitration agreement by which that party is bound, the court is supposed to dismiss the party's request and refer the parties to arbitration.

A caveat to all of these observations is that the New York Convention only applies to arbitrations conducted pursuant to written arbitration agreements. In addition, many individual states (in particular those that are most active commercially) have domestic statutes further facilitating the recognition and enforcement of foreign arbitral awards.

The Reading Exercises for this Chapter 8 focus primarily on the New York Convention and the ICC Rules. These are by far the most influential documents in international private commercial arbitrations.

International arbitration has also gotten an additional boost in recent years with the effectiveness of the North American Free Trade Agreement ("NAFTA") and the World Trade Organization (or "WTO") Agreement. These agreements contain mechanisms for dispute resolution among the contracting parties that very much resemble standard arbitration procedures. However, the features of these procedures are quite particular and tailored to their contexts, and not sufficiently general for discussion in this Chapter.

CHAPTER 8	Part 2: Reading Exercises

Student name: ______________________________

QUESTIONS BASED ON THE NEW YORK CONVENTION

Read and review the New York Convention on the Recognition and Enforcement of Foreign Arbitral Awards, which is included in the "Documents" Unit of this Course Book ("Unit B"). Then answer the following questions based on your reading and review of Part 1 of this Chapter ("Introduction and Overview") and the New York Convention.

1. For each of the following hypothetical fact patterns, indicate whether the facts present primarily an issue of recognition of an arbitral award, an issue of recognition of an arbitral agreement, an issue of enforcement of an arbitral award, or an issue that is outside the scope of the New York Convention.

(a) Recognition of Arbitral Award
Recognition of Arbitration Agreement
Enforcement of Arbitral Award
Outside Scope

A Wisconsin brewery company contracts to purchase from a German manufacturer new brewery equipment for its new brewing facilities in Milwaukee. Pursuant to the contract of sale, the brewery company pays a portion of the purchase price in advance. The contract also contains an arbitration clause providing that all disputes "related to or arising out of" the contract shall be arbitrated in Berlin, using the ICC's Rules of Arbitration. When the equipment is delivered in Milwaukee, the brewery company concludes that it is defective, and sues the German manufacturer of the equipment for the return of the advance payment. The brewery company brings suit in Federal District Court in Milwaukee, but the manufacturer maintains that the suit should be dismissed because of the arbitration clause.

(b) Recognition of Arbitral Award
Recognition of Arbitration Agreement
Enforcement of Arbitral Award
Outside Scope

A sports enthusiast living in New York City decides to rent a mountain chalet in Switzerland for a period of five years. She signs a lease covering that period, pursuant to which she is obligated to pay rent to the Swiss owner at the beginning of every calendar quarter. The lease agreement contains an arbitration clause indicating that all disputes in connection with the terms of the lease shall be subject to arbitration in Berne, Switzerland, pursuant to terms defined in the lease. The sports enthusiast begins defaulting on rent payments beginning in the second year of the lease, and the landlord commences arbitration proceedings in Berne pursuant to the terms of the lease. An arbitral award is issued in Berne to the landlord for the full amount of the arrearages plus interest. The landlord sues the tenant in Federal District court for the Southern District of New York, in an attempt to recover the amount of the award. The tenant files responsive papers indicating that she should not be liable for rent because the landlord failed to make repairs.

(c) Recognition of Arbitral Award
Recognition of Arbitration Agreement
Enforcement of Arbitral Award
Outside Scope

A Japanese manufacturer contracts with a chain of retail jewelry stores in the United Kingdom to supply the British chain with a prescribed number of digital wristwatches every month for two years. The contract contains an arbitration clause that provides that any dispute arising out of the contract shall be settled by arbitration in London. After inspecting the first shipment, the British chain discovers that the shipped watches were of the conventional rotary-hand variety rather than digital watches. Its confidence in its counter-party shaken, the chain commences arbitration proceedings in London, according to the contract, in an effort to rescind the contract. The Japanese manufacturer, at the same time, commences litigation in a court in Tokyo, arguing that the contract actually allowed for the delivery of a certain number of conventional watches. This Tokyo court concededly has jurisdiction over both the parties and the subject matter. The jewelry chain appears before the Tokyo court, intending solely to argue that the manufacturer's claim should be brought before the arbitral tribunal instead of the court.

(d) Recognition of Arbitral Award
Recognition of Arbitration Agreement
Enforcement of Arbitral Award
Outside Scope

During loan negotiations between a commercial bank in San Francisco and an importer from the Philippines, the bank suggests in draft lending documentation that all differences arising under or in connection with the loan be settled by arbitration. However, the Philippine borrower prefers not to submit to arbitration, and agrees instead to submit to the exclusive jurisdiction of all state and federal courts located in California. Three months later the bank declares that the importer has defaulted on repayment of the loan, and accelerates the entire principle amount outstanding. The bank brings an action in a state trial court of appropriate jurisdiction, to obtain a judgment for all amounts due and owing in connection with the loan. The borrower argues in response that under state law it can compel arbitration in California.

(e) Recognition of Arbitral Award
Recognition of Arbitration Agreement
Enforcement of Arbitral Award
Outside Scope

An upscale pet store in Singapore decides to specialize in selling native Australian koala bears as pets. It enters into a contract with an Australian company that operates excursions for tourists in remote regions of Australia. Pursuant to the contract, the Australian tour operator promises to send at least six live koala bears to the Singapore pet store per year, with the timing of each delivery to be on an as-available basis. The contract contains an arbitration clause requiring that all disputes arising out of or related to the contract be arbitrated in Sydney. Shortly after the contract is signed, the tour operator notifies the pet store that the trapping and shipping of koala bears is contrary to Australian law; assume that this is a true statement. The pet store is unconvinced, however, and commences arbitration against the tour operator in Sydney. The arbitral panel ultimately issues a judgment in favor of the tour operator, indicating that the tour operator has no remaining liability to the pet store. Undeterred, the pet store commences litigation in Singapore against the tour operator in a court that has subject-matter jurisdiction and personal jurisdiction over both parties. The tour operator appears in the Singapore court intending to argue solely that the court action is precluded by the arbitral award issued in Australia.

2. "True or False" Questions. For each of the following quoted statements, circle the word "True" above it if you believe it is true, and the word "False" above it if you believe it is false. In each case, in the blank above the statement and after the words, "True" and "False," indicate the provision of the New York Convention on which your selection is based.

(a) True False ______________________________

The New York Convention generally requires each Contracting State to recognize or enforce only those arbitral awards that are made in the territory of other Contracting States.

(b) True False ______________________________

Under the New York Convention, an agreement to arbitrate must be stated in a separate document that expressly contains the agreement to arbitrate and no other extraneous matter. The agreement to arbitrate can not be merely one clause of a larger agreement.

(c) True False ______________________________

Under the conditions of the New York Convention, each Contracting State must recognize arbitral awards as binding and enforce them in accordance of the rules of procedure of the territory where the award is relied upon.

(d) True False ______________________________

The New York Convention by its terms requires that a federal state assure that the Convention applies within the constituent states or provinces of the federal state to the same extent that it applies to the federal state itself.

3. Which of the following is *not* a basis for refusing recognition or enforcement of an arbitral award under the New York Convention?

(a) The parties to the arbitration agreement, under the law applicable to them, are under some incapacity that invalidates the arbitration agreement.

(b) The arbitral award contains decisions on matters beyond the scope of the submission to arbitration.

(c) The arbitral award contains conclusions and judgments that, under the law to which the parties have subjected it, are clearly erroneous as a matter of law.

(d) The party against whom the award is invoked was not given proper notice of the appointment of the arbitration proceedings.

On which provision(s) of the New York Convention are your answers based?

____

____

____

4. Which of the following sets of events is *most likely* to result in the refusal of recognition or enforcement of an arbitral award under the New York Convention?

(a) The competent authority in the country where recognition or enforcement is sought determines of its own accord, *sua sponte* and without any request by either party, that the composition of the arbitral authority was not in accordance with the agreement of the parties.

(b) The competent authority in the country where recognition or enforcement is sought determines, at the request of the party against whom it is invoked but without any evidence offered by that party, that the award has not yet become binding on the parties.

(c) The competent authority in the country where recognition or enforcement is sought determines, *sua sponte* and without any application by either party, that recognition or enforcement of the award would be contrary to the public policy of the country where recognition or enforcement is sought.

On which provision(s) of the New York Convention are your answers based?

____
____
____

QUESTIONS BASED ON THE ICC RULES

Read and review the Rules of Arbitration of the International Chamber of Commerce (the "ICC Rules"). These are included in the "Documents" Unit of this Course Book ("Unit B"). Then answer the following questions based on your reading and review of Part 1 of this Chapter ("Introduction and Overview") and the ICC Rules.

5. "True or False" Questions. For each of the following quoted statements, circle the word "True" above it if you believe it is true, and the word "False" above it if you believe it is false. In each case, in the blank above the statement and after the words, "True" and "False," indicate the provision of the ICC Rules on which your selection is based.

(a) True False ________________________________

The ICC Rules provide that disputes shall be decided by a sole arbitrator or by a panel of three, five or seven arbitrators.

(b) True False ______________________________

Before appointment to an Arbitral Tribunal, a prospective arbitrator must sign a statement of independence and disclose in writing any facts or circumstances which might call into question the arbitrator's independence in the eyes of the parties.

(c) True False ______________________________

In those disputes other than those for which there is a sole arbitrator, the chairman of the Arbitral Tribunal is appointed by the parties to the dispute, unless the parties agree on another procedure for such appointment.

(d) True False ______________________________

If the parties do not agree upon the rules of law to be applied by the Arbitral Tribunal to the merits of the dispute, the Arbitral Tribunal shall apply the rules of law which it determines to be appropriate.

6. Which of the following items is *not* explicitly and specifically required by the ICC Rules to be included in an Arbitral Tribunal's "Terms of Reference"?

(a) The full names and descriptions of the parties.
(b) The full names, descriptions and addresses of the arbitrators.
(c) A statement of the law applicable to the dispute.
(d) The place of arbitration.

On which provision(s) of the ICC Rules is your answer based?

____

____

____

7. Which of the following events would be *least* consistent with the ICC Rules?

(a) None of the parties requests the Arbitral Tribunal to conduct a hearing, so the Arbitral Tribunal decides the case solely on the documents submitted by the parties.

(b) The Arbitral Tribunal summons both parties to a hearing, and (without any prior communication to the Tribunal) neither one appears; the Tribunal proceeds with the hearing anyway.

(c) One of the parties desires that the hearings ordered by the Arbitral Tribunal be open to members of public, but the other party does not consent; the Tribunal then closes the hearings to all persons not involved in the proceedings.

(d) One of the parties, an individual, indicates that she will not be able to attend any of the hearings, and appoints her sister as her duly authorized representative; the Tribunal refuses to conduct the hearings until the party herself can be present.

On which provision(s) of the ICC Rules is your answer based?

____

____

____

8. "True or False" Questions. For each of the following quoted statements, circle the word "True" above it if you believe it is true, and the word "False" above it if you believe it is false. In each case, in the blank above the statement and after the words, "True" and "False," indicate the provision of the ICC Rules on which your selection is based.

(a) True False __________________________

Once an Arbitral Panel has been formed, arbitrators are never replaced unless all parties initially request that the arbitrator be replaced.

(b) True False __________________________

After the Terms of Reference have been signed or approved by the International Court of Arbitration, no party shall make new claims or counterclaims which fall outside the limits of the Terms of Reference unless it has been authorized to do so by the Arbitral Tribunal.

(c) True False ______________________________

The ICC Rules provide that the Arbitral Tribunal may take as much time to render its final award as the complexity of the facts and circumstances of the dispute reasonably require.

CHAPTER 8

Part 3: Guidance for Research

The quantity and importance of commercial arbitration, i.e., arbitration between private parties rather than states, has grown concomitantly with global trade. With this growth has come increased need for practitioners to locate the procedural rules for arbitration in many countries as well as reports of arbitral awards. Over the years, a number of reliable hard-copy sources have been published, but in this area of law (as in others) electronic resources are now available. It is important for students to remember that electronic sources are limited by date—most do not contain data before 1990. Further, some electronic resources are available only to subscribers and can be extremely expensive. The hard-copy resources cited below should be available in most law school and university libraries. Note that these resources are published by not only commercial publishers but also by various public and private organizations.

Collection of ICC arbitral awards = Recueil des sentences arbitrales de la CCI, compiled by Sigvard Jarvin, et al. Paris, New York: ICC Pub.; Deventer; Boston: Kluwer Law and Taxation Publishers, c1990- Published by the International Chamber of Commerce, cumulative five-year indices by subject (termed "Analytical Table") in French and English. Volumes and pages in *Yearbook of Commercial Arbitration* are listed. Note that these volumes are collections of transcriptions of selected cases and are not comprehensive.

Yearbook Commercial Arbitration, Deventer, Netherlands; Cambridge, MA: Kluwer, 1975- Soft cover yearbooks of cases decided by courts, ICSID (see below), UNCITRAL, and the several conventions on arbitration. There are volume indices but see cumulative indices above for ICC awards.

World arbitration reporter, edited by Hans Smit, Vratislav Pechota, Yonkers, NY: Juris Publishing, Inc. 1986. Loose leaf publication containing arbitration legislation of major counties, arbitration rules of procedure, and some awards. Produced at Parker School of Foreign and Comparative Law at Columbia. Contains extensive bibliographies and indices as well as the text of arbitration legislation and a list of arbitration institutions. All eight volumes of this publication are now available online by subscription. http://www.arbitrationlaw.com/books/war.htm.

Another useful commercial resource is *Mealey's International Arbitration Reports* which is available as a loose leaf service or on LexisNexis from 1993.

Some awards are reprinted, but others are cited to federal court reporters. This publication is generally used as an alerting tool. It is extremely useful for very current award decisions.

International Legal Materials can be useful in hard-copy or online in Westlaw or LexisNexis, particularly for early cases. As noted earlier, LexisNexis has ILM from 1962 - ; Westlaw coverage currently starts in 1980.

Several private arbitration associations have very useful websites. Among these is the International Chamber of Commerce which unfortunately lists very recent cases only. However, the site gives access to the ICC rules and other useful information. The site is www.iccwbo.org.

National arbitration associations also have websites. For example, a visit to http://www.arbitrage.org/us/Proceedings/Rules_july2002.pdf will provide the rules used in France. Rules used in Germany can be found at http://www.dis-arb.de/scho/. Although not generally recommended, a Google search for the country and arbitration will often turn up the appropriate website, almost all of which have content in several languages.

UNCITRAL and other public entities also provide information on arbitration programs on their websites. The UNCITRAL website is at http://www.uncitral.org. The International Centre for the Settlement of Investment Disputes (ICSID), an affiliated agency of the World Bank, provides reports of arbitration cases at its website: www.worldbank.org/icsid.

Both proprietary online services, Westlaw and LexisNexis, have databases containing arbitral reports. They are not entirely satisfactory since they are very expensive, ambiguous as to scope of coverage and are composite files from a number of publications. If the case you are seeking is not available on the Internet, these files, e.g. Westlaw's ICA-Cases, are worth searching. Both LexisNexis and Westlaw segregate arbitration awards by country, which can be useful if either the nationality of the parties or the venue of the arbitration proceedings is known.

As with many international law research problems, the best solution is a judicious combination of hard-copy and electronic resources.

CHAPTER 8	Part 4: Research Problems

Student Name: ______________________________

The following Research Problems are designed to help you implement the information contained in Parts 1 and 3 of this Chapter, and experience gained from completing the Reading Exercises in Part 2.

1. The United States experienced steadily worsening political relations with many Arab countries during the late 1980's. These deteriorating circumstances caused difficulties for several high-profile U.S. industrial companies that had entered into major long-term contracts with business counterparties in Arab and Muslim states. Many of these difficulties were ultimately resolved through arbitration. One situation involved Sun Oil Company, a U.S. petroleum corporation, and the National Oil Corporation of Libya ("NOC"). Sun Oil had executed a long-term contract with the NOC, pursuant to which Sun Oil was to explore various areas in Libya for possible oil deposits and then develop the oil fields for commercial production. But the U.S. government, in connection with various accusations it made regarding assertedly hostile actions by the Libyan government, instituted certain limitations on the interaction of U.S. nationals with Libya. Among these were regulations prohibiting the use of U.S. passports for travel to Libya, and sharply limiting the export of certain technical equipment and data to Libya. Sun Oil maintained that these actions of the U.S. government constituted *force majeure* within the meaning of its contract with the NOC, and that Sun Oil was accordingly excused from performing under the contract. The NOC disagreed, and the matter was referred to arbitration. The contract contained an arbitration clause providing for arbitration under the auspices of the ICC, and the panel issued two successive awards: the first was specifically on the *force majeure* issue, and the second was denominated the panel's final award.

(a) Find a report of these two arbitral awards at a source that is suitable for legal citation.

(b) Research Questions. Upon reviewing the report you have retrieved, answer the following questions, in each case indicating the page number(s) on which you found your answer, using the numbering for the pages of the report at the source you used.

(i) What was the actual complete title of the contract between Sun Oil and the NOC?

____

Page(s): _______________

(ii) Was Sun Oil successful in its claim that *force majeure* excused its performance under the contract? (Circle one of the two options below, and write the language from the report that you would cite as support for your answer.)

Successful? Unsuccessful?

Cited Language: ______________________________

____

____

____

____

Page(s): _______________

(iii) In its final award, what monetary amount did the panel fix for damages to be paid by the losing party?

____

Page(s): _______________

(c) Provide a correct bluebook citation to this report.

____

____

____

____

2. Anabolic steroids present a persistent problem for authorities charged with the administration of international sporting competitions. These substances stimulate biological processes in the body that artificially enhance athletic performance. Many athletes around the world are tempted to use them to improve their chances of success, even though using them for this purpose (absent a genuine medical necessity) is illegal in most countries. The private non-governmental sports associations that largely manage international sporting competitions also generally prohibit their use. But what if athletes choose to use other illicit substances that might not necessarily have the effect of enhancing physical performance? Should athletes be penalized by sporting organizations when they ingest certain substances that, although concededly illegal, nevertheless do not necessarily unfairly affect their performance?

The Court of Arbitration for Sport, an arbitral body based in Lausanne, Switzerland, that has no structural connection to the ICC, issued an arbitral award in this connection in 1999. A swimmer had tested positive for the use of marijuana ("cannabinoids"), and had been suspended from international competition by international swimming authorities. The active ingredient in marijuana is a narcotic, rather than an anabolic steroid. The swimmer argued, among other things, that marijuana should not be considered a "banned substance" under relevant sporting regulations.

(a) Find a report of this award at an authoritative source.

(b) Research Questions. Upon reviewing the report you have retrieved, answer the following questions, in each case indicating the page number(s) on which you found your answer, using the numbering for the pages of the report at the source you used.

(i) What was the name of the swimmer, and what was his nationality?

______________________; __________

Page(s): __________

(ii) Did the panel concur that marijuana should not be considered a banned substance for these purposes? (Circle one of the two options below, and write the language from the report that you would cite as support for your answer.)

Yes? No?

Cited Language: ______________________________
____
____
____
____

Page(s): ______________

(iii) The panel awarded costs to the prevailing party. What was the monetary amount of the costs so awarded?

____

Page(s): ______________

(c) Provide a correct Bluebook citation to this report.

____
____
____
____

3. Distributorship agreements are a common feature of international business transactions. Usually, a distributor in one country engages in a long-term contract with a manufacturer or supplier in another country. Pursuant to this distributorship contract, the distributor actually purchases and takes title to the goods manufactured or supplied by its counterparty, and then sells them at retail in the distributor's country. (If the foreign seller doesn't take title in this way, the foreign seller is usually called merely a "sales agent.") The parties to international distributorship contracts (both suppliers and distributors) have a famous tendency to become disenchanted with each others' services, and the annals of arbitration and litigation are a rich trove of disputes in this area of business law. The distributors are usually smaller and less wealthy than their suppliers, and apparently it is easy for resentments to

develop on the part of distributors against their more economically powerful suppliers. The distributorship agreements are often drafted in ways that favor the supplier, and when difficulties develop distributors often attempt to be released, on one theory or another, from the requirements of their distributorship agreements.

Suppose your law firm represents the U.S. manufacturer of certain automobile parts, which has a distributorship agreement with a small company in Argentina. Under the agreement, the Argentine company has the exclusive right over a period of five years to sell the U.S. manufacturer's parts in Argentina. Problems develop with the distributor, who begins asserting that the distributorship contract is invalid, because it is allegedly a contract of adhesion. Your supervising attorney is certain she remembers an arbitration award "a few years back" involving a U.S. exporter and an Argentine distributor, in which the arbitral tribunal determined that the distributorship agreement there involved was not an adhesion contract. She is certain, however, that the arbitration was conducted under ICC auspices.

(a) See if you can find, at an authoritative source, a report of an arbitration award conforming to the description provided by the supervising attorney.

(b) Research Questions. Upon reviewing the report you have retrieved, answer the following questions, in each case indicating the page number(s) on which you found your answer, using the numbering for the pages of the report at the source you used.

(i) In what year was the award issued, and what was its ICC case number?

_______________; ______________________________
Page: _______________

(ii) What state's law was held by the arbitral tribunal in that award as being the law validly governing the contract? (Write the name of the state in the first blank below, then write the language from the report that you would cite as support for your answer.)

Name of State: ______________________

Cited Language: ______________________________
____
____
____

Page: ____________

(iii) The arbitral award partially relied, on the choice-of-law point, on a federal circuit court of appeals case. What was this case? (Provide a correct Bluebook citation.)

____
____
____

Page: ____________

(c) Provide a correct Bluebook citation to this report.

____
____
____
____

4. You are negotiating a contract on behalf of a "celebrity chef" who performs on a weekly television cooking program that is syndicated to individually-owned television stations across the U.S. The chef has received an offer from a French manufacturer of cooking utensils. Pursuant to the offer, the manufacturer will pay to the chef each quarter a fee that will vary according to the number of times during that quarter's shows the chef uses and praises the manufacturer's utensils. The manufacturer insists that there be a written agreement for this fee arrangement, and that it contain an arbitration clause. The chef is agreeable to the arbitration clause, but is absolutely determined that arbitration be by a sole arbitrator (rather than a panel of arbitrators), and that the arbitrator must himself or herself be a professional chef. The French manufacturer was initially insisting that the fee agreement's arbitration clause specify arbitration before the Paris Arbitral Chamber, using that body's Rules of Procedure. However, the manufacturer is owned by a German parent corporation, and after further negotiation you have determined that the manufacturer might instead consent to arbitration before the German Institution of Arbitration, using its Arbitration Rules. Both of these are private arbitral associations,

operating in their respective countries. You have been asked to determine which of these two regimes of arbitral rules would be more advantageous to the chef's position regarding service by a sole arbitrator who is a professional chef.

(a) Locate the Rules of Procedure of the Paris Arbitral Chamber and the Arbitration rules of the German Institution of Arbitration. (Find them in the form of reliable English translations.)

(b) Research Questions. Upon reviewing the two sets of rules, answer the following questions, in each case indicating the page or rule number in each set of rules on which your answer is based.

(i) What is the name of each of these organizations, as written in the language of the state in which it is located?

____

____

Page: ____________________

____

____

Page: ____________________

(ii) Which set of rules is more advantageous for the chef's position?

____

French Rule Citation(s): ____________________

German Rule Citation(s): ____________________

(c) Provide a correct Bluebook citation for each set of rules at the source you used for the above answers:

___

___

___

___

___

___

5. Investment by United States and Western European companies in less developed countries is a multi-faceted issue, particularly when the country involved is essentially a military dictatorship. However attractive the potential profits from the investment, companies have learned that doing business in such countries is truly a "risky business." ICSID, the International Centre for the Settlement of Investment Disputes, attempts to facilitate the resolution of disputes that can arise when investors in one state make active investments in business enterprises operating in other states. In 1980, an American investor, AMCO, which had constructed a hotel in Jakarta, Indonesia, found itself involved in a dispute over management of the hotel. Unfortunately, the opposing party was a cooperative that the government of Indonesian President Suharto had established for the welfare of Indonesian Army personnel. Things did not go well for AMCO and in 1981, AMCO and other investors filed for arbitration with ICSID. Three years later, the ICSID tribunal made its decision.

Find and cite the award on the merits in the arbitration between AMCO ASIA Corp. et al and the Republic of Indonesia, using an authoritative source.

___

___

___

(a) AMCO ASIA and its partners raised three issues in their brief: (1) a recent management takeover, (2) the revocation of its investment license, and (3) the actions of the Jakarta Courts.
How was the "takeover" achieved?

___

___

___

(b) How did both the Indonesian trial and appellate courts rule on this method of management takeover?

____

____

(c) What was the amount of the damages requested from the Indonesian government?

____

6. The United Nations Commission on International Trade Law (or "UNCITRAL") has, as one of its more significant activities, the drafting of model laws for adoption by national governments that are designed to stimulate international trade. UNCITRAL has developed Model Arbitration Rules, analogous to the rules discussed earlier in this Chapter by groups such as the ICC and the American Arbitration Association. However, UNCITRAL has also developed a "Model Law on International Commercial Arbitration." This Model Law is designed, among other purposes, to make the enforcement of arbitral awards by the various countries of the world more effective by providing a domestic-law mechanism governing arbitration and enforcement. Many countries around the world have adopted the UNCITRAL model law as domestic law. The United States Federal Government has not done so, however. This is probably because the Federal Arbitration Act, already in effect when the UNCITRAL text was promulgated and largely compatible with the New York Convention, has been judged adequate. However, several States within the United States have adopted the UNCITRAL model law. See if you can determine whether each of the following States has adopted the UNCITRAL Model Law on International Commercial Arbitration. For each State, indicate "Yes" for adoption and "No" if the State has not adopted the UNCITRAL model. Provide the citation to the State law for those States that have adopted the UNCITRAL model.

(a) California: Yes No

____

____

____

(b) Illinois: Yes No

____
____
____

(c) New York: Yes No

____
____
____

(d) Oregon: Yes No

____
____
____

CHAPTER 9

BASIC INTERNATIONAL CRIMINAL LAW

Part 1: Introduction and Overview

International Criminal Law is a field that is currently undergoing a period of significant development. Many of those who are already interested in International Law are aware of the establishment of the International Criminal Court (or "ICC"). While the ICC is a significant step forward in this area, it does not mark the beginning of International Criminal Law.

For many generations there had been the general social and political idea that some kinds of behavior that occurred in an international context were criminal in character and punishable at international law. The most dramatic and probably most established of these was piracy. However, for the most part the tribunals that heard piracy cases were the domestic courts of the states of the nationality of either the victims or the accused. Also, the criminality inherent in the act of piracy involved damage of a primarily private character: the injured individuals in each case were those who suffered the primary harm from the criminal act.

With the beginning of the twentieth century, these features of the idea of international criminality began to expand. The 1907 Hague Convention Respecting the Laws and Customs of War on Land, for example, reflected the beginning of the development of International Criminal Law in the modern era. This Convention began to refine in a modern context the concept that the behavior of states during wartime must meet certain standards in order to be consistent with law. Although no multilateral forum was envisioned to deal with violations, it contained the seed of the idea that the injured party could be the community of states, or even humanity as a whole, rather than merely the individuals most directly victimized by the behavior involved.

These broader perspectives were even more directly implicated in the 1948 Convention on the Prevention and Punishment of the Crime of Genocide and the 1949 Geneva Conventions. These treaties clearly conveyed the idea that the entire world had an interest in the minimally humane treatment of prisoners of war and civilian populations that are exposed to warfare and ethnic hostility. Although the treaties themselves did not provide for a multilateral tribunal for their enforcement, they were adopted in the shadow of the Nürnberg tribunals that tried and sentenced Nazi war criminals following the Second World War. These were multilateral fora for the trial of criminal charges that would serve as important precedents for the later development and construction of international criminal tribunals.

The Nürnberg tribunals, although multilateral, were of an ad hoc character, established for the single set of circumstances arising out of the Nazi genocide. This ad hoc character of multilateral criminal tribunals continued into the last decade of the twentieth century. In the early 1990's, the United Nations Security Council created two criminal tribunals to deal with war crimes and genocidal behavior in two distinct areas of the world. These were the International Criminal Tribunal for the Former Yugoslavia (often referred to by the acronym, "ICTY"), and the International Criminal Tribunal for Rwanda (often referred to as the "ICTR"). Although these tribunals were formed by the U.N. Security Council, and therefor were multilateral in origin, they were still designed to address only the particular situations within the geographical areas for which there were created. They accordingly continued the pattern of ad hoc tribunals for international criminal proceedings.

The ICC was created through the "Rome Statute for the International Criminal Court," signed in 1998 and entered into force in 2002. For the first time, the international community had created a permanent international criminal tribunal with extensive international jurisdiction that recognized the broad humanitarian character of the issues at stake and provided for the punishment of individual perpetrators.

CHAPTER 9	Part 2: Reading Exercises

Student Name: ______________________________

Read and review the Rome Statute of the International Criminal Court (the "ICC"), included in Unit B of this Course Book. Then answer the following questions.

1. The Rome Statute provides that the ICC has jurisdiction over only four crimes. What are they?

   ____
   ____
   ____
   ____

   Which provision of the Rome Statue is the basis for your answers above?

   ____

2. The provisions of the Rome Statute that define of the crimes over which the ICC has jurisdiction are among the most significant provisions of the Statute.

   (a) For which of these crimes does the Rome Statute provide the *most* textually complex definition?

   ____

   In which Article of the Statute does this definition appear?

   ____

(b) For which of these crimes does the Rome Statute provide the *least* textually complex definition?

____

In which Article of the Statute does this definition appear?

____

3. Which of the following is *not* a sufficient precondition to the exercise of jurisdiction by the ICC?

(a) The State on the territory of which the conduct in question occurred is a State Party to the Rome Statute.

(b) The State of the nationality of the victim or victims of the conduct in question is a State Party to the Rome Statute.

(c) The State of the nationality of the person accused of the crime is a State Party to the Rome Statute.

Which provision of the Rome Statute serves as the basis for your answer?

____

4. True or False Questions. With respect to each of the following statements, circle the word, "True" if you believe the statement is true and the word "False" if you believe it is false. In each case write the Article number (and paragraph number, if applicable) that corresponds to the provision of the Rome Statute on which your answer is based.

(a) True False ______________________________________

The crimes within the jurisdiction of the ICC are subject to a statute of limitations that varies with the severity of each crime alleged.

(b) True False ______________________________

The Rome Statute of the ICC accords full diplomatic immunity to ambassadors, consuls and other diplomatic officers who may be charged with crimes otherwise included within its scope.

(c) True False ______________________________

The ICC has no jurisdiction over any person who was under the age of 18 at the time of the alleged commission of a crime.

(d) True False ______________________________

If a State becomes a Party to the Rome Statute after its entry into force, the Court has jurisdiction only with respect to crimes in connection with such State committed after the entry into force of the Statute.

5. The titles of some of the Articles of the Rome Statute make liberal use of certain Latin phrases. The Statute never explicitly translates the phrases, but their meanings can be understood by reading the text of the Articles for which these titles are used. For each of the following Latin phrases, supply the Article number in which the phrase is used in the title, and its approximate meaning, as you derive it from your review of that Article.

(a) Nullum Crimen Sine Lege

Article: ________________

Meaning: ______________________________
____

(b) Nulla Poena Sine Lege

Article: ________________

Meaning: ______________________________
____

(c) Ne Bis In Idem

Article: ________________

Meaning: ____
____

(d) Ratione Personae

Article: ________________

Meaning: ____
____

6. Much has been made of the "complementary" character of the ICC's jurisdiction. Broadly speaking, this means that the ICC's jurisdiction over the crimes described in the Rome Statute is neither appellate over, nor preliminary to, criminal jurisdiction exercised by the courts of individual states. Rather, the ICC's jurisdiction with respect to these crimes is in a sense co-equal to the jurisdiction that might be exercised by national courts. In two provisions the Rome Statute refers to "complementary" jurisdiction explicitly. On the other hand, at other times the Statute references this concept by speaking in terms of a case being "inadmissible" before the ICC when it is already being investigated or prosecuted by a State having jurisdiction over the case.

(a) Which are the two provisions of the Rome Statute that explicitly refer to "complementary jurisdiction" in this sense? [*Hint:* You won't need to read very far into the Rome Statute to find them.]

____
____

(b) Which Article of the Rome Statute speaks most directly of the issue of "admissibility" of a case? [*Hint:* This Article includes the indicative language in its title.]

____

7. Part 4 of the Rome Statute deals with the composition and administration of the ICC. The primary element of the ICC's

composition, of course, consists of the judges who sit on the Court. Answer each of the following questions concerning the ICC's judges in the first blank line following the question. Indicate in the second blank line following each question which Article number (and paragraph number, if applicable) serves as the basis for your answer.

(a) According to the Rome Statute as initially effective, of how many judges is the ICC composed?

____

____

(b) In general, for how long does each judge hold office on the ICC?

____

____

(c) How many of the ICC judges constitute the presidency of the ICC?

____

____

(d) What is the minimum number of judges that must be assigned to each of the three divisions of the ICC?

___________________ Division: __________
___________________ Division: __________
___________________ Division: __________;

____

8. The Rome Statute requires that several personal characteristics be taken into account in the selection of judges. Which of the following personal characteristics are explicitly included in the Rome Statute as required considerations for the selection of judges? (For each characteristic that *is* explicitly included, provide the Article and paragraph number at which it is referenced; for each characteristic that is *not* explicitly included, indicate "not included.")

(a) Male or female.

____

(b) Representation of principal legal systems of the world.

____

(c) Age.

____

(d) Geographical representation.

____

(e) Legal expertise on specific issues.

____

9. True or False Questions. With respect to each of the following statements, circle the word, "True" if you believe the statement is true and the word "False" if you believe it is false. In each case write the Article number (and paragraph number, if applicable) that corresponds to the provision of the Rome Statute on which your answer is based.

(a) True False ________________________

According to the Rome Statute, the Office of the Prosecutor must consist of one Prosecutor and two Deputy Prosecutors.

(b) True False ________________________

The Prosecutor and Deputy Prosecutors are elected by secret ballot by an absolute majority of the members of the Assembly of States Parties.

(c) True False ________________________

A decision to remove a Prosecutor or Deputy Prosecutor is made by at least a two-thirds majority of the Assembly of States Parties, voting by secret ballot.

(d) True False ____________________

The judges, the Prosecutor and the Deputy Prosecutors of the ICC enjoy immunity from legal process of every kind in respect of their acts performed in their official capacity for so long as they are on the Court; this immunity terminates upon the termination of their service on the Court.

(e) True False ____________________

The salaries of the judges, the Prosecutor and the Deputy Prosecutors may only be reduced during their terms of office by a vote of an absolute majority of the Assembly of States parties, on a secret ballot.

10. (a) How many working languages does the Court have?

____

(b) Which provision of the Rome Statute is the basis of your answer?

____

(c) What are these languages?

____

____

(d) Which provision of the Rome Statute is the basis for your answer?

____

International criminal tribunals are increasing in number and importance in today's turbulent world as pointed out in this Chapter's overview. This trend creates new problems for the researcher. Fortunately, there are a number of excellent resources available, particularly on the Internet.

Electronic Resources

Each of the three major modern tribunals has its own website:

The International Criminal Tribunal for the Former Yugoslavia (ICTY) site may be accessed at http://www.un.org/icty.

The link for the International Criminal Tribunal for Rwanda (ICTR) site is http://www.ictr.org.

The newest tribunal, the International Criminal Court, has a site at http://www.icc-cpi.int/.

International Legal Materials, which contains pleadings and case decisions, is available via Westlaw and LexisNexis, as well as in hard-copy format.

Since these tribunals are ancillary entities of the United Nations, case documents may be found using *accessUN* from the Readex Corporation. Searching this database is less efficient than using some of the other sources listed, but this database does contain miscellaneous court documents not found in ILM.

Documents relating to the 1945 Nürnberg War Crimes Tribunal are available online at several sites retrieved by a Google search. A particularly good one is the Yale Law School's Avalon Project, www.yale.edu/lawweb/avalon.

Print Resources

There are many volumes covering the historic Nürnberg trials, not all of which contain the foundation documents. One of the more interesting titles is *The Nürnberg Case /as presented by Robert H. Jackson.* New York: A.A.

Knopf, 1947. Jackson was the chief prosecutor at the trial. Another is *The Nuremberg war crimes trial, 1945-46: a documentary history.* Michael Marrus, comp., Boston: Bedford Books, c1997. One of the most comprehensive and authoritative sources is the 15 volume *Trials of the Major War Criminals before the Nuremberg Military Tribunals under Control Council Law No. 10.* Washington, D.C., U.S. Gov. Print. Off, 1949. This series should be available at any major federal depository library.

The proceedings of the more modern international criminal tribunals may be found in a multi-volume serial set: *Global war crimes tribunal collection. The Yugoslav Tribunal* and *Global war crimes tribunal collection. The Rwanda Tribunal.* The set is published by the Global Law Association in Nijmegan, The Netherlands.

Two resources for information on the International Criminal Court are: *The International Criminal Court: elements of crimes and rules of procedure and evidence*, edited by Roy S. Lee. Ardsley, NY: Transnational Publishers, 2001 and the two volume, *The Rome Statute of the International Criminal Court: a commentary*, edited by Antonio Cassese, et al. Oxford, New York: Oxford University Press, 2002. The full text of the statute, rules of procedure and evidence, etc. are published in a separate volume.

A well recognized casebook which contains decisions and pleadings is Paust, Jordan, *International criminal law: cases and materials,* Durham, N.C.: Carolina Academic Press, 1996.

Finally it should be noted that resources discussed in earlier chapters such as treaties, resolutions of the U.N. General Assembly, restatements and works on customary law can be useful in researching international criminal law. These resources are available in both hard copy and electronic form.

CHAPTER 9	Part 4: Research Problems

Student Name: ______________________________

The following Research Problems are designed to help you implement the information contained in Parts 1 and 3 of this Chapter, and experience gained from completing the Reading Exercises in Part 2.

1. On August 8, 1945, the four principal victorious states of the Second World War executed an international agreement in London providing for the establishment of what became known as the Nürnberg War Crimes Tribunal. The legal constitutive document for this tribunal (what became known as the "Nürnberg Charter") was appended to the agreement. As indicated earlier in this Chapter, the Nürnberg Tribunal was in many important respects the precursor to today's ICTY, ICTR and ICC.

    (a) Find a copy of this international agreement, and its appended Nürnberg Charter, at an authoritative source.

    (b) Research Questions:

        (i) The Nürnberg Charter provided for the punishment of three international crimes. What were they?

        ____
        ____
        ____

Which provisions of the Charter provide for them, and on which page(s) of this source do the provisions appear?

________________________; _______________

(ii) A later protocol was adopted among the signatory countries for this agreement that had the sole effect of adjusting the punctuation of one of the provisions of the Nürnberg Charter. Which punctuation marks were affected, and in which provision of the Charter was the adjustment made?

________________________; _______________

What was the date of the Protocol, and what was its citation in the U.S. Statutes at Large?

____

(c) Provide a correct Bluebook citation for the 1945 international agreement.

____
____
____

2. The International Criminal Tribunal for the Former Yugoslavia ("ICTY") was established by a resolution of the United Nations Security Council in May 1993. The mere establishment of the ICTY was extremely significant in the field of International Human Rights, because no such criminal tribunal had ever before been convened by the international community as a whole to prosecute individuals for human rights violations. (It can be said that since the Nürnberg and Tokyo tribunals after World War II were convened by the victorious allied forces, they did not represent the same kind of action by the general international community.) Proceedings before the ICTY have been deliberative and marked by a notable regard for the procedural rights of defendants. The proceedings have attracted significant international public attention, and in the eyes of critics, they are painstakingly and unnecessarily slow. The first case in which the ICTY has ultimately determined the guilt or innocence of an individual

prosecuted through its procedures was that of Dusko Tadic, who was indicted on various counts of rape, murder, torture and other inhumane acts.

(a) Find a copy of the text of the "Opinion and Judgment" of the ICTY's Trial Chamber, that was the first ICTY judgment definitively determining the extent of Tadic's guilt or innocence.

(b) Research Questions:

(i) Under this Opinion and Judgment, of how many of the counts of his indictment was Mr. Tadic adjudged:

guilty? __________
not guilty? __________
partially guilty and partially not guilty? __________

Indicate the page of the originally published U.N. document at which this information appears:

____

(ii) In one part of this Opinion and Judgment, the Trial Chamber discusses whether the prohibition of Crimes Against Humanity has become a rule of Customary International Law. Does the Trial Chamber find that this prohibition is, or is not, a rule of Customary International Law?

Provide the language of the Opinion and Judgment that serves as the basis for your answer; indicate also the page of the originally published U.N. document, and the paragraph number on it, at which this language appears:

____
____;
____

(c) Provide a correct "Bluebook" citation to this case at the source you used.

____
____
____
____

3. Using the publication, *International Legal Materials*, find the text of the U.N. Security Council resolution that established the ICTY.

(a) Research Questions:

(i) Was the Security Council resolution establishing the ICTY passed unanimously? If not, which countries voted against it?

____

(ii) Which paragraph of the resolution in substance actually establishes the ICTY?

____

(b) Provide a correct "Bluebook" citation to the resolution at this source.

____
____
____

4. The International Criminal Tribunal for Rwanda ("ICTR") is sitting in the city of Arusha, in the Republic of Tanzania. The U.N. Security Council established the ICTR in 1994. Among the decisions the Tribunal has issued are several with quite diverse results. For example, the cases of two defendants brought before the ICTR resulted in quite different outcomes before the Tribunal: Messrs. Jean Kambanda and Bernard Ntuyahaga.

(a) Find, at an authoritative source, the definitive decisional documents ultimately stating the legal outcome for these two defendants before the ICTR.

(b) Research Questions:

(i) What is the name and date of the decisional document for Mr. Kambanda?

____;
____

What was the Tribunal's ultimate disposition in the case against Mr. Kambanda?

____
____

Using this source, at which page do you find support for your immediately preceding answer?

____

(ii) What is the name and date of the decisional document for Mr. Ntuyahaga?

____;
____

What was the Tribunal's ultimate disposition in the case against Mr. Ntuyahaga?

____
____

Using this source, at which page do you find support for your immediately preceding answer?

____

(c) Provide correct Bluebook citations to each of these decisional documents at this source.

____

____

____

____

5. For Part 2 of this Chapter, we reviewed the Rome Statute of the International Criminal Court. We saw that while the Statute contains specific definitions of most of the crimes within its jurisdiction, Article 9(1) of the Statute directs the Assembly of States Parties to adopt "Elements of Crimes." Such Elements are necessary to provide precise and detailed criteria for determining whether any particular individual's conduct satisfies the definitions of the crimes involved. In September of 2002, the Assembly of States Parties adopted its "Elements of Crimes" pursuant to the Statute's directive.

(a) Find a text of the ICC's "Elements of Crimes."

(b) Research Questions:

(i) Within these "Elements," criminal behavior amounting to "torture" is explicitly dealt with for three different delineated crimes. What is the Article number assigned to each of these three different definitions?

____

____

____

The three sets of elements for the three crimes are quite different, except that they contain one element that is identical as between the three of them. Provide below the identical element.

____

____

____

(ii) Two of the delineated crimes specifically depend upon the status of their victims as children, and so indicate in their titles. Which two of the delineated crimes are these, and which Article number is assigned to each?

_______________________________; ______
_______________________________; ______

Interestingly, the minimum age required for the status of being a child is different as between the two provisions. Which age is required for each?

____________; Article __________________
____________; Article __________________

(c) Provide a complete citation to this document.

____
____
____

6. The ICC has also issued a detailed set of "Rules of Procedure and Evidence." These were adopted by the Assembly of States Parties also in September of 2002.

(a) Find a copy of the text of these Rules of Procedure and Evidence.

(b) Research Questions:

(i) Many jurisdictions in the United States have adopted certain evidentiary rules for rape cases, pursuant to which the use of evidence tending to show the prior sexual activities of the alleged victim is sharply curtailed at trial. These Rules also contain a similar provision.

Which rule (including the specific sub-paragraph or "sub-rule") contains this safeguard?

____

Under this rule, prior sexual conduct of a victim cannot be used to infer three issues. What are these three issues?

____

____

____

(ii) According to these Rules, can the ICC ever require a witness to answer a question that is self-incriminating?

Circle One: Yes No

Which rule (including the specific sub-paragraph or "sub-rule") is the most *direct* authority for your answer?

____

(c) Provide a complete citation to this document.

____

____

____

UNIT	BACKGROUND DOCUMENT FOR CHAPTER 1
B	Document: The United Nations Charter

CHARTER OF THE UNITED NATIONS

June 26, 1945, 59 Stat. 1031, 3 Bevans 1153 (Oct. 24, 1945).

We the Peoples Of The United Nations Determined

to save succeeding generations from the scourge of war, which twice in our lifetime has brought untold sorrow to mankind, and

to reaffirm faith in fundamental human rights, in the dignity and worth of the human person, in the equal rights of men and women and of nations large and small, and

to establish conditions under which justice and respect for the obligations arising from treaties and other sources of international law can be maintained, and

to promote social progress and better standards of life in larger freedom,

And for these Ends

to practice tolerance and live together in peace with one another as good neighbours, and

to unite our strength to maintain international peace and security, and

to ensure, by the acceptance of principles and the institution of methods, that armed force shall not be used, save in the common interest, and to employ international machinery for the promotion of the economic and social advancement of all peoples,

Have Resolved to Combine our Efforts to Accomplish these Aims

accordingly, our respective Governments, through representatives assembled in the city of San Francisco, who have exhibited their full powers found to be in good and due form, have agreed to the present Charter of the United Nations and do hereby establish an international organization to be known as the United Nations.

CHAPTER I

PURPOSES AND PRINCIPLES

Article 1

The Purposes of the United Nations are:

1. To maintain international peace and security, and to that end: to take effective collective measures for the prevention and removal of threats to the peace, and for the suppression of acts of aggression or other breaches of the peace, and to bring about by peaceful means, and in conformity with the principles of justice and international law, adjustment or settlement of international disputes or situations which might lead to a breach of the peace;

2. To develop friendly relations among nations based on respect for the principle of equal rights and self-determination of peoples, and to take other appropriate measures to strengthen universal peace;

3. To achieve international co-operation in solving international problems of an economic, social, cultural, or humanitarian character, and in promoting and encouraging respect for human rights and for fundamental freedoms for all without distinction as to race, sex, language, or religion; and

4. To be a centre for harmonizing the actions of nations in the attainment of these common ends.

Article 2

The Organization and its Members, in pursuit of the Purposes stated in Article 1, shall act in accordance with the following Principles.

1. The Organization is based on the principle of the sovereign equality of all its Members.
2. All Members, in order to ensure to all of them the rights and benefits resulting from membership, shall fulfill in good faith the obligations assumed by them in accordance with the present Charter.
3. All Members shall settle their international disputes by peaceful means in such a manner that international peace and security, and justice, are not endangered.
4. All Members shall refrain in their international relations from the threat or use of force against the territorial integrity or political independence of any state, or in any other manner inconsistent with the Purposes of the United Nations.
5. All Members shall give the United Nations every assistance in any action it takes in accordance with the present Charter, and shall refrain from giving assistance to any state against which the United Nations is taking preventive or enforcement action.
6. The Organization shall ensure that states which are not Members of the United Nations act in accordance with these Principles so far as may be necessary for the maintenance of international peace and security.
7. Nothing contained in the present Charter shall authorize the United Nations to intervene in matters which are essentially within the domestic jurisdiction of any state or shall require the Members to submit such matters to settlement under the present Charter; but this principle shall not prejudice the application of enforcement measures under Chapter VII.

CHAPTER II

MEMBERSHIP

Article 3

The original Members of the United Nations shall be the states which, having participated in the United Nations Conference on International Organization at San Francisco, or having previously signed the Declaration by United Nations of 1 January 1942, sign the present Charter and ratify it in accordance with Article 110.

Article 4

1. Membership in the United Nations is open to all other peace-loving states which accept the obligations contained in the present Charter and, in the judgment of the Organization, are able and willing to carry out these obligations.
2. The admission of any such state to membership in the United Nations will be effected by a decision of the General Assembly upon the recommendation of the Security Council.

Article 5

A Member of the United Nations against which preventive or enforcement action has been taken by the Security Council may be suspended from the exercise of the rights and privileges of membership by the General Assembly upon the recommendation of the Security Council. The exercise of these rights and privileges may be restored by the Security Council.

Article 6

A Member of the United Nations which has persistently violated the Principles contained in the present Charter may be expelled from the Organization by the General Assembly upon the recommendation of the Security Council.

CHAPTER III

ORGANS

Article 7

1. There are established as the principal organs of the United Nations: a General Assembly, a Security Council, an Economic and Social Council, a Trusteeship Council, an International Court of Justice, and a Secretariat.
2. Such subsidiary organs as may be found necessary may be established in accordance with the present Charter.

Article 8

The United Nations shall place no restrictions on the eligibility of men and women to participate in any capacity and under conditions of equality in its principal and subsidiary organs.

CHAPTER IV

THE GENERAL ASSEMBLY

Composition

Article 9

1. The General Assembly shall consist of all the Members of the United Nations.
2. Each Member shall have not more than five representatives in the General Assembly.

Functions and Powers

Article 10

The General Assembly may discuss any questions or any matters within the scope of the present Charter or relating to the powers and functions of any organs provided for in the present Charter, and, except as provided in Article 12, may make recommendations to the Members of the United Nations or to the Security Council or to both on any such questions or matters.

Article 11

1. The General Assembly may consider the general principles of co-operation in the maintenance of international peace and security, including the principles governing disarmament and the regulation of armaments, and may make recommendations with regard to such principles to the Members or to the Security Council or to both.
2. The General Assembly may discuss any questions relating to the maintenance of international peace and security brought before it by any Member of the United Nations, or by the Security Council, or by a state which is not a Member of the United Nations in accordance with Arti-

cle 35, paragraph 2, and, except as provided in Article 12, may make recommendations with regard to any such questions to the state or states concerned or to the Security Council or to both. Any such question on which action is necessary shall be referred to the Security Council by the General Assembly either before or after discussion.

3. The General Assembly may call the attention of the Security Council to situations which are likely to endanger international peace and security.

4. The powers of the General Assembly set forth in this Article shall not limit the general scope of Article 10.

Article 12

1. While the Security Council is exercising in respect of any dispute or situation the functions assigned to it in the present Charter, the General Assembly shall not make any recommendation with regard to that dispute or situation unless the Security Council so requests.

2. The Secretary-General, with the consent of the Security Council, shall notify the General Assembly at each session of any matters relative to the maintenance of international peace and security which are being dealt with by the Security Council and similarly notify the General Assembly, or the Members of the United Nations if the General Assembly is not in session, immediately the Security Council ceases to deal with such matters.

Article 13

1. The General Assembly shall initiate studies and make recommendations for the purpose of:

    a. promoting international co-operation in the political field and encouraging the progressive development of international law and its codification;

    b. promoting international co-operation in the economic, social, cultural, educational, and health fields, and assisting in the realization of human rights and fundamental freedoms for all without distinction as to race, sex, language, or religion.

2. The further responsibilities, functions and powers of the General with respect to matters mentioned in paragraph 1(b) above are set forth in Chapters IX and X.

Article 14

Subject to the provisions of Article 12, the General Assembly may recommend measures for the peaceful adjustment of any situation, regardless of origin, which it deems likely to impair the general welfare or friendly relations among nations, including situations resulting from a violation of the provisions of the present Charter setting forth the Purposes and Principles of the United Nations.

Article 15

1. The General Assembly shall receive and consider annual and special reports from the Security Council; these reports shall include an account of the measures that the Security Council has decided upon or taken to maintain international peace and security.
2. The General Assembly shall receive and consider reports from the other organs of the United Nations.

Article 16

The General Assembly shall perform such functions with respect to the international trusteeship system as are assigned to it under Chapters XII and XIII, including the approval of the trusteeship agreements for areas not designated as strategic.

Article 17

1. The General Assembly shall consider and approve the budget of the Organization.
2. The expenses of the Organization shall be borne by the Members as apportioned by the General Assembly.
3. The Assembly shall consider and approve any financial and budgetary arrangements with specialize agencies referred to in Article 57 and shall examine the administrative budgets of such specialized agencies with a view to making recommendations to the agencies concerned.

Voting

Article 18

1. Each member of the General Assembly shall have one vote.

2. Decisions of the General Assembly on important questions shall be made by a two-thirds majority of the members present and voting. These questions shall include: recommendations with respect to the maintenance of international peace and security, the election of the non-permanent members of the Security Council, the election of the members of the Economic and Social Council, the election of members of the Trusteeship Council in accordance with paragraph 1(c) of Article 86, the admission of new Members to the United Nations, the suspension of the rights and privileges of membership, the expulsion of Members, questions relating to the operation of the trusteeship system, and budgetary questions.
3. Decisions on other questions, including the determination of additional categories of questions to be decided by a two-thirds majority, shall be made by a majority of the members present and voting.

Article 19

A Member of the United Nations which is in arrears in the payment of its financial contributions to the Organization shall have no vote in the General Assembly if the amount of its arrears equals or exceeds the amount of the contributions due from it for the preceding two full years. The General Assembly may, nevertheless, permit such a Member to vote if it is satisfied that the failure to pay is due to conditions beyond the of the Member.

Procedure

Article 20

The General Assembly shall meet in regular annual sessions and in such special sessions as occasion may require. Special sessions shall be convoked by the Secretary-General at the request of the Security Council or of a majority of the Members of the United Nations.

Article 21

The General Assembly shall adopt its own rules of procedure. It shall elect its President for each session.

Article 22

The General Assembly may establish such subsidiary organs as it deems necessary for the performance of its functions.

CHAPTER V

THE SECURITY COUNCIL

Composition

Article 23

1. The Security Council shall consist of fifteen Members of the United Nations. The Republic of China, France, the Union of Soviet Socialist Republics, the United Kingdom of Great Britain and Northern Ireland, and the United States of America shall be permanent members of the Security Council. The General Assembly shall elect ten other Members of the United Nations to be non-permanent members of the Security Council, due regard being specially paid, in the first instance to the contribution of Members of the United Nations to the maintenance of international peace and security and to the other purposes of the Organization, and also to equitable geographical distribution.
2. The non-permanent members of the Security Council shall be elected for a term of two years. In the first election of the non-permanent members after the increase of the membership of the Security Council from eleven to fifteen, two of the four additional members shall be chosen for a term of one year. A retiring member shall not be eligible for immediate re-election.
3. Each member of the Security Council shall have one representative.

Functions and Powers

Article 24

1. In order to ensure prompt and effective action by the United Nations, its Members confer on the Security Council primary responsibility for the maintenance of international peace and security, and agree that in carrying out its duties under this responsibility the Security Council acts on their behalf.

2. In discharging these duties the Security Council shall act in accordance with the Purposes and Principles of the United Nations. The specific powers granted to the Security Council for the discharge of these duties are laid down in Chapters VI, VII, VIII, and XII.
3. The Security Council shall submit annual and, when necessary, special reports to the General Assembly for its consideration.

Article 25

The Members of the United Nations agree to accept and carry out the decisions of the Security Council in accordance with the present Charter.

Article 26

In order to promote the establishment and maintenance of international peace and security with the least diversion for armaments of the world's human and economic resources, the Security Council shall be responsible for formulating, with the assistance of the Military Staff Committee referred to in Article 47, plans to be submitted to the Members of the United-Nations for the establishment of a system for the regulation of armaments.

Voting

Article 27

1. Each member of the Security Council shall have one vote.
2. Decisions of the Security Council on procedural matters shall be made by an affirmative vote of nine members.
3. Decisions of the Security Council on all other matters shall be made by an affirmative vote of nine members including the concurring votes of the permanent members; provided that, in decisions under Chapter VI, and under paragraph 3 of Article 52, a party to a dispute shall abstain from voting.

Procedure

Article 28

1. The Security Council shall be so organized as to be able to function continuously. Each member of the Security Council shall for this purpose be represented at times at the seat of the Organization.
2. The Security Council shall hold periodic meetings at which each of its members may, if it so desires, be represented by a member of the government or by some other specially designated representative.
3. The Security Council may hold meetings at such places other than the seat of the Organization as in its judgment will best facilitate its work.

Article 29

The Security Council may establish such subsidiary organs as it deems necessary for the performance of its functions.

Article 30

The Security Council shall adopt its own rules of procedure, including the method of selecting its President.

Article 31

Any Member of the United Nations which is not a member of the Security Council may participate, without vote, in the discussion of any question brought before the Security Council whenever the latter considers that the interests of that Member are specially affected.

Article 32

Any Member of the United Nations which is not a member of the Security Council or any state which is not a Member of the United Nations, if it is a party to a dispute under consideration by the Security Council, shall be invited to participate, without vote, in the discussion relating to the dispute. The Security Council shall lay down such conditions as it deems just for the participation of a state which is not a Member of the United Nations.

CHAPTER VI

PACIFIC SETTLEMENT OF DISPUTES

Article 33

1. The parties to any dispute, the continuance of which is likely to endanger the maintenance of international peace and security, shall, first of all, seek a solution by negotiation, enquiry, mediation, conciliation, arbitration, judicial settlement, resort to regional agencies or arrangements, or other peaceful means of their own choice.
2. The Security Council shall, when it deems necessary, call upon the parties to settle their dispute by such means.

Article 34

The Security Council may investigate any dispute, or any situation which might lead to international friction or give rise to a dispute, in order to determine whether the continuance of the dispute or situation is likely to endanger the maintenance of international peace and security.

Article 35

1. l. Any Member of the United Nations may bring any dispute, or any situation of the nature referred to in Article 34, to the attention of the Security Council or of the General Assembly.
2. A state which is not a Member of the United Nations may bring to the attention of the Security Council or of the General Assembly any dispute to which it is a party if it accepts in advance, for the purposes of the dispute, the obligations of pacific settlement provided in the present Charter.
3. The proceedings of the General Assembly in respect of matters brought to its attention under this Article will be subject to the provisions of Articles 11 and 12.

Article 36

1. The Security Council may, at any stage of a dispute of the nature referred to in Article 33 or of a situation of like nature, recommend appropriate procedures or methods of adjustment.

2. The Security Council should take into consideration any procedures for the settlement of the dispute which have already been adopted by the parties.
3. In making recommendations under this Article the Security Council should also take into consideration that legal disputes should as a general rule be referred by the parties to the International Court of Justice in accordance with the provisions of the Statute of the Court.

Article 37

1. Should the parties to a dispute of the nature referred to in Article 33 fail to settle it by the means indicated in that Article, they shall refer it to the Security Council.
2. If the Security Council deems that the continuance of the dispute is in fact likely to endanger the maintenance of international peace and security, it shall decide whether to take action under Article 36 or to recommend such terms of settlement as it may consider appropriate.

Article 38

Without prejudice to the provisions of Articles 33 to 37, the Security Council may, if all the parties to any dispute so request, make recommendations to the parties with a view to a pacific settlement of the dispute.

CHAPTER VII

ACTION WITH RESPECT TO THREATS TO THE PEACE, BREACHES OF THE PEACE, AND ACTS OF AGGRESSION

Article 39

The Security Council shall determine the existence of any threat to the peace, breach of the peace, or act of aggression and shall make recommendations, or decide what measures shall be taken in accordance with Articles 41 and 42, to maintain or restore international peace and security.

Article 40

In order to prevent an aggravation of the situation, the Security Council may, before making the recommendations or deciding upon the measures provided for in Article 39, call upon the parties concerned to comply with such provisional measures as it deems necessary or desirable. Such provisional measures shall be without prejudice to the rights, claims, or position of the parties concerned. The Security Council shall duly take account of failure to comply with such provisional measures.

Article 41

The Security Council may decide what measures not involving the use of armed force are to be employed to give effect to its decisions, and it may call upon the Members of the United Nations to apply such measures. These may include complete or partial interruption of economic relations and of rail, sea, air, postal, telegraphic, radio, and other means of communication, and the severance of diplomatic relations.

Article 42

Should the Security Council consider that measures provided for in Article 41 would be inadequate or have proved to be inadequate, it may take such action by air, sea, or land forces as may be necessary to maintain or restore international peace and security. Such action may include demonstrations, blockade, and other operations by air, sea, or land forces of Members of the United Nations.

Article 43

1. All Members of the United Nations, in order to contribute to the maintenance of international peace and security, undertake to make available to the Security Council, on its and in accordance with a special agreement or agreements, armed forces, assistance, and facilities, including rights of passage, necessary for the purpose of maintaining international peace and security.
2. Such agreement or agreements shall govern the numbers and types of forces, their degree of readiness and general location, and the nature of the facilities and assistance to be provided.
3. The agreement or agreements shall be negotiated as soon as possible on the initiative of the Security Council. They shall be concluded between the Security Council and Members or between the Security Council and groups of Members and shall be subject to ratification by the signatory states in accordance with their respective constitutional processes.

Article 44

When the Security Council has decided to use force it shall, before calling upon a Member not represented on it to provide armed forces in fulfillment of the obligations assumed under Article 43, invite that Member, if the Member so desires, to participate in the decisions of the Security Council concerning the employment of contingents of that Member's armed forces.

Article 45

In order to enable the United Nations to take urgent military measures, Members shall hold immediately available national air-force contingents for combined international enforcement action. The strength and degree of readiness of these contingents and plans for their combined action shall be determined within the limits laid down in the special agreement or agreements referred to in Article 43, by the Security Council with the assistance of the Military Staff Committee.

Article 46

Plans for the application of armed force shall be made by the Security Council with the assistance of the Military Staff Committee.

Article 47

1. There shall be established a Military Staff Committee to advise and assist the Security Council on all questions relating to the Security Council's military requirements for the maintenance of international peace and security, the employment and command of forces placed at its disposal, the regulation of armaments, and possible disarmament.
2. The Military Staff Committee shall consist of the Chiefs of Staff of the permanent members of the Security Council or their representatives. Any Member of the United Nations not permanently represented on the Committee shall be invited by the Committee to be associated with it when the efficient discharge of the Committee's responsibilities requires the participation of that Member in its work.
3. The Military Staff Committee shall be responsible under the Security Council for the strategic direction of any armed forces placed at the disposal of the Security Council. Questions relating to the command of such forces shall be worked out subsequently.

4. The Military Staff Committee, with the authorization of the Security Council and after consultation with appropriate regional agencies, may establish regional sub-committees.

Article 48

1. The action required to carry out the decisions of the Security Council for the maintenance of international peace and security shall be taken by all the Members of the United Nations or by some of them, as the Security Council may determine.
2. Such decisions shall be carried out by the Members of the United Nations directly and through their action in the appropriate international agencies of which they are members.

Article 49

The Members of the United Nations shall join in affording mutual assistance in carrying out the measures decided upon by the Security Council.

Article 50

If preventive or enforcement measures against any state are taken by the Security Council, any other state, whether a Member of the United Nations or not, which finds itself confronted with special economic problems arising from the carrying out of those measures shall have the right to consult the Security Council with regard to a solution of those problems.

Article 51

Nothing in the present Charter shall impair the inherent right of individual or collective self-defence if an armed attack occurs against a Member of the United Nations, until the Security Council has taken measures necessary to maintain international peace and security. Measures taken by Members in the exercise of this right of self-defence shall be immediately reported to the Security Council and shall not in any way affect the authority and responsibility of the Security Council under the present Charter to take at any time such action as it deems necessary in order to maintain or restore international peace and security.

CHAPTER VIII

REGIONAL ARRANGEMENTS

Article 52

1. Nothing in the present Charter precludes the existence of regional arrangements or agencies for dealing with such matters relating to the maintenance of international peace and security as are appropriate for regional action provided that such arrangements or agencies and their activities are consistent with the Purposes and Principles of the United Nations.
2. The Members of the United Nations entering into such arrangements or constituting such agencies shall make every effort to achieve pacific settlement of local disputes through such regional arrangements or by such regional agencies before referring them to the Security Council.
3. The Security Council shall encourage the development of pacific settlement of local disputes through such regional arrangements or by such regional agencies either on the initiative of the states concerned or by reference from the Security Council.
4. This Article in no way impairs the application of Articles 34 and 35.

Article 53

1. The Security Council shall, where appropriate, utilize such regional arrangements or agencies for enforcement action under its authority. But no enforcement action shall be taken under regional arrangements or by regional agencies without the authorization of the Security Council, with the exception of measures against any enemy state, as defined in paragraph 2 of this Article, provided for pursuant to Article 107 or in regional arrangements directed against renewal of aggressive policy on the part of any such state, until such time as the Organization may, on request of the Governments concerned, be charged with the responsibility for preventing further aggression by such a state.
2. The term enemy state as used in paragraph 1 of this Article applies to any state which during the Second World War has been an enemy of any signatory of the present Charter.

Article 54

The Security Council shall at all times be kept fully informed of activities undertaken or in contemplation under regional arrangements or by regional agencies for the maintenance of international peace and security.

CHAPTER IX

INTERNATIONAL ECONOMIC AND SOCIAL CO-OPERATION

Article 55

With a view to the creation of conditions of stability and well-being which are necessary for peaceful and friendly relations among nations based on respect for the principle of equal rights and self-determination of peoples, the United Nations shall promote:

a. higher standards of living, full employment, and conditions of economic and social progress and development;

b. solutions of international economic, social, health, and related problems; and international cultural and educational co-operation; and

c. universal respect for, and observance of, human rights and fundamental freedoms for all without distinction as to race, sex, language, or religion.

Article 56

All Members pledge themselves to take joint and separate action in co-operation with the Organization for the achievement of the purposes set forth in Article 55.

Article 57

1. The various specialized agencies, established by intergovernmental agreement and having wide international responsibilities, as defined in their basic instruments, in economic, social, cultural, educational, health, and related fields, shall be brought into relationship with the United Nations in accordance with the provisions of Article 63.

2. Such agencies thus brought into relationship with the United Nations are hereinafter referred to as specialized agencies.

Article 58

The Organization shall make recommendations for the co-ordination of the policies and activities of the specialized agencies.

Article 59

The Organization shall, where appropriate, initiate negotiations among the states concerned for the creation of any new specialized agencies required for the accomplishment of the purposes set forth in Article 55.

Article 60

Responsibility for the discharge of the functions of the Organization set forth in this Chapter shall be vested in the General Assembly and, under the authority of the General Assembly, in the Economic and Social Council, which shall have for this purpose the powers set forth in Chapter X.

CHAPTER X

THE ECONOMIC AND SOCIAL COUNCIL

Composition

Article 61

1. The Economic and Social Council shall consist of fifty-four Members of the United Nations elected by the General Assembly.
2. Subject to the provisions of paragraph 3, eighteen members of the Economic and Social Council shall be elected each year for a term of three years. A retiring member shall be eligible for immediate re-election.
3. At the first election after the increase in the membership of the Economic and Social Council from twenty-seven to fifty-four members, in addition to the members elected in place of the nine members whose term of office expires at the end of that year, twenty-seven additional members shall be elected. Of these twenty-seven additional members, the term of office of nine members so elected shall expire at the end of

one year, and of nine other members at the end of two years, in accordance with arrangements made by the General Assembly.

4. Each member of the Economic and Social Council shall have one representative.

Functions and Powers

Article 62

1. The Economic and Social Council may make or initiate studies and reports with respect to international economic, social, cultural, educational, health, and related matters and may make recommendations with respect to any such matters to the General Assembly to the Members of the United Nations, and to the specialized agencies concerned.
2. It may make recommendations for the purpose of promoting respect for, and observance of, human rights and fundamental freedoms for all.
3. It may prepare draft conventions for submission to the General Assembly, with respect to matters falling within its competence.
4. It may call, in accordance with the rules prescribed by the United Nations, international conferences on matters falling within its competence.

Article 63

1. The Economic and Social Council may enter into agreements with any of the agencies referred to in Article 57, defining the terms on which the agency concerned shall be brought into relationship with the United Nations. Such agreements shall be subject to approval by the General Assembly.
2. It may co-ordinate the activities of the specialized agencies through consultation with and recommendations to such agencies and through recommendations to the General Assembly and to the Members of the United Nations.

Article 64

1. The Economic and Social Council may take appropriate steps to obtain regular reports from the specialized agencies. It may make arrangements with the Members of the United Nations and with the specialized

agencies to obtain reports on the steps taken to give effect to its own recommendations and to recommendations on matters falling within its competence made by the General Assembly.

2. It may communicate its observations on these reports to the General Assembly.

Article 65

The Economic and Social Council may furnish information to the Security Council and shall assist the Security Council upon its request.

Article 66

1. The Economic and Social Council shall perform such functions as fall within its competence in connexion with the carrying out of the recommendations of the General Assembly.
2. It may, with the approval of the General Assembly, perform services at the request of Members of the United Nations and at the request of specialized agencies.
3. It shall perform such other functions as are specified elsewhere in the present Charter or as may be assigned to it by the General Assembly.

Voting

Article 67

1. Each member of the Economic and Social Council shall have one vote.
2. Decisions of the Economic and Social Council shall be made by a majority of the members present and voting.

Procedure

Article 68

The Economic and Social Council shall set up commissions in economic and social fields and for the promotion of human rights, and such other commissions as may required for the performance of its functions.

Article 69

The Economic and Social Council shall invite any Member of the United Nations to participate, without vote, in its deliberations on any matter of particular concern to that Member.

Article 70

The Economic and Social Council may make arrangements for representatives of the specialized agencies to participate, without vote, in its deliberations and in those of the commissions established by it, and for its representatives to participate in the deliberations of the specialized agencies.

Article 71

The Economic and Social Council may make suitable arrangements for consultation with non-governmental organizations which are concerned with matters within its competence. Such arrangements may be made with international organizations and, where appropriate, with national organizations after consultation with the Member of the United Nations concerned.

Article 72

1. The Economic and Social Council shall adopt its own rules of procedure, including the method of selecting its President.
2. The Economic and Social Council shall meet as required in accordance with its rules, which shall include provision for the convening of meetings on the request of a majority of its members.

CHAPTER XI

DECLARATION REGARDING NON-SELF-GOVERNING TERRITORIES

Article 73

Members of the United Nations which have or assume responsibilities for the administration of territories whose peoples have not yet attained a full measure of self-government recognize the principle that the interests of the inhabitants of these territories are paramount, and accept as a sacred trust the obligation to promote to the utmost, within the system of international peace and security established by the present Charter, the well-being of the inhabitants of these territories, and, to this end:

a. to ensure, with due respect for the culture of the peoples concerned, their political, economic, social, and educational advancement, their just treatment, and their protection against abuses;

b. to develop self-government, to take due account of the political aspirations of the peoples, and to assist them in the progressive development of their free political institutions, according to the particular circumstances of each territory and its peoples and their varying stages of advancement;

c. to further international peace and security;

d. to promote constructive measures of development, to encourage research, and to co-operate with one another and, when and where appropriate, with specialized international bodies with a view to the practical achievement of the social, economic, and scientific purposes set forth in this Article; and

e. to transmit regularly to the Secretary-General for information purposes, subject to such limitation as security and constitutional considerations may require, statistical and other information of a technical nature relating to economic, social, and educational conditions in the territories for which they are respectively responsible other than those territories to which Chapters XII and XIII apply.

Article 74

Members of the United Nations also agree that their policy in respect of the territories to which this Chapter applies, no less than in respect of their metropolitan areas, must be based on the general principle of good-neighbourliness, due account being taken of the interests and well-being of the rest of the world, in social, economic, and commercial matters.

CHAPTER XII

INTERNATIONAL TRUSTEESHIP SYSTEM

Article 75

The United Nations shall establish under its authority an international trusteeship system for the administration and supervision of such territories as may be placed thereunder by subsequent individual agreements. These territories are hereinafter referred to as trust territories.

Article 76

The basic objectives of the trusteeship system, in accordance with the Purposes of the United Nations laid down in Article 1 of the present Charter, shall be:

a. to further international peace and security;

b. to promote the political, economic, social, and educational advancement of the inhabitants of the trust territories, and their progressive development towards self-government or independence as may be appropriate to the particular circumstances of each territory and its peoples and the freely expressed wishes of the peoples concerned, and as may be provided by the terms of each trusteeship agreement;

c. to encourage respect for human rights and for fundamental freedoms for all without distinction as to race, sex, language, or religion, and to encourage recognition of the interdependence of the peoples of the world; and

d. to ensure equal treatment in social, economic, and commercial matters for all Members of the United Nations and their nationals, and also equal treatment for the latter in the administration of justice, without prejudice to the attainment of the foregoing objectives and subject to the provisions of Article 80.

Article 77

1. The trusteeship system shall apply to such territories in the following categories as may be placed thereunder by means of trusteeship agreements:

   a. territories now held under mandate;

   b. territories which may be detached from enemy states as a result of the Second World War; and

   c. territories voluntarily placed under the system by states responsible for their administration.

2. It will be a matter for subsequent agreement as to which territories in the foregoing categories will be brought under the trusteeship system and upon what terms.

Article 78

The trusteeship system shall not apply to territories which have become Members of the United Nations, relationship among which shall be based on respect for the principle of sovereign equality.

Article 79

The terms of trusteeship for each territory to be placed under the trusteeship system, including any alteration or amendment, shall be agreed upon by the states directly concerned, including the mandatory power in the case of territories held under mandate by a Member of the United Nations, and shall be approved as provided for in Articles 83 and 85.

Article 80

1. Except as may be agreed upon in individual trusteeship agreements, made under Articles 77, 79, and 81, placing each territory under the trusteeship system, and until such agreements have been concluded, nothing in this Chapter shall be construed in or of itself to alter in any manner the rights whatsoever of any states or any peoples or the terms of existing international instruments to which Members of the United Nations may respectively be parties.

2. Paragraph 1 of this Article shall not be interpreted as giving grounds for delay or postponement of the negotiation and conclusion of agree-

ments for placing mandated and other territories under the trusteeship system as provided for in Article 77.

Article 81

The trusteeship agreement shall in each case include the terms under which the trust territory will be administered and designate the authority which will exercise the administration of the trust territory. Such authority, hereinafter called the administering authority, may be one or more states or the Organization itself.

Article 82

There may be designated, in any trusteeship agreement, a strategic area or areas which may include part or all of the trust territory to which the agreement applies, without prejudice to any special agreement or agreements made under Article 43.

Article 83

1. All functions of the United Nations relating to strategic areas, including the approval of the terms of the trusteeship agreements and of their alteration or amendment, shall be exercised by the Security Council.
2. The basic objectives set forth in Article 76 shall be applicable to the people of each strategic area.
3. The Security Council shall, subject to the provisions of the trusteeship agreements and without prejudice to security considerations, avail itself of the assistance of the Trusteeship Council to perform those functions of the United Nations under the trusteeship system relating to political, economic, social, and educational matters in the strategic areas.

Article 84

It shall be the duty of the administering authority to ensure that the trust territory shall play its part in the maintenance of international peace and security. To this end the administering authority may make use of volunteer forces, facilities, and assistance from the trust territory in carrying out the obligations towards the Security Council undertaken in this regard by the administering authority, as well as for local defence and the maintenance of law and order within the trust territory.

Article 85

1. The functions of the United Nations with regard to trusteeship agreements for all areas not designated as strategic, including the approval of the terms of the trusteeship agreements and of their alteration or amendment, shall be exercised by the General Assembly.
2. The Trusteeship Council, operating under the authority of the General Assembly, shall assist the General Assembly in carrying out these functions.

CHAPTER XIII

THE TRUSTEESHIP COUNCIL

Composition

Article 86

1. The Trusteeship Council shall consist of the following Members of the United Nations:
    a. those Members administering trust territories;
    b. such of those Members mentioned by name in Article 23 as are not administering trust territories; and
    c. as many other Members elected for three-year terms by the General Assembly as may be necessary to ensure that the total number of members of the Trusteeship Council is equally divided between those Members of the United Nations which administer trust territories and those which do not.
2. Each member of the Trusteeship Council shall designate one specially qualified person to represent it therein.

Functions and Powers

Article 87

The General Assembly and, under its authority, the Trusteeship Council, in carrying out their functions, may:

a. consider reports submitted by the administering authority;

b. accept petitions and examine them in consultation with the administering authority;

c. provide for periodic visits to the respective trust territories at times agreed upon with the administering authority; and

d. take these and other actions in conformity with the terms of the trusteeship agreements.

Article 88

The Trusteeship Council shall formulate a questionnaire on the political, economic, social, and educational advancement of the inhabitants of each trust territory, and the administering authority for each trust territory within the competence of the General Assembly shall make an annual report to the General Assembly upon the basis of such questionnaire.

Voting

Article 89

1. Each member of the Trusteeship Council shall have one vote.
2. Decisions of the Trusteeship Council shall be made by a majority of the members present and voting.

Procedure

Article 90

1. The Trusteeship Council shall adopt its own rules of procedure, including the method of selecting its President.
2. The Trusteeship Council shall meet as required in accordance with its rules, which shall include provision for the convening of meetings on the request of a majority of its members.

Article 91

The Trusteeship Council shall, when appropriate, avail itself of the assistance of the Economic and Social Council and of the specialized agencies in regard to matters with which they are respectively concerned.

CHAPTER XIV

THE INTERNATIONAL COURT OF JUSTICE

Article 92

The International Court of Justice shall be the principal judicial organ of the United Nations. It shall function in accordance with the annexed Statute, which is based upon the Statute of the Permanent Court of International Justice and forms an integral part of the present Charter.

Article 93

1. All Members of the United Nations are *ipso facto* parties to the Statute of the International Court of Justice.
2. A state which is not a Member of the United Nations may become a party to the Statute of the International Court of Justice conditions to be determined in each case by the General Assembly upon the recommendation of the Security Council.

Article 94

1. Each Member of the United Nations undertakes to comply with the decision of the International Court of Justice in any case to which it is a party.
2. If any party to a case fails to perform the obligations incumbent upon it under a judgment rendered by the Court, the other party may have recourse to the Security Council, which may, if it deems necessary, make recommendations or decide upon measures to be taken to give to the judgment.

Article 95

Nothing in the present Charter shall prevent Members of the United Nations from entrusting the solution of their differences to other tribunals by virtue of agreements already in existence or which may be concluded in the future.

Article 96

1. The General Assembly or the Security Council may request the International Court of Justice to give an advisory opinion on any legal question.
2. Other organs of the United Nations and specialized agencies, which may at any time be so authorized by the General Assembly, may also request advisory opinions of the Court on legal questions arising within the scope of their activities.

CHAPTER XV

THE SECRETARIAT

Article 97

The Secretariat shall comprise a Secretary-General and such staff as the Organization may require. The Secretary-General shall be appointed by the General Assembly upon the recommendation of the Security Council. He shall be the chief administrative officer of the Organization.

Article 98

The Secretary-General shall act in that capacity in all meetings of the General Assembly, of the Security Council, of the Economic and Social Council, and of the Trusteeship Council, and shall perform such other functions as are entrusted to him by these organs. The Secretary-General shall make an annual report to the General Assembly on the work of the Organization.

Article 99

The Secretary-General may bring to the attention of the Security Council any matter which in his opinion may threaten the maintenance of international peace and security.

Article 100

1. In the performance of their duties the Secretary-General and the staff shall not seek or receive instructions from any government or from any other authority external to the Organization. They shall refrain from

any action which might reflect on their position as international officials responsible only to the Organization.

2. Each Member of the United Nations undertakes to respect the exclusively international character of the responsibilities of the Secretary-General and the staff and not to seek to influence them in the discharge of their responsibilities.

Article 101

1. The staff shall be appointed by the Secretary-General under regulations established by the General Assembly.
2. Appropriate staffs shall be permanently assigned to the Economic and Social Council, the Trusteeship Council, and, as required, to other organs of the United Nations. These staffs shall form a part of the Secretariat.
3. The paramount consideration in the employment of the staff and in the determination of the conditions of service shall be the necessity of securing the highest standards of efficiency, competence, and integrity. Due regard shall be paid to the importance of recruiting the staff on as wide a geographical basis as possible.

CHAPTER XVI

MISCELLANEOUS PROVISIONS

Article 102

1. Every treaty and every international agreement entered into by any Member of the United Nations after the present Charter comes into force shall as soon as possible be registered with the Secretariat and published by it.
2. No party to any such treaty or international agreement which has not been registered in accordance with the provisions of paragraph 1 of this Article may invoke that treaty or agreement before any organ of the United Nations.

Article 103

In the event of a conflict between the obligations of the Members of the United Nations under the present Charter and their obligations under any other international agreement, their obligations under the present Charter shall prevail.

Article 104

The Organization shall enjoy in the territory of each of its Members such legal capacity as may be necessary for the exercise of its functions and the fulfillment of its purposes.

Article 105

1. The Organization shall enjoy in the territory of each of its Members such privileges and immunities as are necessary for the fulfillment of its purposes.
2. Representatives of the Members of the United Nations and officials of the Organization shall similarly enjoy such privileges and immunities as are necessary for the independent exercise of their functions in connexion with the Organization.
3. The General Assembly may make recommendations with a view to determining the details of the application of paragraphs 1 and 2 of this Article or may propose conventions to the Members of the United Nations for this purpose.

CHAPTER XVII

TRANSITIONAL SECURITY ARRANGEMENTS

Article 106

Pending the coming into force of such special agreements referred to in Article 43 as in the opinion of the Security Council enable it to begin the exercise of its responsibilities under Article 42, the parties to the Four-Nation Declaration, signed at Moscow, 30 October 1943, and France, shall, in accordance with the provisions of paragraph 5 of that Declaration, consult with one another and as occasion requires with other Members of the United Nations with a view to such joint action on behalf of the Organization as may be necessary for the purpose of maintaining international peace and security.

Article 107

Nothing in the present Charter shall invalidate or preclude action, in relation to any state which during the Second World War has been an enemy of any signatory to the present Charter, taken or authorized as a result of that war by the Governments having responsibility for such action.

CHAPTER XVIII

AMENDMENTS

Article 108

Amendments to the present Charter shall come into force for all Members of the United Nations when they have been adopted by a vote of two thirds of the members of the General Assembly and ratified in accordance with their respective constitutional processes by two thirds of the Members of the United Nations, including all the permanent members of the Security Council.

Article 109

1. A General Conference of the Members of the United Nations for the purpose of reviewing the present Charter may be held at a date and place to be fixed by a two-thirds vote of the members of the General Assembly and by a vote of any nine members of the Security Council. Each Member of the United Nations shall have one vote in the conference.
2. Any alteration of the present Charter recommended by a two-thirds vote of the conference shall take effect when ratified in accordance with their respective constitutional processes by two thirds of the Members of the United Nations including the permanent members of the Security Council.
3. If such a conference has not been held before the tenth annual session of the General Assembly following the coming into force of the present Charter, the proposal to call such a conference shall be placed on the agenda of that session of the General Assembly, and the conference shall be held if so decided by a majority vote of the members of the General Assembly and by a vote of any seven members of the Security Council.

CHAPTER XIX

RATIFICATION AND SIGNATURE

Article 110

1. The present Charter shall be ratified by the signatory states in accordance with their respective constitutional processes.
2. The ratifications shall be deposited with the Government of the United States of America, which shall notify all the signatory states of each deposit as well as the Secretary-General of the Organization when he has been appointed.
3. The present Charter shall come into force upon the deposit of ratifications by the Republic of China, France, the Union of Soviet Socialist Republics, the United Kingdom of Great Britain and Northern Ireland, and the United States of America, and by a majority of the other signatory states. A protocol of the ratifications deposited shall thereupon be drawn up by the Government of the United States of America which shall communicate copies thereof to all the signatory states.
4. The states signatory to the present Charter which ratify it after it has come into force will become original Members of the United Nations on the date of the deposit of their respective ratifications.

Article 111

The present Charter, of which the Chinese, French, Russian, English, and Spanish texts are equally authentic, shall remain deposited in the archives of the Government of the United States of America. Duly certified copies thereof shall be transmitted by that Government to the Governments of the other signatory states.

IN FAITH WHEREOF the representatives of the Governments of the United Nations have signed the present Charter.

DONE at the city of San Francisco the twenty-sixth day of June, one thousand nine hundred and forty-five.

UNIT

B

BACKGROUND DOCUMENTS FOR CHAPTER 2

Document 1: UNCTAD Document

ESTABLISHMENT OF THE UNITED NATIONS CONFERENCE ON TRADE AND DEVELOPMENT AS AN ORGAN OF THE GENERAL ASSEMBLY

General Assembly resolution 1995 (XIX) of 30 December 1964, as amended.

The General Assembly

Convinced that sustained efforts are necessary to raise the standards of living in all countries and to accelerate the economic growth of the developing countries,

Considering that international trade is an important instrument for economic development,

Recognizing that the United Nations Conference on Trade and Development has provided a unique opportunity to make a comprehensive review of the problems of trade and of trade in relation to economic development, particularly those problems affecting the developing countries,

Convinced that adequate and effectively functioning organizational arrangements are essential if the full contribution of international trade to the accelerated economic growth of the developing countries is to be successfully realized through the formulation and implementation of the necessary policies,

Taking into account that the operation of existing international institutions was examined by the United Nations Conference on Trade and Development, which recognized both their contributions and their limitations in dealing with all the problems of trade and related problems of development,

Believing that all States participating in the United Nations Conference on Trade and Development should make the most effective use of institutions and arrangements to which they are or may become parties,

Convinced that, at the same time, there should be a further review of both the present and the proposed institutional arrangements, in the light of the experience of their work and activities,

Taking note of the widespread desire among developing countries for a comprehensive trade organization,

Recognizing that further institutional arrangements are necessary in order to continue the work initiated by the Conference and to implement its recommendations and conclusions,

I.

Establishes the United Nations Conference on Trade and Development as an organ of the General Assembly in accordance with the provisions set forth in section II below;

II.

1. The members of the United Nations Conference on Trade and Development (hereinafter referred to as the Conference) shall be those States which are Members of the United Nations or members of the specialized agencies or of the International Atomic Energy Agency.
2. The Conference shall normally be convened at intervals of not more than four years. The General Assembly shall determine the date and location of the sessions of the Conference, taking into account the recommendations of the Conference or of the Trade and Development Board, established under paragraph 4 below.
3. The principal functions of the Conference shall be:
    (a) To promote international trade, especially with a view to accelerating economic development, particularly trade between

countries at different stages of development, between developing countries and between countries with different systems of economic and social organization, taking into account the functions performed by existing international organizations;

(b) To formulate principles and policies on international trade and related problems of economic development;

(c) To make proposals for putting the said principles and policies into effect and to take such other steps within its competence as may be relevant to this end, having regard to differences in economic systems and stages of development;

(d) Generally, to review and facilitate the co-ordination of activities of other institutions within the United Nations system in the field of international trade and related problems of economic development, and in this regard to cooperate with the General Assembly and the Economic and Social Council with respect to the performance of their responsibilities for co-ordination under the Charter of the United Nations;

(e) To initiate action, where appropriate, in co-operation with the competent organs of the United Nations for the negotiation and adoption of multilateral legal instruments in the field of trade, with due regard to the adequacy of existing organs of negotiation and without duplication of their activities;

(f) To be available as a centre for harmonizing the trade and related development policies of Governments and regional economic groupings in pursuance of Article 1 of the Charter:

(g) To deal with any other matters within the scope of its competence.

Trade and Development Board

Composition

4. A permanent organ of the Conference, the Trade and Development Board (hereinafter referred to as the Board), shall be established as part of the United Nations machinery in the economic field.

5. Membership of the Board shall be open to all members of the Conference. Those members of the Conference wishing to become members

of the Board shall communicate their intention to do so, in writing, to the Secretary-General of the Conference.

6. The lists of States contained in the annex shall be reviewed periodically by the Conference in the light of changes in membership of the Conference and other factors.

7. The Secretary-General of the Conference shall bring the communications referred to in paragraph 5 above to the attention of the President of the Board who, at the commencement of the following regular, special or resumed session of the Board, or during such sessions as the case may be, shall announce the membership of the Board. Membership of the Board shall be for an indefinite period, subject to the provisions of paragraph 8 below.

8. Any member of the Board wishing to relinquish its membership shall inform the Secretary-General of the Conference, in writing, of its intention to do so. The Secretary-General of the Conference shall bring such communications to the attention of the President of the Board who, at the commencement of the following regular, special or resumed session, or during such session as the case may be, shall announce the revised membership of the Board.

9. Each member of the Board shall have one representative with such alternates and advisers as may be required.

10. Any member of the Conference shall be entitled to participate in the deliberations of the Board on any item on its agenda of particular concern to that member, with all the rights and privileges of a Board member except the right to vote.

11. The Board may make arrangements for representatives of the intergovernmental bodies referred to in paragraphs 18 and 19 below to participate, without vote, in its deliberations and in those of the subsidiary bodies and working groups established by it. Such participation may also be offered to non-governmental organizations concerned with matters of trade and of trade as related to development.

12. The Board shall adopt its own rules of procedure.

13. The Board shall meet as required in accordance with its rules. It shall normally meet twice in any particular year.

Functions

14. When the Conference is not in session, the Board shall carry out the functions that fall within the competence of the Conference.

15. In particular, the Board shall keep under review and take appropriate action within its competence for the implementation of the recommendations, declarations, resolutions and other decisions of the Conference and to ensure the continuity of its work.

16. The Board may make or initiate studies and reports in the field of trade and related problems of development.

17. The Board may request the Secretary-General of the United Nations to prepare such reports, studies or other documents as it may deem appropriate.

18. The Board shall, as required, make arrangements to obtain reports from and establish links with intergovernmental bodies whose activities are relevant to its functions. In order to avoid duplication it shall avail itself, whenever possible, of the relevant reports made to the Economic and Social Council and other United Nations bodies.

19. The Board shall establish close and continuous links with the regional economic commissions of the United Nations and it may establish such links with other relevant regional intergovernmental bodies.

20. In its relations with organs and agencies within the United Nations system, the Board shall act in conformity with the responsibilities of the Economic and Social Council under the Charter, particularly those of co-ordination, and with the relationship agreements with the agencies concerned.

21. The Board shall serve as a preparatory committee for future sessions of the Conference. To that end, it shall initiate the preparation of documents, including a provisional agenda, for consideration by the Conference, as well as make recommendations as to the appropriate date and place for its convening.

22. The Board shall report to the Conference and it shall also report annually on its activities to the General Assembly through the Economic and Social Council. The Council may transmit to the Assembly such comments on the reports as it may deem necessary.

23. The Board shall establish such subsidiary organs as may be necessary to the effective discharge of its functions. It shall establish, in particular, the following committees:

(a) A committee on commodities which, inter alia, will carry out the functions which are now performed by the Commission on International Commodity Trade and the Interim Co-ordinating Committee for International Commodity Arrangements;

(b) A committee on manufactures;

(c) A committee on invisibles and financing related to trade. The Board shall give special consideration to the appropriate institutional means for dealing with problems of shipping, and shall take into account the recommendations contained in annexes A.IV.21 and A.IV.22 of the Final Act of the Conference.

The terms of reference of the latter two subsidiary bodies and other subsidiary organs established by the Board shall be adopted after consultation with the appropriate organs of the United Nations and shall take fully into account the desirability of avoiding duplication and overlapping of responsibilities. In determining the size of the subsidiary organs and in electing their members, the Board shall take fully into account the desirability of including in the membership of these bodies member States with a special interest in the subject matter to be dealt with by them. It may include any State member of the Conference, whether or not that State is represented on the Board. The Board will determine the terms of reference and rules of procedure of its subsidiary organs.

Voting

24. Each State represented at the Conference shall have one vote. Decisions of the Conference on matters of substance shall be taken by a two-thirds majority of the representatives present and voting. Decisions of the Conference on matters of procedure shall be taken by a majority of the representatives present and voting. Decisions of the Board shall be taken by a simple majority of the representatives present and voting.

Procedures

25. The procedures set forth in the present paragraph are designed to provide a process of conciliation to take place before voting and to provide an adequate basis for the adoption of recommendations with regard to

proposals of a specific nature for action substantially affecting the economic or financial interests of particular countries.

(a) Levels of conciliation

The process of conciliation within the meaning of the present paragraph may take place under the conditions stated with regard to proposals which are before the Conference, the Board or Committees of the Board. In the case of the Committees of the Board, the process of conciliation shall apply only to those matters, if any, with respect to which a Committee has been authorized to submit, without further approval, recommendations for action.

(b) Request for conciliation

A request for conciliation within the meaning of the present paragraph may be made:

(i) In the case of proposals before the Conference, by at least 10 members of the Conference;

(ii) In the case of proposals before the Board, by at least five members of the Conference, whether or not they are members of the Board;

(iii) In the case of proposals before Committees of the Board, by three members of the Committee.

The request for conciliation under the present paragraph shall be submitted, as appropriate, to the President of the Conference or to the President of the Board. In the case of a request relating to a proposal before a Committee of the Board, the Chairman of the Committee concerned shall submit the request to the President of the Board.

(c) Initiation of conciliation by a presiding officer

The process of conciliation within the meaning of the present paragraph may also be initiated whenever the President of the Conference, the President of the Board or the Chairman of the Committee concerned is satisfied that the required number of countries as specified in subparagraph (b) above are in favour of such conciliation. In cases where the process of conciliation is initiated at the level of a Committee, the Chairman of the Committee concerned shall refer the matter to the President of the Board for action to be taken in accordance with subparagraph (f) below.

(d) Time for request or initiation of conciliation

The request for conciliation (or the initiation of conciliation by the President of the Conference or the President of the Board, as the case may be) may be made only after the debate on the proposal has been concluded within the organ concerned and prior to the vote on that proposal. For the purposes of this provision, the presiding officer of the organ concerned shall, at the conclusion of the debate on any proposal, afford an appropriate interval for the submission of requests for conciliation before proceeding to the vote on the proposal in question. In the event that conciliation is requested or initiated, voting on the proposal in question shall be suspended and the procedures provided for below shall be followed.

(e) Subjects in regard to which conciliation is appropriate or excluded

The institution of the process of conciliation shall be automatic under the conditions stated in subparagraphs (b) and (c) above. The categories in (i) and (ii) below shall serve as guidelines:

(i) Appropriate for conciliation shall be proposals of a specific nature for action substantially affecting the economic or financial interests of particular countries in the following fields:

Economic plans or programmes or economic or social readjustments;

Trade, monetary or tariff policies, or balance of payments;

Policies of economic assistance or transfer of resources;

Levels of employment, income, revenue or investment;

Rights or obligations under international agreements or treaties.

(ii) Proposals in the following fields shall not require conciliation:

Any procedural matter;

Any proposal for study or investigation, including such proposals related to the preparation of legal instruments in the field of trade;

Establishment of subsidiary bodies of the Board within the scope of its competence;

Recommendations and declarations of a general character not calling for specific actions;

Proposals involving action proposed in pursuance of recommendations which were unanimously adopted by the Conference.

(f) Nomination of a conciliation committee

When a request for conciliation is made or initiated, the presiding officer of the organ concerned shall immediately inform the organ. The President of the Conference or the President of the Board shall, as soon as possible, after consultation with the members of the organ concerned, nominate the members of a conciliation committee and submit the nominations for the approval of the Conference or the Board, as appropriate.

(g) Size and composition of the conciliation committee

The conciliation committee shall, as a rule, be small in size. Its members shall include countries especially interested in the matter with respect to which such conciliation was initiated and shall be selected on an equitable geographical basis.

(h) Procedure within the conciliation committee and submission of its report

The conciliation committee shall begin its work as soon as possible and it shall endeavour to reach agreement during the same session of the Conference or the Board. No vote shall take place in the conciliation committee. In the event that the conciliation committee is unable to conclude its work or fails to reach agreement at the same session of the Conference or the Board, it shall report to the next session of the Board or to the next session of the Conference, whichever meets earlier. However, the Conference may instruct the conciliation committee appointed by it to submit its report to the following session of the Conference in the event that the committee shall not have concluded its work or shall have failed to reach agreement during the same session of the Conference.

(i) Extension of the mandate of the conciliation committee

A proposal to continue a conciliation committee beyond the session at which it is required to report shall be decided by a simple majority.

(j) Report of the conciliation committee

The report of the conciliation committee shall indicate whether or not the committee was able to reach an agreement and whether or not the committee recommends a further period of conciliation. The report of the committee shall be made available to the members of the Conference.

(k) Action on the report of the conciliation committee

The report of the conciliation committee shall have priority on the agenda of the organ to which it is submitted. If the organ adopts a resolution on the proposal which was the subject of the report of the conciliation committee, that resolution shall refer explicitly to the report of the conciliation committee and to the conclusion reached by the conciliation committee in the following form, as appropriate:

"Noting the report of the Conciliation Committee appointed on (date) (document number),

"Noting also that the Conciliation Committee [was able to reach an agreement] [recommends a further period of conciliation] [was unable to reach agreement],"

(l) Reports of the Board and the Conference

The reports of the Board to the Conference and to the General Assembly and the reports of the Conference to the Assembly shall include, inter alia:

(i) The texts of all recommendations, resolutions and declarations adopted by the Board or the Conference during the period covered by the report;

(ii) In respect of recommendations and resolutions which are adopted after a process of conciliation, there shall also be included a record of the voting on each recommendation or resolution, together with the texts of the reports of the conciliation committees concerned. In the report, the record of voting and the texts of the reports shall normally follow the resolution to which they pertain.

(m) Good offices of the Secretary-General of the Conference

The good offices of the Secretary-General of the Conference shall be utilized as fully as practicable in connection with the process of conciliation.

Egypt
Equatorial Guinea
Ethiopia
Fiji
Gabon
Gambia
Ghana
Guinea
Guinea-Bissau
India
Indonesia
Iran, Islamic Republic of
Iraq
Israel
Jordan
Kenya
Kuwait
Lao People's Democratic Republic
Lebanon
Lesotho
Liberia
Libyan Arab Jamahiriya
Madagascar
Malawi
Malaysia
Maldives
Mali
Mauritania
Mauritius
Mongolia
Morocco
Mozambique
Myanmar
Namibia
Nepal
Niger
Nigeria
Oman
Pakistan
Papua New Guinea
Philippines
Qatar
Republic of Korea
Rwanda
Samoa
Sao Tome and Principe
Saudi Arabia
Senegal
Seychelles
Sierra Leone
Singapore
Solomon Islands
Somalia
South Africa
Sri Lanka
Sudan
Swaziland
Syrian Arab Republic
Thailand
Togo

Tonga
Tunisia
Uganda
United Arab Emirates
Vanuatu
Zambia
Zimbabwe

B

Australia
Austria
Belgium
Canada
Cyprus
Denmark
Finland
France
Germany
Greece
Holy See
Iceland
Ireland
Italy
Japan
Liechtenstein
Luxembourg
Malta
Monaco
Netherlands
New Zealand
Norway
Portugal
San Marino
Spain
Sweden
Switzerland
Turkey
United Kingdom of Great Britain and Northern Ireland
United States of America

C

Antigua and Barbuda
Argentina
Bahamas
Barbados
Belize
Bolivia
Brazil
Chile
Colombia
Costa Rica
Cuba
Dominica

Dominican Republic
Ecuador
El Salvador
Grenada
Guatemala
Guyana
Haiti
Honduras
Jamaica
Mexico
Nicaragua
Panama
Paraguay
Peru
Saint Kitts and Nevis
Saint Lucia
Saint Vincent and the Grenadines
Suriname
Trinidad and Tobago
Uruguay
Venezuela

D

Albania
Bulgaria
Belarus
Hungary
Poland
Romania
Ukraine
Russian Federation

UNIT

B

BACKGROUND DOCUMENTS FOR CHAPTER 2

Document 2: UNESCO Document

CONSTITUTION OF THE UNITED NATIONS EDUCATIONAL, SCIENTIFIC, AND CULTURAL ORGANIZATION

Adopted in London on 16 November 1945 and amended by the General Conference at its second, third, fourth, fifth, sixth, seventh, eighth, ninth, tenth, twelfth, fifteenth, seventeenth, nineteenth, twentieth, twenty-first, twenty-fourth, and twenty-fifth sessions.

The Governments of the States Parties to this Constitution on behalf of their peoples declare:

That since wars begin in the minds of men, it is in the minds of men that the defenses of peace must be constructed;

That ignorance of each other's ways and lives has been a common cause, throughout the history of mankind, of that suspicion and mistrust between the peoples of the world through which their differences have all too often broken into war;

That the great and terrible war which has now ended was a war made possible by the denial of the democratic principles of the dignity, equality and mutual respect of men, and by the propagation, in their place, through ignorance and prejudice, of the doctrine of the inequality of men and races;

That the wide diffusion of culture, and the education of humanity for justice and liberty and peace are indispensable to the dignity of man and constitute a sacred duty which all the nations must fulfil in a spirit of mutual assistance and concern;

That a peace based exclusively upon the political and economic arrangements of governments would not be a peace which could secure the unanimous, lasting and sincere support of the peoples of the world, and that the peace must therefore be founded, if it is not to fail, upon the intellectual and moral solidarity of mankind.

For these reasons, the States Parties to this Constitution, believing in full and equal opportunities for education for all, in the unrestricted pursuit of objective truth, and in the free exchange of ideas and knowledge, are agreed and determined to develop and to increase the means of communication between their peoples and to employ these means for the purposes of mutual understanding and a truer and more perfect knowledge of each other's lives;

In consequence whereof they do hereby create the United Nations Educational, Scientific and Cultural Organization for the purpose of advancing, through the educational and scientific and cultural relations of the peoples of the world, the objectives of international peace and of the common welfare of mankind for which the United Nations Organization was established and which its Charter proclaims.

Article I

Purposes and Functions

1. The purpose of the Organization is to contribute to peace and security by promoting collaboration among the nations through education, science and culture in order to further universal respect for justice, for the rule of law and for the human rights and fundamental freedoms which are affirmed for the peoples of the world, without distinction of race, sex, language or religion, by the Charter of the United Nations.
2. To realize this purpose the Organization will:
    a. Collaborate in the work of advancing the mutual knowledge and understanding of peoples, through all means of mass communication and to that end recommend such international agreements as may be necessary to promote the free flow of ideas by word and image;
    b. Give fresh impulse to popular education and to the spread of culture;
    By collaborating with Members, at their request, in the development of educational activities;

By instituting collaboration among the nations to advance the ideal of equality of educational opportunity without regard to race, sex or any distinctions, economic or social;

By suggesting educational methods best suited to prepare the children of the world for the responsibilities of freedom;

c. Maintain, increase and diffuse knowledge;
By assuring the conservation and protection of the world's inheritance of books, works of art and monuments of history and science, and recommending to the nations concerned the necessary international conventions;

By encouraging co-operation among the nations in all branches of intellectual activity, including the international exchange of persons active in the fields of education, science and culture and the exchange of publications, objects of artistic and scientific interest and other materials of information;

By initiating methods of international co-operation calculated to give the people of all countries access to the printed and published materials produced by any of them.

3. With a view to preserving the independence, integrity and fruitful diversity of the cultures and educational systems of the States members of this Organization, the Organization is prohibited from intervening in matters which are essentially within their domestic jurisdiction.

Article II

Membership

1. Membership of the United Nations Organization shall carry with it the right to membership of the United Nations Educational, Scientific and Cultural Organization.

2. Subject to the conditions of the Agreement between this Organization and the United Nations Organization, approved pursuant to Article X of this Constitution, States not members of the United Nations Organization may be admitted to membership of the Organization, upon recommendation of the Executive Board, by a two-thirds majority vote of the General Conference.

3. Territories or groups of territories which are not responsible for the conduct of their international relations may be admitted as Associate Members by the General Conference by a two-thirds majority of Mem-

bers present and voting, upon application made on behalf of such territory or group of territories by the Member or other authority having responsibility for their international relations. The nature and extent of the rights and obligations of Associate Members shall be determined by the General Conference.

4. Members of the Organization which are suspended from the exercise of the rights and privileges of membership of the United Nations Organization shall, upon the request of the latter, be suspended from the rights and privileges of this Organization.

5. Members of the Organization which are expelled from the United Nations Organization shall automatically cease to be members of this Organization.

6. Any Member State or Associate Member of the Organization may withdraw from the Organization by notice addressed to the Director-General. Such notice shall take effect on 31 December of the year following that during which the notice was given. No such withdrawal shall affect the financial obligations owed to the Organization on the date the withdrawal takes effect. Notice of withdrawal by an Associate Member shall be given on its behalf by the Member State or other authority having responsibility for its international relations.

Article III

Organs

The Organization shall include a General Conference, an Executive Board and a Secretariat.

Article IV

The General Conference

A. Composition

1. The General Conference shall consist of the representatives of the States members of the Organization. The Government of each Member State shall appoint not more than five delegates, who shall be selected after consultation with the National Commission if established, or with educational, scientific and cultural bodies.

B. Functions

2. The General Conference shall determine the policies and the main lines of work of the Organization. It shall take decisions on programmes submitted to it by the Executive Board.

3. The General Conference shall, when it deems desirable and in accordance with the regulations to be made by it, summon international conferences of States on education, the sciences and humanities or the dissemination of knowledge; non-governmental conferences on the same subjects may be summoned by the General Conference or by the Executive Board in accordance with such regulations.

4. The General Conference shall, in adopting proposals for submission to the Member States, distinguish between recommendations and international conventions submitted for their approval. In the former case a majority vote shall suffice; in the latter case a two-thirds majority shall be required. Each of the Member States shall submit recommendations or conventions to its competent authorities within a period of one year from the close of the session of the General Conference at which they were adopted.

5. Subject to the provisions of Article V, paragraph 5(c), the General Conference shall advise the United Nations Organization on the educational, scientific and cultural aspects of matters of concern to the latter; in accordance with the terms and procedure agreed upon between the appropriate authorities of the two Organizations.

6. The General Conference shall receive and consider the reports sent to the Organization by Member States on the action taken upon the recommendations and conventions referred to in paragraph 4 above or, if it so decides, analytical summaries of these reports.

7. The General Conference shall elect the members of the Executive Board and, on the recommendation of the Board, shall appoint the Director-General.

C. Voting

a. Each Member State shall have one vote in the General Conference. Decisions shall be made by a simple majority except in cases in which a two-thirds majority is required by the provisions of this Constitution, or of the Rules of Procedure of the General Conference. A majority shall be a majority of the Members present and voting.

b. A Member State shall have no vote in the General Conference if the total amount of contributions due from it exceeds the total amount of contributions payable by it for the current year and the immediately preceding calendar year.

c. The General Conference may nevertheless permit such a Member State to vote, if it is satisfied that failure to pay is due to conditions beyond the control of the Member State.

D. Procedure

d. The General Conference shall meet in ordinary session every two years. It may meet in extraordinary session if it decides to do so itself or if summoned by the Executive Board, or on the demand of at least one-third of the Member States.

e. At each session the location of its next ordinary session shall be designated by the General Conference. The location of an extraordinary session shall be decided by the General Conference if the session is summoned by it, or otherwise by the Executive Board.

8. The General Conference shall adopt its own rules of procedure. It shall at each session elect a President and other officers.

9. The General Conference shall set up special and technical committees and such other subordinate organs as may be necessary for its purposes.

10. The General Conference shall cause arrangements to be made for public access to meetings, subject to such regulations as it shall prescribe.

E. Observers

11. The General Conference, on the recommendation of the Executive Board and by a two-thirds majority may, subject to its rules of procedure, invite as observers at specified sessions of the Conference or of its Commissions representatives of international organizations, such as those referred to in Article XI, paragraph 4.

12. When consultative arrangements have been approved by the Executive Board for such international non-governmental or semi-governmental organizations in the manner provided in Article XI, paragraph 4, those organizations shall be invited to send observers to sessions of the General Conference and its Commissions.

Article V
Executive Board

A. Composition

1. The Executive Board shall be elected by the General Conference from among the delegates appointed by the Member States and shall consist of fifty-one members each of whom shall represent the Government of the Member State of which he is a national. The President of the General Conference shall sit ex officio in an advisory capacity on the Executive Board.
2. In electing the members of the Executive Board the General Conference shall endeavour to include persons competent in the arts, the humanities, the sciences, education and the diffusion of ideas, and qualified by their experience and capacity to fulfil the administrative and executive duties of the Board. It shall also have regard to the diversity of cultures and a balanced geographical distribution. Not more than one national of any Member State shall serve on the Board at any one time, the President of the Conference excepted.
3. Members of the Board shall serve from the close of the session of the General Conference which elected them until the close of the second ordinary session of the General Conference following that election. They shall not be immediately eligible for a second term. The General Conference shall, at each of its ordinary sessions, elect the number of members required to fill vacancies occurring at the end of the session.
    a. In the event of the death or resignation of a member of the Executive Board, his replacement for the remainder of his term shall be appointed by the Executive Board on the nomination of the Government of the Member State the former member of the Board represented.
    b. The Government making the nomination and the Executive Board shall have regard to the factors set forth in paragraph 2 of this Article.
    c. When exceptional circumstances arise, which, in the considered opinion of the represented State, make it indispensable for its representative to be replaced, even if he does not tender his resignation, measures shall be taken in accordance with the provisions of sub-paragraph (a) above.
    d. In the event of the withdrawal from the Organization of a Member State a national of which is a member of the Execu-

tive Board, that member's term of office shall be terminated on the date the withdrawal becomes effective.

B. Functions

e. The Executive Board shall prepare the agenda for the General Conference. It shall examine the programme of work for the Organization and corresponding budget estimates submitted to it by the Director-General in accordance with paragraph 3 of Article VI and shall submit them with such recommendations as it considers desirable to the General Conference.

f. The Executive Board, acting under the authority of the General Conference, shall be responsible for the execution of the programme adopted by the Conference. In accordance with the decisions of the General Conference and having regard to circumstances arising between two ordinary sessions, the Executive Board shall take all necessary measures to ensure the effective and rational execution of the programme by the Director-General.

g. Between ordinary sessions of the General Conference, the Board may discharge the functions of adviser to the United Nations, set forth in Article IV, paragraph 5, whenever the problem upon which advice is sought has already been dealt with in principle by the Conference, or when the solution is implicit in decisions of the Conference.

4. The Executive Board shall recommend to the General Conference the admission of new Members to the Organization.

5. Subject to decisions of the General Conference, the Executive Board shall adopt its own rules of procedure. It shall elect its officers from among its members.

6. The Executive Board shall meet in regular session at least twice a year and may meet in special session if convoked by the Chairman on his own initiative or upon the request of six members of the Board.

7. The Chairman of the Executive Board shall present, on behalf of the Board, to each ordinary session of the General Conference, with or without comments, the reports on the activities of the Organization which the Director-General is required to prepare in accordance with the provisions of Article VI.3(b).

8. The Executive Board shall make all necessary arrangements to consult the representatives of international organizations or qualified persons concerned with questions within its competence.

9. Between sessions of the General Conference, the Executive Board may request advisory opinions from the International Court of Justice on legal questions arising within the field of the Organization's activities.

10. Although the members of the Executive Board are representative of their respective Governments they shall exercise the powers delegated to them by the General Conference on behalf of the Conference as a whole.

Article VI

Secretariat

1. The Secretariat shall consist of a Director-General and such staff as may be required.

2. The Director-General shall be nominated by the Executive Board and appointed by the General Conference for a period of six years, under such conditions as the Conference may approve. The Director-General may be appointed for a further term of six years but shall not be eligible for reappointment for a subsequent term. The Director-General shall be the chief administrative officer of the Organization.

    a. The Director-General, or a deputy designated by him, shall participate, without the right to vote, in all meetings of the General Conference, of the Executive Board, and of the Committees of the Organization. He shall formulate proposals for appropriate action by the Conference and the Board, and shall prepare for submission to the Board a draft programme of work for the Organization with corresponding budget estimates.

    b. The Director-General shall prepare and communicate to Member States and to the Executive Board periodical reports on the activities of the Organization. The General Conference shall determine the periods to be covered by these reports.

3. The Director-General shall appoint the staff of the Secretariat in accordance with staff regulations to be approved by the General Conference. Subject to the paramount consideration of securing the highest standards of integrity, efficiency and technical competence, appointment to the staff shall be on as wide a geographical basis as possible.

4. The responsibilities of the Director-General and of the staff shall be exclusively international in character. In the discharge of their duties they shall not seek or receive instructions from any Government or from any

authority external to the Organization. They shall refrain from any action which might prejudice their position as international officials. Each State member of the Organization undertakes to respect the international character of the responsibilities of the Director-General and the staff, and not to seek to influence them in the discharge of their duties.

5. Nothing in this Article shall preclude the Organization from entering into special arrangements within the United Nations Organization for common services and staff and for the interchange of personnel.

Article VII

National Co-operating Bodies

1. Each Member State shall make such arrangements as suit its particular conditions for the purpose of associating its principal bodies interested in educational, scientific and cultural matters with the work of the Organization, preferably by the formation of a National Commission broadly representative of the Government and such bodies.
2. National Commissions or National Co-operating Bodies, where they exist, shall act in an advisory capacity to their respective delegations to the General Conference and to their Governments in matters relating to the Organization and shall function as agencies of liaison in all matters of interest to it.
3. The Organization may, on the request of a Member State, delegate, either temporarily or permanently, a member of its Secretariat to serve on the National Commission of that State, in order to assist in the development of its work.

Article VIII

Reports by Member States

Each Member State shall submit to the Organization, at such times and in such manner as shall be determined by the General Conference, reports on the laws, regulations and statistics relating to its educational, scientific and cultural institutions and activities, and on the action taken upon the recommendations and conventions referred to in Article IV, paragraph 4.

Article IX
Budget

1. The Budget shall be administered by the Organization.
2. The General Conference shall approve and give final effect to the budget and to the apportionment of financial responsibility among the States members of the Organization subject to such arrangement with the United Nations as may be provided in the agreement to be entered into pursuant to Article X.
3. The Director-General may accept voluntary contributions, gifts, bequests, and subventions directly from Governments, public and private institutions, associations and private persons, subject to the conditions specified in the Financial Regulations.

Article X
Relations with the United Nations Organization

This Organization shall be brought into relation with the United Nations Organization, as soon as practicable, as one of the Specialized Agencies referred to in Article 57 of the Charter of the United Nations. This relationship shall be effected through an agreement with the United Nations Organization under Article 63 of the Charter, which agreement shall be subject to the approval of the General Conference of this Organization. The agreement shall provide for effective co-operation between the two Organizations in the pursuit of their common purposes, and at the same time shall recognize the autonomy of this Organization, within the fields of its competence as defined in this Constitution. Such agreement may, among other matters, provide for the approval and financing of the budget of the Organization by the General Assembly of the United Nations.

Article XI
Relations with other Specialized International Organizations and Agencies

1. This Organization may cooperate with other specialized inter governmental organizations and agencies whose interests and activities are related to its purposes. To this end the Director-General, acting under the general authority of the Executive Board, may establish effective working relationships with such organizations and agencies and establish

such joint committees as may be necessary to assure effective co-operation. Any formal arrangements entered into with such organizations or agencies shall be subject to the approval of the Executive Board.

2. Whenever the General Conference of this Organization and the competent authorities of any other specialized intergovernmental organizations or agencies whose purpose and functions lie within the competence of this Organization, deem it desirable to effect a transfer of their resources and activities to this Organization, the Director-General, subject to the approval of the Conference, may enter into mutually acceptable arrangements for this purpose.
3. This Organization may make appropriate arrangements with other intergovernmental organizations for reciprocal representation at meetings.
4. The United Nations Educational, Scientific and Cultural Organization may make suitable arrangements for consultation and co-operation with non-governmental international organizations concerned with matters within its competence, and may invite them to undertake specific tasks. Such co-operation may also include appropriate participation by representatives of such organizations on advisory committees set up by the General Conference.

Article XII

Legal status of the Organization

The provisions of Articles 104 and 105 of the Charter of the United Nations Organization concerning the legal status of that Organization, its privileges and immunities, shall apply in the same way to this Organization.

Article XIII

Amendments

1. Proposals for amendments to this Constitution shall become effective upon receiving the approval of the General Conference by a two-thirds majority; provided, however, that those amendments which involve fundamental alterations in the aims of the Organization or new obligations for the Member States shall require subsequent acceptance on the part of two-thirds of the Member States before they come into force.

The draft texts of proposed amendments shall be communicated by the Director-General to the Member States at least six months in advance of their consideration by the General Conference.

2. The General Conference shall have power to adopt by a two-thirds majority rules of procedure for carrying out the provisions of this Article.

Article XIV

Interpretation

1. The English and French texts of this Constitution shall be regarded as equally authoritative.
2. Any question or dispute concerning the interpretation of this Constitution shall be referred for determination to the International Court of Justice or to an arbitral tribunal, as the General Conference may determine under its rules of procedure.

Article XV

Entry into force

1. This Constitution shall be subject to acceptance. The instrument of acceptance shall be deposited with the Government of the United Kingdom.
2. This Constitution shall remain open for signature in the archives of the Government of the United Kingdom. Signature may take place either before or after the deposit of the instrument of acceptance. No acceptance shall be valid unless preceded or followed by signature. However, a State that has withdrawn from the Organization shall simply deposit a new instrument of acceptance in order to resume membership.
3. This Constitution shall come into force when it has been accepted by twenty of its signatories. Subsequent acceptances shall take effect immediately.
4. The Government of the United Kingdom will inform all Members of the United Nations of the receipt of all instruments of acceptance and of the date on which the Constitution comes into force in accordance with the preceding paragraph.

In faith whereof, the undersigned, duly authorized to that effect, have signed this Constitution in the English and French languages, both texts being equally authentic.

Done in London the sixteenth day of November, one thousand nine hundred and forty-five, in a single copy, in the English and French languages, of which certified copies will be communicated by the Government of the United Kingdom to the Governments of all the Members of the United Nations.

UNIT	BACKGROUND DOCUMENTS FOR CHAPTER 2
B	Document 3: OPCW Document

CONVENTION ON THE PROHIBITION OF THE DEVELOPMENT, PRODUCTION, STOCKPILING AND USE OF CHEMICAL WEAPONS AND ON THEIR DISTRUCTION

Jan. 13, 1993, 1974 U.N.T.S. 45 (Apr. 29, 1997).

Article VIII

THE ORGANIZATION

A. GENERAL PROVISIONS

1. The States Parties to this Convention hereby establish the Organization for the Prohibition of Chemical Weapons to achieve the object and purpose of this Convention, to ensure the implementation of its provisions, including those for international verification of compliance with it, and to provide a forum for consultation and cooperation among States Parties.
2. All States Parties to this Convention shall be members of the Organization. A State Party shall not be deprived of its membership in the Organization.
3. The seat of the Headquarters of the Organization shall be The Hague, Kingdom of the Netherlands.

4. There are hereby established as the organs of the Organization: the Conference of the States Parties, the Executive Council, and the Technical Secretariat.
5. The Organization shall conduct its verification activities provided for under this Convention in the least intrusive manner possible consistent with the timely and efficient accomplishment of their objectives. It shall request only the information and data necessary to fulfil its responsibilities under this Convention. It shall take every precaution to protect the confidentiality of information on civil and military activities and facilities coming to its knowledge in the implementation of this Convention and, in particular, shall abide by the provisions set forth in the Confidentiality Annex.
6. In undertaking its verification activities the Organization shall consider measures to make use of advances in science and technology.
7. The costs of the Organization's activities shall be paid by States Parties in accordance with the United Nations scale of assessment adjusted to take into account differences in membership between the United Nations and this Organization. . . . Financial contributions of States Parties to the Preparatory Commission shall be deducted in an appropriate way from their contributions to the regular budget. The budget of the Organization shall comprise two separate chapters, one relating to administrative and other costs, and one relating to verification costs.
8. A member of the Organization which is in arrears in the payment of its financial contribution to the Organization shall have no vote in the Organization if the amount of its arrears equals or exceeds the amount of the contribution due from it for the preceding two full years. The Conference of the States Parties may, nevertheless, permit such a member to vote if it is satisfied that the failure to pay is due to conditions beyond the control of the member.

B. THE CONFERENCE OF THE STATES PARTIES

Composition, procedures and decision-making

9. The Conference of the States Parties (hereinafter referred to as "the Conference") shall be composed of all members of this Organization. Each member shall have one representative in the Conference, who may be accompanied by alternates and advisers.
10. The first session of the Conference shall be convened by the depositary not later than 30 days after the entry into force of this Convention.

11. The Conference shall meet in regular sessions which shall be held annually unless it decides otherwise.

12. Special sessions of the Conference shall be convened:

    (a) When decided by the Conference;

    (b) When requested by the Executive Council;

    (c) When requested by any member and supported by one third of the members; or

    (d) In accordance with paragraph 22 to undertake reviews of the operation of this Convention.

    Except in the case of subparagraph (d), the special session shall be convened not later than 30 days after receipt of the request by the Director-General of the Technical Secretariat, unless specified otherwise in the request.

13. The Conference shall also be convened in the form of an Amendment Conference in accordance with [this Convention].

14. Sessions of the Conference shall take place at the seat of the Organization unless the Conference decides otherwise.

15. The Conference shall adopt its rules of procedure. At the beginning of each regular session, it shall elect its Chairman and such other officers as may be required. They shall hold office until a new Chairman and other officers are elected at the next regular session.

16. A majority of the members of the Organization shall constitute a quorum for the Conference.

17. Each member of the Organization shall have one vote in the Conference.

18. The Conference shall take decisions on questions of procedure by a simple majority of the members present and voting. Decisions on matters of substance should be taken as far as possible by consensus. If consensus is not attainable when an issue comes up for decision, the Chairman shall defer any vote for 24 hours and during this period of deferment shall make every effort to facilitate achievement of consensus, and shall report to the Conference before the end of this period. If consensus is not possible at the end of 24 hours, the Conference shall take the decision by a two-thirds majority of members present and voting unless specified otherwise in this Convention. When the issue arises as to whether the question is one of substance or not, that question shall be treated as a matter of substance unless otherwise decided

by the Conference by the majority required for decisions on matters of substance.

Powers and functions

19. The Conference shall be the principal organ of the Organization. It shall consider any questions, matters or issues within the scope of this Convention, including those relating to the powers and functions of the Executive Council and the Technical Secretariat. It may make recommendations and take decisions on any questions, matters or issues related to this Convention raised by a State Party or brought to its attention by the Executive Council.

20. The Conference shall oversee the implementation of this Convention, and act in order to promote its object and purpose. The Conference shall review compliance with this Convention. It shall also oversee the activities of the Executive Council and the Technical Secretariat and may issue guidelines in accordance with this Convention to either of them in the exercise of their functions.

21. The Conference shall:

    (a) Consider and adopt at its regular sessions the report, programme and budget of the Organization, submitted by the Executive Council, as well as consider other reports;

    (b) Decide on the scale of financial contributions to be paid by States Parties in accordance with paragraph 7;

    (c) Elect the members of the Executive Council;

    (d) Appoint the Director-General of the Technical Secretariat (hereinafter referred to as "the Director-General");

    (e) Approve the rules of procedure of the Executive Council submitted by the latter;

    (f) Establish such subsidiary organs as it finds necessary for the exercise of its functions in accordance with this Convention;

    (g) Foster international cooperation for peaceful purposes in the field of chemical activities;

    (h) Review scientific and technological developments that could affect the operation of this Convention and, in this context, direct the Director-General to establish a Scientific Advisory Board to enable him, in the performance of his functions, to render specialized advice in areas of science and technology relevant to this Convention, to the Conference, the Executive Council or States Parties. The Scientific Advisory Board shall be composed of independent experts appointed in accordance with terms of reference adopted by the Conference;

(i) Consider and approve at its first session any draft agreements, provisions and guidelines developed by the Preparatory Commission;

(j) Establish at its first session the voluntary fund for assistance in accordance with [this Convention];

(k) Take the necessary measures to ensure compliance with this Convention and to redress and remedy any situation which contravenes the provisions of this Convention....

22. The Conference shall not later than one year after the expiry of the fifth and the tenth year after the entry into force of this Convention, and at such other times within that time period as may be decided upon, convene in special sessions to undertake reviews of the operation of this Convention. Such reviews shall take into account any relevant scientific and technological developments. At intervals of five years thereafter, unless otherwise decided upon, further sessions of the Conference shall be convened with the same objective.

C. THE EXECUTIVE COUNCIL

Composition, procedure and decision-making

23. The Executive Council shall consist of 41 members. Each State Party shall have the right, in accordance with the principle of rotation, to serve on the Executive Council. The members of the Executive Council shall be elected by the Conference for a term of two years. In order to ensure the effective functioning of this Convention, due regard being specially paid to equitable geographical distribution, to the importance of chemical industry, as well as to political and security interests, the Executive Council shall be composed as follows:

(a) Nine States Parties from Africa to be designated by States Parties located in this region. As a basis for this designation it is understood that, out of these nine States Parties, three members shall, as a rule, be the States Parties with the most significant national chemical industry in the region as determined by internationally reported and published data; in addition, the regional group shall agree also to take into account other regional factors in designating these three members;

(b) Nine States Parties from Asia to be designated by States Parties located in this region. As a basis for this designation it is understood that, out of these nine States Parties, four members shall, as a rule, be the States Parties with the most significant national chemical industry in the region as determined by internationally reported and published data; in addition, the regional group shall agree also to take into account other regional factors in designating these four members;

(c) Five States Parties from Eastern Europe to be designated by States Parties located in this region. As a basis for this designation it is understood that, out of these five States Parties, one member shall, as a rule, be the State Party with the most significant national chemical industry in the region as determined by internationally reported and published data; in addition, the regional group shall agree also to take into account other regional factors in designating this one member;

(d) Seven States Parties from Latin America and the Caribbean to be designated by States Parties located in this region. As a basis for this designation it is understood that, out of these seven States Parties, three members shall, as a rule, be the States Parties with the most significant national chemical industry in the region as determined by internationally reported and published data; in addition, the regional group shall agree also to take into account other regional factors in designating these three members;

(e) Ten States Parties from among Western European and other States to be designated by States Parties located in this region. As a basis for this designation it is understood that, out of these 10 States Parties, 5 members shall, as a rule, be the States Parties with the most significant national chemical industry in the region as determined by internationally reported and published data; in addition, the regional group shall agree also to take into account other regional factors in designating these five members;

(f) One further State Party to be designated consecutively by States Parties located in the regions of Asia and Latin

America and the Caribbean. As a basis for this designation it is understood that this State Party shall be a rotating member from these regions.

24. For the first election of the Executive Council 20 members shall be elected for a term of one year, due regard being paid to the established numerical proportions as described in paragraph 23.

25. After the full implementation of [the other provisions of this Covention] the Conference may, upon the request of a majority of the members of the Executive Council, review the composition of the Executive Council taking into account developments related to the principles specified in paragraph 23 that are governing its composition.

26. The Executive Council shall elaborate its rules of procedure and submit them to the Conference for approval.

27. The Executive Council shall elect its Chairman from among its members.

28. The Executive Council shall meet for regular sessions. Between regular sessions it shall meet as often as may be required for the fulfilment of its powers and functions.

29. Each member of the Executive Council shall have one vote. Unless otherwise specified in this Convention, the Executive Council shall take decisions on matters of substance by a two-thirds majority of all its members. The Executive Council shall take decisions on questions of procedure by a simple majority of all its members. When the issue arises as to whether the question is one of substance or not, that question shall be treated as a matter of substance unless otherwise decided by the Executive Council by the majority required for decisions on matters of substance.

Powers and functions

30. The Executive Council shall be the executive organ of the Organization. It shall be responsible to the Conference. The Executive Council shall carry out the powers and functions entrusted to it under this Convention, as well as those functions delegated to it by the Conference. In so doing, it shall act in conformity with the recommendations, decisions and guidelines of the Conference and assure their proper and continuous implementation.

31. The Executive Council shall promote the effective implementation of, and compliance with, this Convention. It shall supervise the activities of the Technical Secretariat, cooperate with the National Authority of

each State Party and facilitate consultations and cooperation among States Parties at their request.

32. The Executive Council shall:

    (a) Consider and submit to the Conference the draft programme and budget of the Organization;

    (b) Consider and submit to the Conference the draft report of the Organization on the implementation of this Convention, the report on the performance of its own activities and such special reports as it deems necessary or which the Conference may request;

    (c) Make arrangements for the sessions of the Conference including the preparation of the draft agenda.

33. The Executive Council may request the convening of a special session of the Conference.

34. The Executive Council shall:

    (a) Conclude agreements or arrangements with States and international organizations on behalf of the Organization, subject to prior approval by the Conference;

    (b) Conclude agreements with States Parties on behalf of the Organization in connection with [specified provisions of the Convention];

    (c) Approve agreements or arrangements relating to the implementation of verification activities, negotiated by the Technical Secretariat with States Parties.

35. The Executive Council shall consider any issue or matter within its competence affecting this Convention and its implementation, including concerns regarding compliance, and cases of non-compliance, and, as appropriate, inform States Parties and bring the issue or matter to the attention of the Conference.

36. In its consideration of doubts or concerns regarding compliance and cases of non-compliance, including, inter alia, abuse of the rights provided for under this Convention, the Executive Council shall consult with the States Parties involved and, as appropriate, request the State Party to take measures to redress the situation within a specified time. To the extent that the Executive Council considers further action to be necessary, it shall take, inter alia, one or more of the following measures:

    (a) Inform all States Parties of the issue or matter;

(b) Bring the issue or matter to the attention of the Conference;

(c) Make recommendations to the Conference regarding measures to redress the situation and to ensure compliance.

The Executive Council shall, in cases of particular gravity and urgency, bring the issue or matter, including relevant information and conclusions, directly to the attention of the United Nations General Assembly and the United Nations Security Council. It shall at the same time inform all States Parties of this step.

D. THE TECHNICAL SECRETARIAT

37. The Technical Secretariat shall assist the Conference and the Executive Council in the performance of their functions. The Technical Secretariat shall carry out the verification measures provided for in this Convention. It shall carry out the other functions entrusted to it under this Convention as well as those functions delegated to it by the Conference and the Executive Council.

38. The Technical Secretariat shall:

(a) Prepare and submit to the Executive Council the draft programme and budget of the Organization;

(b) Prepare and submit to the Executive Council the draft report of the Organization on the implementation of this Convention and such other reports as the Conference or the Executive Council may request;

(c) Provide administrative and technical support to the Conference, the Executive Council and subsidiary organs;

(d) Address and receive communications on behalf of the Organization to and from States Parties on matters pertaining to the implementation of this Convention;

(e) Provide technical assistance and technical evaluation to States Parties in the implementation of the provisions of this Convention, including evaluation of scheduled and unscheduled chemicals.

39. The Technical Secretariat shall:

(a) Negotiate agreements or arrangements relating to the implementation of verification activities with States Parties, subject to approval by the Executive Council;

(b) Not later than 180 days after entry into force of this Convention, coordinate the establishment and maintenance of permanent stockpiles of emergency and humanitarian assistance by States Parties in accordance with [other specified provisions of the Convention]. The Technical Secretariat may inspect the items maintained for serviceability. Lists of items to be stockpiled shall be considered and approved by the Conference pursuant to paragraph 21 (i) above;

(c) Administer the voluntary fund referred to in [other specified provisions of the Convention], compile declarations made by the States Parties and register, when requested, bilateral agreements concluded between States Parties or between a State Party and the Organization. . . .

40. The Technical Secretariat shall inform the Executive Council of any problem that has arisen with regard to the discharge of its functions, including doubts, ambiguities or uncertainties about compliance with this Convention that have come to its notice in the performance of its verification activities and that it has been unable to resolve or clarify through its consultations with the State Party concerned.

41. The Technical Secretariat shall comprise a Director-General, who shall be its head and chief administrative officer, inspectors and such scientific, technical and other personnel as may be required.

42. The Inspectorate shall be a unit of the Technical Secretariat and shall act under the supervision of the Director-General.

43. The Director-General shall be appointed by the Conference upon the recommendation of the Executive Council for a term of four years, renewable for one further term, but not thereafter.

44. The Director-General shall be responsible to the Conference and the Executive Council for the appointment of the staff and the organization and functioning of the Technical Secretariat. The paramount consideration in the employment of the staff and in the determination of the conditions of service shall be the necessity of securing the highest standards of efficiency, competence and integrity. Only citizens of States Parties shall serve as the Director-General, as inspectors or as other members of the professional and clerical staff. Due regard shall be paid to the importance of recruiting the staff on as wide a geographical basis as possible. Recruitment shall be guided by the principle that the staff shall be kept to a minimum necessary for the proper discharge of the responsibilities of the Technical Secretariat.

45. The Director-General shall be responsible for the organization and functioning of the Scientific Advisory Board. . . . The Director-General shall, in consultation with States Parties, appoint members of the Scientific Advisory Board, who shall serve in their individual capacity. The members of the Board shall be appointed on the basis of their expertise in the particular scientific fields relevant to the implementation of this Convention. The Director-General may also, as appropriate, in consultation with members of the Board, establish temporary working groups of scientific experts to provide recommendations on specific issues. In regard to the above, States Parties may submit lists of experts to the Director-General.

46. In the performance of their duties, the Director-General, the inspectors and the other members of the staff shall not seek or receive instructions from any Government or from any other source external to the Organization. They shall refrain from any action that might reflect on their positions as international officers responsible only to the Conference and the Executive Council.

47. Each State Party shall respect the exclusively international character of the responsibilities of the Director-General, the inspectors and the other members of the staff and not seek to influence them in the discharge of their responsibilities.

E. PRIVILEGES AND IMMUNITIES

48. The Organization shall enjoy on the territory and in any other place under the jurisdiction or control of a State Party such legal capacity and such privileges and immunities as are necessary for the exercise of its functions.

49. Delegates of States Parties, together with their alternates and advisers, representatives appointed to the Executive Council together with their alternates and advisers, the Director-General and the staff of the Organization shall enjoy such privileges and immunities as are necessary in the independent exercise of their functions in connection with the Organization.

50. The legal capacity, privileges, and immunities referred to in this Article shall be defined in agreements between the Organization and the States Parties as well as in an agreement between the Organization and the State in which the headquarters of the Organization is seated. These agreements shall be considered and approved by the Conference pursuant to paragraph 21 (i).

51. Notwithstanding paragraphs 48 and 49, the privileges and immunities enjoyed by the Director-General and the staff of the Technical Secretariat during the conduct of verification activities shall be those set forth in Part II, Section B, of the Verification Annex [appended to the Convention].

UNIT B

BACKGROUND DOCUMENT FOR CHAPTER 3

Document: Statute of the International Court of Justice

STATUTE OF THE INTERNATIONAL COURT OF JUSTICE

June 26, 1945, 59 Stat. 1055, 3 Bevans 1179 (Oct. 24, 1945).

Article 1

The International Court of Justice established by the Charter of the United Nations as the principal judicial organ of the United Nations shall be constituted and shall function in accordance with the provisions of the present Statute.

CHAPTER I—ORGANIZATION OF THE COURT

Article 2

The Court shall be composed of a body of independent judges, elected regardless of their nationality from among persons of high moral character, who possess the qualifications required in their respective countries for appointment to the highest judicial offices, or are jurisconsults of recognized competence in international law.

Article 3

1. The Court shall consist of fifteen members, no two of whom may be nationals of the same state.
2. A person who for the purposes of membership in the Court could be regarded as a national of more than one state shall be deemed to be a na-

tional of the one in which he ordinarily exercises civil and political rights.

Article 4

1. The members of the Court shall be elected by the General Assembly and by the Security Council from a list of persons nominated by the national groups in the Permanent Court of Arbitration, in accordance with the following provisions.
2. In the case of Members of the United Nations not represented in the Permanent Court of Arbitration, candidates shall be nominated by national groups appointed for this purpose by their governments under the same conditions as those prescribed for members of the Permanent Court of Arbitration by Article 44 of the Convention of The Hague of 1907 for the pacific settlement of international disputes.
3. The conditions under which a state which is a party to the present Statute but is not a Member of the United Nations may participate in electing the members of the Court shall, in the absence of a special agreement, be laid down by the General Assembly upon recommendation of the Security Council.

Article 5

1. At least three months before the date of the election, the Secretary-General of the United Nations shall address a written request to the members of the Permanent Court of Arbitration belonging to the states which are parties to the present Statute, and to the members of the national groups appointed under Article 4, paragraph 2, inviting them to undertake, within a given time, by national groups, the nomination of persons in a position to accept the duties of a member of the Court.
2. No group may nominate more than four persons, not more than two of whom shall be of their own nationality. In no case may the number of candidates nominated by a group be more than double the number of seats to be filled.

Article 6

Before making these nominations, each national group is recommended to consult its highest court of justice, its legal faculties and schools of law, and its national academies and national sections of international academies devoted to the study of law.

Article 7

1. The Secretary-General shall prepare a list in alphabetical order of all the persons thus nominated. Save as provided in Article 12, paragraph 2, these shall be the only persons eligible.
2. The Secretary-General shall submit this list to the General Assembly and to the Security Council.

Article 8

The General Assembly and the Security Council shall proceed independently of one another to elect the members of the Court.

Article 9

At every election, the electors shall bear in mind not only that the persons to be elected should individually possess the qualifications required, but also that in the body as a whole the representation of the main forms of civilization and of the principal legal systems of the world should be assured.

Article 10

1. Those candidates who obtain an absolute majority of votes in the General Assembly and in the Security Council shall be considered as elected.
2. Any vote of the Security Council, whether for the election of judges or for the appointment of members of the conference envisaged in Article 12, shall be taken without any distinction between permanent and non-permanent members of the Security Council.
3. In the event of more than one national of the same state obtaining an absolute majority of the votes both of the General Assembly and of the Security Council, the eldest of these only shall be considered as elected.

Article 11

If, after the first meeting held for the purpose of the election, one or more seats remain to be filled, a second and, if necessary, a third meeting shall take place.

Article 12

1. If, after the third meeting, one or more seats still remain unfilled, a joint conference consisting of six members, three appointed by the General Assembly and three by the Security Council, may be formed at any time at the request of either the General Assembly or the Security Council, for the purpose of choosing by the vote of an absolute majority one name for each seat still vacant, to submit to the General Assembly and the Security Council for their respective acceptance.
2. If the joint conference is unanimously agreed upon any person who fulfills the required conditions, he may be included in its list, even though he was not included in the list of nominations referred to in Article 7.
3. If the joint conference is satisfied that it will not be successful in procuring an election, those members of the Court who have already been elected shall, within a period to be fixed by the Security Council, proceed to fill the vacant seats by selection from among those candidates who have obtained votes either in the General Assembly or in the Security Council.
4. In the event of an equality of votes among the judges, the eldest judge shall have a casting vote.

Article 13

1. The members of the Court shall be elected for nine years and may be re-elected; provided, however, that of the judges elected at the first election, the terms of five judges shall expire at the end of three years and the terms of five more judges shall expire at the end of six years.
2. The judges whose terms are to expire at the end of the above-mentioned initial periods of three and six years shall be chosen by lot to be drawn by the Secretary-General immediately after the first election has been completed.

3. The members of the Court shall continue to discharge their duties until their places have been filled. Though replaced, they shall finish any cases which they may have begun.

4. In the case of the resignation of a member of the Court, the resignation shall be addressed to the President of the Court for transmission to the Secretary-General. This last notification makes the place vacant.

Article 14

Vacancies shall be filled by the same method as that laid down for the first election subject to the following provision: the Secretary-General shall, within one month of the occurrence of the vacancy, proceed to issue the invitations provided for in Article 5, and the date of the election shall be fixed by the Security Council.

Article 15

A member of the Court elected to replace a member whose term of office has not expired shall hold office for the remainder of his predecessor's term.

Article 16

1. No member of the Court may exercise any political or administrative function, or engage in any other occupation of a professional nature.
2. Any doubt on this point shall be settled by the decision of the Court.

Article 17

1. No member of the Court may act as agent, counsel, or advocate in any case.
2. No member may participate in the decision of any case in which he has previously taken part as agent, counsel, or advocate for one of the parties, or as a member of a national or international court, or of a commission of enquiry, or in any other capacity.
3. Any doubt on this point shall be settled by the decision of the Court.

Article 18

1. No member of the Court can be dismissed unless, in the unanimous opinion of the other members, he has ceased to fulfill the required conditions.
2. Formal notification thereof shall be made to the Secretary-General by the Registrar.
3. This notification makes the place vacant.

Article 19

The members of the Court, when engaged on the business of the Court, shall enjoy diplomatic privileges and immunities.

Article 20

Every member of the Court shall, before taking up his duties, make a solemn declaration in open court that he will exercise his powers impartially and conscientiously.

Article 21

1. The Court shall elect its President and Vice-President for three years; they may be re-elected.
2. The Court shall appoint its Registrar and may provide for the appointment of such other officers as may be necessary.

Article 22

1. The seat of the Court shall be established at The Hague. This, however, shall not prevent the Court from sitting and exercising its functions elsewhere whenever the Court considers it desirable.
2. The President and the Registrar shall reside at the seat of the Court.

Article 23

1. The Court shall remain permanently in session, except during the judicial vacations, the dates and duration of which shall be fixed by the Court.

2. Members of the Court are entitled to periodic leave, the dates and duration of which shall be fixed by the Court, having in mind the distance between The Hague and the home of each judge.
3. Members of the Court shall be bound, unless they are on leave or prevented from attending by illness or other serious reasons duly explained to the President, to hold themselves permanently at the disposal of the Court.

Article 24

1. If, for some special reason, a member of the Court considers that he should not take part in the decision of a particular case, he shall so inform the President.
2. If the President considers that for some special reason one of the members of the Court should not sit in a particular case, he shall give him notice accordingly.
3. If in any such case the member Court and the President disagree, the matter shall be settled by the decision of the Court.

Article 25

1. The full Court shall sit except when it is expressly provided otherwise in the present Statute.
2. Subject to the condition that the number of judges available to constitute the Court is not thereby reduced below eleven, the Rules of the Court may provide for allowing one or more judges, according to circumstances and in rotation, to be dispensed from sitting.
3. A quorum of nine judges shall suffice to constitute the Court.

Article 26

1. The Court may from time to time form one or more chambers, composed of three or more judges as the Court may determine, for dealing with particular categories of cases; for example, labour cases and cases relating to transit and communications.
2. The Court may at any time form a chamber for dealing with a particular case. The number of judges to constitute such a chamber shall be determined by the Court with the approval of the parties.

3. Cases shall be heard and determined by the chambers provided for in this article if the parties so request.

Article 27

A judgment given by any of the chambers provided for in Articles 26 and 29 shall be considered as rendered by the Court.

Article 28

The chambers provided for in Articles 26 and 29 may, with the consent of the parties, sit and exercise their functions elsewhere than at The Hague.

Article 29

With a view to the speedy dispatch of business, the Court shall form annually a chamber composed of five judges which, at the request of the parties, may hear and determine cases by summary procedure. In addition, two judges shall be selected for the purpose of replacing judges who find it impossible to sit.

Article 30

1. The Court shall frame rules for carrying out its functions. In particular, it shall lay down rules of procedure.
2. The Rules of the Court may provide for assessors to sit with the Court or with any of its chambers, without the right to vote.

Article 31

1. Judges of the nationality of each of the parties shall retain their right to sit in the case before the Court.
2. If the Court includes upon the Bench a judge of the nationality of one of the parties, any other party may choose a person to sit as judge. Such person shall be chosen preferably from among those persons who have been nominated as candidates as provided in Articles 4 and 5.
3. If the Court includes upon the Bench no judge of the nationality of the parties, each of these parties may proceed to choose a judge as provided in paragraph 2 of this Article.

4. The provisions of this Article shall apply to the case of Articles 26 and 29. In such cases, the President shall request one or, if necessary, two of the members of the Court forming the chamber to give place to the members of the Court of the nationality of the parties concerned, and, failing such, or if they are unable to be present, to the judges specially chosen by the parties.

5. Should there be several parties in the same interest, they shall, for the purpose of the preceding provisions, be reckoned as one party only. Any doubt upon this point shall be settled by the decision of the Court.

6. Judges chosen as laid down in paragraphs 2, 3, and 4 of this Article shall fulfill the conditions required by Articles 2, 17 (paragraph 2), 20, and 24 of the present Statute. They shall take part in the decision on terms of complete equality with their colleagues.

Article 32

1. Each member of the Court shall receive an annual salary.

2. The President shall receive a special annual allowance.

3. The Vice-President shall receive a special allowance for every day on which he acts as President.

4. The judges chosen under Article 31, other than members of the Court, shall receive compensation for each day on which they exercise their functions.

5. These salaries, allowances, and compensation shall be fixed by the General Assembly. They may not be decreased during the term of office.

6. The salary of the Registrar shall be fixed by the General Assembly on the proposal of the Court.

7. Regulations made by the General Assembly shall fix the conditions under which retirement pensions may be given to members of the Court and to the Registrar, and the conditions under which members of the Court and the Registrar shall have their travelling expenses refunded.

8. The above salaries, allowances, and compensation shall be free of all taxation.

Article 33

The expenses of the Court shall be borne by the United Nations in such a manner as shall be decided by the General Assembly.

CHAPTER II—COMPETENCE OF THE COURT

Article 34

1. Only states may be parties in cases before the Court.
2. The Court, subject to and in conformity with its Rules, may request of public international organizations information relevant to cases before it, and shall receive such information presented by such organizations on their own initiative.
3. Whenever the construction of the constituent instrument of a public international organization or of an international convention adopted thereunder is in question in a case before the Court, the Registrar shall so notify the public international organization concerned and shall communicate to it copies of all the written proceedings.

Article 35

1. The Court shall be open to the states parties to the present Statute.
2. The conditions under which the Court shall be open to other states shall, subject to the special provisions contained in treaties in force, be laid down by the Security Council, but in no case shall such conditions place the parties in a position of inequality before the Court.
3. When a state which is not a Member of the United Nations is a party to a case, the Court shall fix the amount which that party is to contribute towards the expenses of the Court. This provision shall not apply if such state is bearing a share of the expenses of the Court

Article 36

1. The jurisdiction of the Court comprises all cases which the parties refer to it and all matters specially provided for in the Charter of the United Nations or in treaties and conventions in force.
2. The states parties to the present Statute may at any time declare that they recognize as compulsory ipso facto and without special agreement,

in relation to any other state accepting the same obligation, the jurisdiction of the Court in all legal disputes concerning:

a. the interpretation of a treaty;

b. any question of international law;

c. the existence of any fact which, if established, would constitute a breach of an international obligation;

d. the nature or extent of the reparation to be made for the breach of an international obligation.

3. The declarations referred to above may be made unconditionally or on condition of reciprocity on the part of several or certain states, or for a certain time.

4. Such declarations shall be deposited with the Secretary-General of the United Nations, who shall transmit copies thereof to the parties to the Statute and to the Registrar of the Court.

5. Declarations made under Article 36 of the Statute of the Permanent Court of International Justice and which are still in force shall be deemed, as between the parties to the present Statute, to be acceptances of the compulsory jurisdiction of the International Court of Justice for the period which they still have to run and in accordance with their terms.

6. In the event of a dispute as to whether the Court has jurisdiction, the matter shall be settled by the decision of the Court.

Article 37

Whenever a treaty or convention in force provides for reference of a matter to a tribunal to have been instituted by the League of Nations, or to the Permanent Court of International Justice, the matter shall, as between the parties to the present Statute, be referred to the International Court of Justice.

Article 38

1. The Court, whose function is to decide in accordance with international law such disputes as are submitted to it, shall apply:

a. international conventions, whether general or particular, establishing rules expressly recognized by the contesting states;

b. international custom, as evidence of a general practice accepted as law;

c. the general principles of law recognized by civilized nations;

d. subject to the provisions of Article 59, judicial decisions and the teachings of the most highly qualified publicists of the various nations, as subsidiary means for the determination of rules of law.

2. This provision shall not prejudice the power of the Court to decide a case *ex aequo et bono*, if the parties agree thereto.

CHAPTER III—PROCEDURE

Article 39

1. The official languages of the Court shall be French and English. If the parties agree that the case shall be conducted in French, the judgment shall be delivered in French. If the parties agree that the case shall be conducted in English, the judgment shall be delivered in English.

2. In the absence of an agreement as to which language shall be employed, each party may, in the pleadings, use the language which it prefers; the decision of the Court shall be given in French and English. In this case the Court shall at the same time determine which of the two texts shall be considered as authoritative.

3. The Court shall, at the request of any party, authorize a language other than French or English to be used by that party.

Article 40

1. Cases are brought before the Court, as the case may be, either by the notification of the special agreement or by a written application addressed to the Registrar. In either case the subject of the dispute and the parties shall be indicated.

2. The Registrar shall forthwith communicate the application to all concerned.

3. He shall also notify the Members of the United Nations through the Secretary-General, and also any other states entitled to appear before the Court.

Article 41

1. The Court shall have the power to indicate, if it considers that circumstances so require, any provisional measures which ought to be taken to preserve the respective rights of either party.
2. Pending the final decision, notice of the measures suggested shall forthwith be given to the parties and to the Security Council

Article 42

1. The parties shall be represented by agents.
2. They may have the assistance of counsel or advocates before the Court.
3. The agents, counsel, and advocates of parties before the Court shall enjoy the privileges and immunities necessary to the independent exercise of their duties.

Article 43

1. The procedure shall consist of two parts: written and oral.
2. The written proceedings shall consist of the communication to the Court and to the parties of memorials, counter-memorials and, if necessary, replies; also all papers and documents in support.
3. These communications shall be made through the Registrar, in the order and within the time fixed by the Court.
4. A certified copy of every document produced by one party shall be communicated to the other party.
5. The oral proceedings shall consist of the hearing by the Court of witnesses, experts, agents, counsel, and advocates.

Article 44

1. For the service of all notices upon persons other than the agents, counsel, and advocates, the Court shall apply direct to the government of the state upon whose territory the notice has to be served.
2. The same provision shall apply whenever steps are to be taken to procure evidence on the spot.

Article 45

The hearing shall be under the control of the President or, if he is unable to preside, of the Vice-President; if neither is able to preside, the senior judge present shall preside.

Article 46

The hearing in Court shall be public, unless the Court shall decide otherwise, or unless the parties demand that the public be not admitted .

Article 47

1. Minutes shall be made at each hearing and signed by the Registrar and the President.
2. These minutes alone shall be authentic.

Article 48

The Court shall make orders for the conduct of the case, shall decide the form and time in which each party must conclude its arguments, and make all arrangements connected with the taking of evidence.

Article 49

The Court may, even before the hearing begins, call upon the agents to produce any document or to supply any explanations. Formal note shall be taken of any refusal.

Article 50

The Court may, at any time, entrust any individual, body, bureau, commission, or other organization that it may select, with the task of carrying out an enquiry or giving an expert opinion.

Article 51

During the hearing any relevant questions are to be put to the witnesses and experts under the conditions laid down by the Court in the rules of procedure referred to in Article 30.

Article 52

After the Court has received the proofs and evidence within the time specified for the purpose, it may refuse to accept any further oral or written evidence that one party may desire to present unless the other side consents.

Article 53

1. Whenever one of the parties does not appear before the Court, or fails to defend its case, the other party may call upon the Court to decide in favour of its claim.
2. The Court must, before doing so, satisfy itself, not only that it has jurisdiction in accordance with Articles 36 and 37, but also that the claim is well founded in fact and law.

Article 54

1. When, subject to the control of the Court, the agents, counsel, and advocates have completed their presentation of the case, the President shall declare the hearing closed.
2. The Court shall withdraw to consider the judgment.
3. The deliberations of the Court shall take place in private and remain secret.

Article 55

1. All questions shall be decided by a majority of the judges present.
2. In the event of an equality of votes, the President or the judge who acts in his place shall have a casting vote.

Article 56

1. The judgment shall state the reasons on which it is based.
2. It shall contain the names of the judges who have taken part in the decision.

Article 57

If the judgment does not represent in whole or in part the unanimous opinion of the judges, any judge shall be entitled to deliver a separate opinion.

Article 58

The judgment shall be signed by the President and by the Registrar. It shall be read in open court, due notice having been given to the agents.

Article 59

The decision of the Court has no binding force except between the parties and in respect of that particular case.

Article 60

The judgment is final and without appeal. In the event of dispute as to the meaning or scope of the judgment, the Court shall construe it upon the request of any party.

Article 61

1. An application for revision of a judgment may be made only when it is based upon the discovery of some fact of such a nature as to be a decisive factor, which fact was, when the judgment was given, unknown to the Court and also to the party claiming revision, always provided that such ignorance was not due to negligence.
2. The proceedings for revision shall be opened by a judgment of the Court expressly recording the existence of the new fact, recognizing that it has such a character as to lay the case open to revision, and declaring the application admissible on this ground.
3. The Court may require previous compliance with the terms of the judgment before it admits proceedings in revision.
4. The application for revision must be made at latest within six months of the discovery of the new fact.

5. No application for revision may be made after the lapse of ten years from the date of the judgment.

Article 62

1. Should a state consider that it has an interest of a legal nature which may be affected by the decision in the case, it may submit a request to the Court to be permitted to intervene.
2. It shall be for the Court to decide upon this request.

Article 63

1. Whenever the construction of a convention to which states other than those concerned in the case are parties is in question, the Registrar shall notify all such states forthwith.
2. Every state so notified has the right to intervene in the proceedings; but if it uses this right, the construction given by the judgment will be equally binding upon it.

Article 64

Unless otherwise decided by the Court, each party shall bear its own costs.

CHAPTER IV—ADVISORY OPINIONS

Article 65

1. The Court may give an advisory opinion on any legal question at the request of whatever body may be authorized by or in accordance with the Charter of the United Nations to make such a request.
2. Questions upon which the advisory opinion of the Court is asked shall be laid before the Court by means of a written request containing an exact statement of the question upon which an opinion is required, and accompanied by all documents likely to throw light upon the question.

Article 66

1. The Registrar shall forthwith give notice of the request for an advisory opinion to all states entitled to appear before the Court.
2. The Registrar shall also, by means of a special and direct communication, notify any state entitled to appear before the Court or international organization considered by the Court, or, should it not be sitting, by the President, as likely to be able to furnish information on the question, that the Court will be prepared to receive, within a time limit to be fixed by the President, written statements, or to hear, at a public sitting to be held for the purpose, oral statements relating to the question.
3. Should any such state entitled to appear before the Court have failed to receive the special communication referred to in paragraph 2 of this Article, such state may express a desire to submit a written statement or to be heard; and the Court will decide.
4. States and organizations having presented written or oral statements or both shall be permitted to comment on the statements made by other states or organizations in the form, to the extent, and within the time limits which the Court, or, should it not be sitting, the President, shall decide in each particular case. Accordingly, the Registrar shall in due time communicate any such written statements to states and organizations having submitted similar statements.

Article 67

The Court shall deliver its advisory opinions in open court, notice having been given to the Secretary-General and to the representatives of Members of the United Nations, of other states and of international organizations immediately concerned.

Article 68

In the exercise of its advisory functions the Court shall further be guided by the provisions of the present Statute which apply in contentious cases to the extent to which it recognizes them to be applicable.

CHAPTER V—AMENDMENT

Article 69

Amendments to the present Statute shall be effected by the same procedure as is provided by the Charter of the United Nations for amendments to that Charter, subject however to any provisions which the General Assembly upon recommendation of the Security Council may adopt concerning the participation of states which are parties to the present Statute but are not Members of the United Nations.

Article 70

The Court shall have power to propose such amendments to the present Statute as it may deem necessary, through written communications to the Secretary-General, for consideration in conformity with the provisions of Article 69.

UNIT	BACKGROUND DOCUMENT FOR CHAPTER 4
B	**Document: Pacific Settlement of Disputes**

CONVENTION FOR THE PACIFIC SETTLEMENT OF INTERNATIONAL DISPUTES

Oct. 18, 1907, 1 Bevans 577 (Jan. 26, 1910).

His Majesty the German Emperor, King of Prussia; the President of the United States of America; the President of the Argentine Republic; His Majesty the Emperor of Austria, King of Bohemia, etc., and Apostolic King of Hungary; His Majesty the King of the Belgians; the President of the Republic of Bolivia; the President of the Republic of the United States of Brazil; His Royal Highness the Prince of Bulgaria; the President of the Republic of Chile; His Majesty the Emperor of China; the President of the Republic of Colombia; the Provisional Governor of the Republic of Cuba; His Majesty the King of Denmark; the President of the Dominican Republic; the President of the Republic of Ecuador; His Majesty the King of Spain; the President of the French Republic; His Majesty the King of the United Kingdom of Great Britain and Ireland and of the British Dominions beyond the Seas, Emperor of India; His Majesty the King of the Hellenes; the President of the Republic of Guatemala; the President of the Republic of Haiti; His Majesty the King of Italy; His Majesty the Emperor of Japan; His Royal Highness the Grand Duke of Luxembourg, Duke of Nassau; the President of the United States of Mexico; His Royal Highness the Prince of Montenegro; the President of the Republic of Nicaragua; His Majesty the King of Norway; the President of the Republic of Panama; the President of the Republic of Paraguay; Her Majesty the Queen of the Netherlands; the President of the Republic of Peru; His Imperial Majesty the Shah of Persia; His Majesty the King of Roumania; His Majesty the Emperor of All the Russias; the President of the Republic of Salvador; His Majesty the King of Serbia; His Majesty the King of Siam; His Majesty the King of Sweden; the Swiss Federal Council; His Majesty the

Emperor of the Ottomans; the President of the Oriental Republic of Uruguay; the President of the United States of Venezuela;

Animated by the sincere desire to work for the maintenance of general peace;

Resolved to promote by all the efforts in their power the friendly settlement of international disputes;

Recognizing the solidarity uniting the members of the society of civilized nations;

Desirous of extending the empire of law and of strengthening the appreciation of international justice;

Convinced that the permanent institution of a Tribunal of Arbitration accessible to all, in the midst of independent Powers, will contribute effectively to this result;

Having regard to the advantages attending the general and regular organization of the procedure of arbitration;

Sharing the opinion of the august initiator of the International Peace Conference that it is expedient to record in an International Agreement the principles of equity and right on which are based the security of States and the welfare of peoples;

Being desirous, with this object, of insuring the better working in practice of Commissions of Inquiry and Tribunals of Arbitration, and of facilitating recourse to arbitration in cases which allow of a summary procedure;

Have deemed it necessary to revise in certain particulars and to complete the work of the First Peace Conference for the pacific settlement of international disputes;

The High Contracting Parties have resolved to conclude a new Convention for this purpose, and have appointed the following as their Plenipotentiaries:

(Here follow the names of Plenipotentiaries.)

Who, after having deposited their full powers, found in good and due form, have agreed upon the following:

PART I

THE MAINTENANCE OF GENERAL PEACE

Article 1

With a view to obviating as far as possible recourse to force in the relations between States, the Contracting Powers agree to use their best efforts to ensure the pacific settlement of international differences.

PART II

GOOD OFFICES AND MEDIATION

Article 2

In case of serious disagreement or dispute, before an appeal to arms, the Contracting Powers agree to have recourse, as far as circumstances allow, to the good offices or mediation of one or more friendly Powers.

Article 3

Independently of this recourse, the Contracting Powers deem it expedient and desirable that one or more Powers, strangers to the dispute, should, on their own initiative and as far as circumstances may allow, offer their good offices or mediation to the States at variance.

Powers strangers to the dispute have the right to offer good offices or mediation even during the course of hostilities.

The exercise of this right can never be regarded by either of the parties in dispute as an unfriendly act.

Article 4

The part of the mediator consists in reconciling the opposing claims and appeasing the feelings of resentment which may have arisen between the States at variance.

Article 5

The functions of the mediator are at an end when once it is declared, either by one of the parties to the dispute or by the mediator himself, that the means of reconciliation proposed by him are not accepted.

Article 6

Good offices and mediation undertaken either at the request of the parties in dispute or on the initiative of Powers strangers to the dispute have exclusively the character of advice, and never have binding force.

Article 7

The acceptance of mediation cannot, unless there be an agreement to the contrary, have the effect of interrupting, delaying, or hindering mobilization or other measures of preparation for war.

If it takes place after the commencement of hostilities, the military operations in progress are not interrupted in the absence of an agreement to the contrary.

Article 8

The Contracting Powers are agreed in recommending the application, when circumstances allow, of special mediation in the following form:

In case of a serious difference endangering peace, the States at variance choose respectively a Power, to which they entrust the mission of entering into direct communication with the Power chosen on the other side, with the object of preventing the rupture of pacific relations.

For the period of this mandate, the term of which, unless otherwise stipulated, cannot exceed thirty days, the States in dispute cease from all direct communication on the subject of the dispute, which is regarded as referred exclusively to the mediating Powers, which must use their best efforts to settle it.

In case of a definite rupture of pacific relations, these Powers are charged with the joint task of taking advantage of any opportunity to restore peace.

PART III

INTERNATIONAL COMMISSIONS OF INQUIRY

Article 9

In disputes of an international nature involving neither honour nor vital interests, and arising from a difference of opinion on points of facts, the Contracting Powers deem it expedient and desirable that the parties who have not been able to come to an agreement by means of diplomacy, should, as far as circumstances allow, institute an International Commission of Inquiry, to facilitate a solution of these disputes by elucidating the facts by means of an impartial and conscientious investigation.

Article 10

International Commissions of Inquiry are constituted by special agreement between the parties in dispute.

The Inquiry Convention defines the facts to be examined; it determines the mode and time in which the Commission is to be formed and the extent of the powers of the Commissioners.

It also determines, if there is need, where the Commission is to sit, and whether it may remove to another place, the language the Commission shall use and the languages the use of which shall be authorized before it, as well as the date on which each party must deposit its statement of facts, and, generally speaking, all the conditions upon which the parties have agreed.

If the parties consider it necessary to appoint Assessors, the Convention of Inquiry shall determine the mode of their selection and the extent of their powers.

Article 11

If the Inquiry Convention has not determined where the Commission is to sit, it will sit at The Hague.

The place of meeting, once fixed, cannot be altered by the Commission except with the assent of the parties.

If the Inquiry Convention has not determined what languages are to be employed, the question shall be decided by the Commission.

Article 12

Unless an undertaking is made to the contrary, Commissions of Inquiry shall be formed in the manner determined by Articles 45 and 57 of the present Convention.

Article 13

Should one of the Commissioners or one of the Assessors, should there be any, either die, or resign, or be unable for any reason whatever to discharge his functions, the same procedure is followed for filling the vacancy as was followed for appointing him.

Article 14

The parties are entitled to appoint special agents to attend the Commission of Inquiry, whose duty it is to represent them and to act as intermediaries between them and the Commission.

They are further authorized to engage counsel or advocates, appointed by themselves, to state their case and uphold their interests before the Commission.

Article 15

The International Bureau of the Permanent Court of Arbitration acts as registry for the Commissions which sit at The Hague, and shall place its offices and staff at the disposal of the Contracting Powers for the use of the Commission of Inquiry.

Article 16

If the Commission meets elsewhere than at The Hague, it appoints a Secretary-General, whose office serves as registry.

It is the function of the registry, under the control of the President, to make the necessary arrangements for the sittings of the Commission, the preparation of the Minutes, and, while the inquiry lasts, for the charge of the archives, which shall subsequently be transferred to the International Bureau at The Hague.

Article 17

In order to facilitate the constitution and working of Commissions of Inquiry, the Contracting Powers recommend the following rules, which shall be applicable to the inquiry procedure in so far as the parties do not adopt other rules.

Article 18

The Commission shall settle the details of the procedure not covered by the special Inquiry Convention or the present Convention, and shall arrange all the formalities required for dealing with the evidence.

Article 19

On the inquiry both sides must be heard.

At the dates fixed, each party communicates to the Commission and to the other party the statements of facts, if any, and, in all cases, the instruments, papers, and documents which it considers useful for ascertaining the truth, as well as the list of witnesses and experts whose evidence it wishes to be heard.

Article 20

The Commission is entitled, with the assent of the Powers, to move temporarily to any place where it considers it may be useful to have recourse to this means of inquiry or to send one or more of its members. Permission must be obtained from the State on whose territory it is proposed to hold the inquiry.

Article 21

Every investigation, and every examination of a locality, must be made in the presence of the agents and counsel of the parties or after they have been duly summoned.

Article 22

The Commission is entitled to ask from either party for such explanations and information as it considers necessary.

Article 23

The parties undertake to supply the Commission of Inquiry, as fully as they may think possible, with all means and facilities necessary to enable it to become completely acquainted with, and to accurately understand, the facts in question.

They undertake to make use of the means at their disposal, under their municipal law, to insure the appearance of the witnesses or experts who are in their territory and have been summoned before the Commission.

If the witnesses or experts are unable to appear before the Commission, the parties will arrange for their evidence to be taken before the qualified officials of their own country.

Article 24

For all notices to be served by the Commission in the territory of a third Contracting Power, the Commission shall apply direct to the Government of the said Power. The same rule applies in the case of steps being taken on the spot to procure evidence.

The requests for this purpose are to be executed so far as the means at the disposal of the Power applied to under its municipal law allow. They cannot be rejected unless the Power in question considers they are calculated to impair its sovereign rights or its safety.

The Commission will equally be always entitled to act through the Power on whose territory it sits.

Article 25

The witnesses and experts are summoned on the request of the parties or by the Commission of its own motion, and, in every case, through the Government of the State in whose territory they are.

The witnesses are heard in succession and separately in the presence of the agents and counsel, and in the order fixed by the Commission.

Article 26

The examination of witnesses is conducted by the President.

The members of the Commission may however put to each witness questions which they consider likely to throw light on and complete his evidence, or get information on any point concerning the witness within the limits of what is necessary in order to get at the truth.

The agents and counsel of the parties may not interrupt the witness when he is making his statement, nor put any direct question to him, but they may ask the President to put such additional questions to the witness as they think expedient.

Article 27

The witness must give his evidence without being allowed to read any written draft. He may, however, be permitted by the President to consult notes or documents if the nature of the facts referred to necessitates their employment.

Article 28

A Minute of the evidence of the witness is drawn up forthwith and read to the witness. The latter may make such alterations and additions as he thinks necessary, which will be recorded at the end of his statement.

When the whole of his statement has been read to the witness, he is asked to sign it.

Article 29

The agents are authorized, in the course of or at the close of the inquiry, to present in writing to the Commission and to the other party such statements, requisitions, or summaries of the facts as they consider useful for ascertaining the truth.

Article 30

The Commission considers its decisions in private and the proceedings are secret.

All questions are decided by a majority of the members of the Commission.

If a member declines to vote, the fact must be recorded in the Minutes.

Article 31

The sittings of the Commission are not public, nor the Minutes and documents connected with the inquiry published except in virtue of a decision of the Commission taken with the consent of the parties.

Article 32

After the parties have presented all the explanations and evidence, and the witnesses have all been heard, the President declares the inquiry terminated, and the Commission adjourns to deliberate and to draw up its Report.

Article 33

The Report is signed by all the members of the Commission.

If one of the members refuses to sign, the fact is mentioned; but the validity of the Report is not affected.

Article 34

The Report of the Commission is read at a public sitting, the agents and counsel of the parties being present or duly summoned.

A copy of the Report is given to each party.

Article 35

The Report of the Commission is limited to a statement of facts, and has in no way the character of an Award. It leaves to the parties entire freedom as to the effect to be given to the statement.

Article 36

Each party pays its own expenses and an equal share of the expenses incurred by the Commission.

PART IV

INTERNATIONAL ARBITRATION

Chapter I. The System of Arbitration

Article 37

International arbitration has for its object the settlement of disputes between States by Judges of their own choice and on the basis of respect for law.

Recourse to arbitration implies an engagement to submit in good faith to the Award.

Article 38

In questions of a legal nature, and especially in the interpretation or application of International Conventions, arbitration is recognized by the Contracting Powers as the most effective, and, at the same time, the most equitable means of settling disputes which diplomacy has failed to settle.

Consequently, it would be desirable that, in disputes about the above-mentioned questions, the Contracting Powers should, if the case arose, have recourse to arbitration, in so far as circumstances permit.

Article 39

The Arbitration Convention is concluded for questions already existing or for questions which may arise eventually.

It may embrace any dispute or only disputes of a certain category.

Article 40

Independently of general or private Treaties expressly stipulating recourse to arbitration as obligatory on the Contracting Powers, the said Powers reserve to themselves the right of concluding new Agreements, general or particular, with a view to extending compulsory arbitration to all cases which they may consider it possible to submit to it.

Chapter II. The Permanent Court of Arbitration

Article 41

With the object of facilitating an immediate recourse to arbitration for international differences, which it has not been possible to settle by diplomacy, the Contracting Powers undertake to maintain the Permanent Court of Arbitration, as established by the First Peace Conference, accessible at all times, and operating, unless otherwise stipulated by the parties, in accordance with the rules of procedure inserted in the present Convention.

Article 42

The Permanent Court is competent for all arbitration cases, unless the parties agree to institute a special Tribunal.

Article 43

The Permanent Court sits at The Hague.

An International Bureau serves as registry for the Court. It is the channel for communications relative to the meetings of the Court; it has charge of the archives and conducts all the administrative business.

The Contracting Powers undertake to communicate to the Bureau, as soon as possible, a certified copy of any conditions of arbitration arrived at between them and of any Award concerning them delivered by a special Tribunal.

They likewise undertake to communicate to the Bureau the laws, regulations, and documents eventually showing the execution of the Awards given by the Court.

Article 44

Each Contracting Power selects four persons at the most, of known competency in questions of international law, of the highest moral reputation, and disposed to accept the duties of Arbitrator.

The persons thus elected are inscribed, as Members of the Court, in a list which shall be notified to all the Contracting Powers by the Bureau.

Any alteration in the list of Arbitrators is brought by the Bureau to the knowledge of the Contracting Powers.

Two or more Powers may agree on the selection in common of one or more Members.

The same person can be selected by different Powers. The Members of the Court are appointed for a term of six years. These appointments are renewable.

Should a Member of the Court die or resign, the same procedure is followed for filling the vacancy as was followed for appointing him. In this case the appointment is made for a fresh period of six years.

Article 45

When the Contracting Powers wish to have recourse to the Permanent Court for the settlement of a difference which has arisen between them, the Arbitrators called upon to form the Tribunal with jurisdiction to decide this difference must be chosen from the general list of Members of the Court.

Failing the direct agreement of the parties on the composition of the Arbitration Tribunal, the following course shall be pursued:

Each party appoints two Arbitrators, of whom one only can be its national or chosen from among the persons selected by it as Members of the Permanent Court. These Arbitrators together choose an Umpire.

If the votes are equally divided, the choice of the Umpire is entrusted to a third Power, selected by the parties by common accord.

If an agreement is not arrived at on this subject each party selects a different Power, and the choice of the Umpire is made in concert by the Powers thus selected.

If, within two months' time, these two Powers cannot come to an agreement, each of them presents two candidates taken from the list of Members of the Permanent Court, exclusive of the members selected by the parties and not being nationals of either of them. Drawing lots determines which of the candidates thus presented shall be Umpire.

Article 46

The Tribunal being thus composed, the parties notify to the Bureau their determination to have recourse to the Court, the text of their 'Compromis', and the names of the Arbitrators.

The Bureau communicates without delay to each Arbitrator the 'Compromis', and the names of the other members of the Tribunal.

The Tribunal assembles at the date fixed by the parties. The Bureau makes the necessary arrangements for the meeting.

The members of the Tribunal, in the exercise of their duties and out of their own country, enjoy diplomatic privileges and immunities.

Article 47

The Bureau is authorized to place its offices and staff at the disposal of the Contracting Powers for the use of any special Board of Arbitration.

The jurisdiction of the Permanent Court may, within the conditions laid down in the regulations, be extended to disputes between non-Contracting Powers or between Contracting Powers and non-Contracting Powers, if the parties are agreed on recourse to this Tribunal.

Article 48

The Contracting Powers consider it their duty, if a serious dispute threatens to break out between two or more of them, to remind these latter that the Permanent Court is open to them.

Consequently, they declare that the fact of reminding the parties at variance of the provisions of the present Convention, and the advice given to them, in the highest interests of peace, to have recourse to the Permanent Court, can only be regarded as friendly actions.

In case of dispute between two Powers, one of them can always address to the International Bureau a note containing a declaration that it would be ready to submit the dispute to arbitration.

The Bureau must at once inform the other Power of the declaration.

Article 49

The Permanent Administrative Council, composed of the Diplomatic Representatives of the Contracting Powers accredited to The Hague and of the Netherlands Minister for Foreign Affairs, who will act as President, is charged with the direction and control of the International Bureau.

The Council settles its rules of procedure and all other necessary regulations.

It decides all questions of administration which may arise with regard to the operations of the Court.

It has entire control over the appointment, suspension, or dismissal of the officials and employees of the Bureau.

It fixes the payments and salaries, and controls the general expenditure.

At meetings duly summoned the presence of nine members is sufficient to render valid the discussions of the Council. The decisions are taken by a majority of votes.

The Council communicates to the Contracting Powers without delay the regulations adopted by it. It furnishes them with an annual Report on the labours of the Court, the working of the administration, and the expenditure. The Report likewise contains a résumé of what is important in the documents communicated to the Bureau by the Powers in virtue of Article 43, paragraphs 3 and 4.

Article 50

The expenses of the Bureau shall be borne by the Contracting Powers in the proportion fixed for the International Bureau of the Universal Postal Union.

The expenses to be charged to the adhering Powers shall be reckoned from the date on which their adhesion comes into force.

Chapter III. Arbitration Procedure

Article 51

With a view to encouraging the development of arbitration, the Contracting Powers have agreed on the following rules, which are applicable to arbitration procedure, unless other rules have been agreed on by the parties.

Article 52

The Powers which have recourse to arbitration sign a 'Compromis', in which the subject of the dispute is clearly defined, the time allowed for appointing Arbitrators, the form, order, and time in which the communication referred to in Article 63 must be made, and the amount of the sum which each party must deposit in advance to defray the expenses.

The 'Compromis' likewise defines, if there is occasion, the manner of appointing Arbitrators, any special powers which may eventually belong to the Tribunal, where it shall meet, the language it shall use, and the languages the employment of which shall be authorized before it, and, generally speaking, all the conditions on which the parties are agreed.

Article 53

The Permanent Court is competent to settle the 'Compromis', if the parties are agreed to have recourse to it for the purpose.

It is similarly competent, even if the request is only made by one of the parties, when all attempts to reach an understanding through the diplomatic channel have failed, in the case of:

1. A dispute covered by a general Treaty of Arbitration concluded or renewed after the present Convention has come into force, and providing for a 'Compromis' in all disputes and not either explicitly or implicitly excluding the settlement of the 'Compromis' from the competence of the Court. Recourse cannot, however, be had to the Court if the other party declares that in its opinion the dispute does not belong to the category of disputes which can be submitted to compulsory arbitration, unless the Treaty of Arbitration confers upon the Arbitration Tribunal the power of deciding this preliminary question.

2. A dispute arising from contract debts claimed from one Power by another Power as due to its nationals, and for the settlement of which the offer of arbitration has been accepted. This arrangement is not applicable if acceptance is subject to the condition that the 'Compromis' should be settled in some other way.

Article 54

In the cases contemplated in the preceding Article, the 'Compromis' shall be settled by a Commission consisting of five members selected in the manner arranged for in Article 45, paragraphs 3 to 6.

The fifth member is President of the Commission *ex officio*.

Article 55

The duties of Arbitrator may be conferred on one Arbitrator alone or on several Arbitrators selected by the parties as they please, or chosen by them from the Members of the Permanent Court of Arbitration established by the present Convention.

Failing the constitution of the Tribunal by direct agreement between the parties, the course referred to in Article 45, paragraphs 3 to 6, is followed.

Article 56

When a Sovereign or the Chief of a State is chosen as Arbitrator, the arbitration procedure is settled by him.

Article 57

The Umpire is President of the Tribunal *ex officio*.

When the Tribunal does not include an Umpire, it appoints its own President.

Article 58

When the 'Compromis' is settled by a Commission, as contemplated in Article 54, and in the absence of an agreement to the contrary, the Commission itself shall form the Arbitration Tribunal.

Article 59

Should one of the Arbitrators either die, retire, or be unable for any reason whatever to discharge his functions, the same procedure is followed for filling the vacancy as was followed for appointing him.

Article 60

The Tribunal sits at The Hague, unless some other place is selected by the parties.

The Tribunal can only sit in the territory of a third Power with the latter's consent.

The place of meeting once fixed cannot be altered by the Tribunal, except with the consent of the parties.

Article 61

If the question as to what languages are to be used has not been settled by the 'Compromis', it shall be decided by the Tribunal.

Article 62

The parties are entitled to appoint special agents to attend the Tribunal to act as intermediaries between themselves and the Tribunal.

They are further authorized to retain for the defence of their rights and interests before the Tribunal counsel or advocates appointed by themselves for this purpose.

The Members of the Permanent Court may not act as agents, counsel, or advocates except on behalf of the Power which appointed them Members of the Court.

Article 63

As a general rule, arbitration procedure comprises two distinct phases: pleadings and oral discussions.

The pleadings consist in the communication by the respective agents to the members of the Tribunal and the opposite party of cases, counter-cases, and, if necessary, of replies; the parties annex thereto all papers and documents called for in the case. This communication shall be made either directly or through the intermediary of the International Bureau, in the order and within the time fixed by the 'Compromis'.

The time fixed by the 'Compromis' may be extended by mutual agreement by the parties, or by the Tribunal when the latter considers it necessary for the purpose of reaching a just decision.

The discussions consist in the oral development before the Tribunal of the arguments of the parties.

Article 64

A certified copy of every document produced by one party must be communicated to the other party.

Article 65

Unless special circumstances arise, the Tribunal does not meet until the pleadings are closed.

Article 66

The discussions are under the control of the President. They are only public if it be so decided by the Tribunal, with the assent of the parties.

They are recorded in minutes drawn up by the Secretaries appointed by the President. These minutes are signed by the President and by one of the Secretaries and alone have an authentic character.

Article 67

After the close of the pleadings, the Tribunal is entitled to refuse discussion of all new papers or documents which one of the parties may wish to submit to it without the consent of the other party.

Article 68

The Tribunal is free to take into consideration new papers or documents to which its attention may be drawn by the agents or counsel of the parties.

In this case, the Tribunal has the right to require the production of these papers or documents, but is obliged to make them known to the opposite party.

Article 69

The Tribunal can, besides, require from the agents of the parties the production of all papers, and can demand all necessary explanations. In case of refusal the Tribunal takes note of it.

Article 70

The agents and the counsel of the parties are authorized to present orally to the Tribunal all the arguments they may consider expedient in defence of their case.

Article 71

They are entitled to raise objections and points. The decisions of the Tribunal on these points are final and cannot form the subject of any subsequent discussion.

Article 72

The members of the Tribunal are entitled to put questions to the agents and counsel of the parties, and to ask them for explanations on doubtful points.

Neither the questions put, nor the remarks made by members of the Tribunal in the course of the discussions, can be regarded as an expression of opinion by the Tribunal in general or by its members in particular.

Article 73

The Tribunal is authorized to declare its competence in interpreting the 'Compromis', as well as the other Treaties which may be invoked, and in applying the principles of law.

Article 74

The Tribunal is entitled to issue rules of procedure for the conduct of the case, to decide the forms, order, and time in which each party must conclude its arguments, and to arrange all the formalities required for dealing with the evidence.

Article 75

The parties undertake to supply the Tribunal, as fully as they consider possible, with all the information required for deciding the case.

Article 76

For all notices which the Tribunal has to serve in the territory of a third Contracting Power, the Tribunal shall apply direct to the Government of that Power. The same rule applies in the case of steps being taken to procure evidence on the spot.

The requests for this purpose are to be executed as far as the means at the disposal of the Power applied to under its municipal law allow. They cannot be rejected unless the Power in question considers them calculated to impair its own sovereign rights or its safety.

The Court will equally be always entitled to act through the Power on whose territory it sits.

Article 77

When the agents and counsel of the parties have submitted all the explanations and evidence in support of their case the President shall declare the discussion closed.

Article 78

The Tribunal considers its decisions in private and the proceedings remain secret.

All questions are decided by a majority of the members of the Tribunal.

Article 79

The Award must give the reasons on which it is based. It contains the names of the Arbitrators; it is signed by the President and Registrar or by the Secretary acting as Registrar.

Article 80

The Award is read out in public sitting, the agents and counsel of the parties being present or duly summoned to attend.

Article 81

The Award, duly pronounced and notified to the agents of the parties, settles the dispute definitively and without appeal.

Article 82

Any dispute arising between the parties as to the interpretation and execution of the Award shall, in the absence of an Agreement to the contrary, be submitted to the Tribunal which pronounced it.

Article 83

The parties can reserve in the 'Compromis' the right to demand the revision of the Award.

In this case and unless there be an Agreement to the contrary, the demand must be addressed to the Tribunal which pronounced the Award. It can only be made on the ground of the discovery of some new fact calculated to exercise a decisive influence upon the Award and which was unknown to the Tribunal and to the party which demanded the revision at the time the discussion was closed.

Proceedings for revision can only be instituted by a decision of the Tribunal expressly recording the existence of the new fact, recognizing in it the character described in the preceding paragraph, and declaring the demand admissible on this ground.

The 'Compromis' fixes the period within which the demand for revision must be made.

Article 84

The Award is not binding except on the parties in dispute.

When it concerns the interpretation of a Convention to which Powers other than those in dispute are parties, they shall inform all the Signatory Powers in good time. Each of these Powers is entitled to intervene in the case. If one or more avail themselves of this right, the interpretation contained in the Award is equally binding on them.

Article 85

Each party pays its own expenses and an equal share of the expenses of the Tribunal.

Chapter IV. Arbitration by Summary Procedure

Article 86

With a view to facilitating the working of the system of arbitration in disputes admitting of a summary procedure, the Contracting Powers adopt the following rules, which shall be observed in the absence of other arrangements and subject to the reservation that the provisions of Chapter III apply so far as may be.

Article 87

Each of the parties in dispute appoints an Arbitrator. The two Arbitrators thus selected choose an Umpire. If they do not agree on this point, each of them proposes two candidates taken from the general list of the Members of the Permanent Court exclusive of the members appointed by either of the parties and not being nationals of either of them; which of the candidates thus proposed shall be the Umpire is determined by lot.

The Umpire presides over the Tribunal, which gives its decisions by a majority of votes.

Article 88

In the absence of any previous agreement the Tribunal, as soon as it is formed, settles the time within which the two parties must submit their respective cases to it.

Article 89

Each party is represented before the Tribunal by an agent, who serves as intermediary between the Tribunal and the Government who appointed him.

Article 90

The proceedings are conducted exclusively in writing. Each party, however, is entitled to ask that witnesses and experts should be called. The Tribunal has, for its part, the right to demand oral explanations from the agents of the two parties, as well as from the experts and witnesses whose appearance in Court it may consider useful.

PART V

FINAL PROVISIONS

Article 91

The present Convention, duly ratified, shall replace, as between the Contracting Powers, the Convention for the Pacific Settlement of International Disputes of the 29th July, 1899.

Article 92

The present Convention shall be ratified as soon as possible.

The ratifications shall be deposited at The Hague.

The first deposit of ratifications shall be recorded in a *procès-verbal* signed by the Representatives of the Powers which take part therein and by the Netherlands Minister for Foreign Affairs.

The subsequent deposits of ratifications shall be made by means of a written notification, addressed to the Netherlands Government and accompanied by the instrument of ratification.

A duly certified copy of the *procès-verbal* relative to the first deposit of ratifications, of the notifications mentioned in the preceding paragraph, and of the instruments of ratification, shall be immediately sent by the Netherlands Government, through the diplomatic channel, to the Powers invited to the Second Peace Conference, as well as to those Powers which have adhered to the Convention. In the cases contemplated in the preceding paragraph, the said Government shall at the same time inform the Powers of the date on which it received the notification.

Article 93

Non-Signatory Powers which have been invited to the Second Peace Conference may adhere to the present Convention.

The Power which desires to adhere notifies its intention in writing to the Netherlands Government, forwarding to it the act of adhesion, which shall be deposited in the archives of the said Government.

This Government shall immediately forward to all the other Powers invited to the Second Peace Conference a duly certified copy of the notification as well as of the act of adhesion, mentioning the date on which it received the notification.

Article 94

The conditions on which the Powers which have not been invited to the Second Peace Conference may adhere to the present Convention shall form the subject of a subsequent Agreement between the Contracting Powers.

Article 95

The present Convention shall take effect, in the case of the Powers which were not a party to the first deposit of ratifications, sixty days after the date of the *procès-verbal* of this deposit, and, in the case of the Powers which ratify subsequently or which adhere, sixty days after the notification of their ratification or of their adhesion has been received by the Netherlands Government.

Article 96

In the event of one of the Contracting Parties wishing to denounce the present Convention, the denunciation shall be notified in writing to the Netherlands Government, which shall immediately communicate a duly certified copy of the notification to all the other Powers informing them of the date on which it was received.

The denunciation shall only have effect in regard to the notifying Power, and one year after the notification has reached the Netherlands Government.

Article 97

A register kept by the Netherlands Minister for Foreign Affairs shall give the date of the deposit of ratifications effected in virtue of Article 92, paragraphs 3 and 4, as well as the date on which the notifications of adhesion (Article 93, paragraph 2) or of denunciation (Article 96, paragraph 1) have been received.

Each Contracting Power is entitled to have access to this register and to be supplied with duly certified extracts from it.

In faith whereof the Plenipotentiaries have appended their signatures to the present Convention.

Done at The Hague, the 18th October, 1907, in a single copy, which shall remain deposited in the archives of the Netherlands Government, and duly certified copies of which shall be sent, through the diplomatic channel, to the Contracting Powers.

UNIT	BACKGROUND DOCUMENT FOR CHAPTER 5
B	Document: Vienna Convention on the Law of Treaties

VIENNA CONVENTION ON THE LAW OF TREATIES

May 23, 1969, 1155 U.N.T.S. 331 (Jan. 27, 1980).

The States Parties to the present Convention,

Considering the fundamental role of treaties in the history of international relations,

Recognizing the ever-increasing importance of treaties as a source of international law and as a means of developing peaceful co-operation among nations, whatever their constitutional and social systems,

Noting that the principles of free consent and of good faith and the *pacta sunt servanda* rule are universally recognized,

Affirming that disputes concerning treaties, like other international disputes, should be settled by peaceful means and in conformity with the principles of justice and international law,

Recalling the determination of the peoples of the United Nations to establish conditions under which justice and respect for the obligations arising from treaties can be maintained,

Having in mind the principles of international law embodied in the Charter of the United Nations, such as the principles of the equal rights and self-determination of peoples, of the sovereign equality and independence of all States, of non-interference in the domestic affairs of States, of the prohibition of the threat or use of force and of universal respect for, and observance of, human rights and fundamental freedoms for all,

Believing that the codification and progressive development of the law of treaties achieved in the present Convention will promote the purposes of the United Nations set forth in the Charter, namely, the maintenance of international peace and security, the development of friendly relations and the achievement of co-operation among nations,

Affirming that the rules of customary international law will continue to govern questions not regulated by the provisions of the present Convention,

Have agreed as follows:

PART I

INTRODUCTION

Article 1. Scope of the Present Convention

The present Convention applies to treaties between States.

Article 2. Use of Terms

1. For the purposes of the present Convention:

   (a) "Treaty" means an international agreement concluded between States in written form and governed by international law, whether embodied in a single instrument or in two or more related instruments and whatever its particular designation;

   (b) "Ratification", "acceptance", "approval" and "accession" mean in each case the international act so named whereby a State establishes on the international plane its consent to be bound by a treaty;

   (c) "Full powers" means a document emanating from the competent authority of a State designating a person or persons to represent the State for negotiating, adopting or authenticating the text of a treaty, for expressing the consent of the State to be bound by a treaty, or for accomplishing any other act with respect to a treaty;

(d) "Reservation" means a unilateral statement, however phrased or named, made by a State, when signing, ratifying, accepting, approving or acceding to a treaty, whereby it purports to exclude or to modify the legal effect of certain provisions of the treaty in their application to that State;

(e) "Negotiating State" means a State which took part in the drawing up and adoption of the text of the treaty;

(f) "Contracting State" means a State which has consented to be bound by the treaty, whether or not the treaty has entered into force;

(g) "Party" means a State which has consented to be bound by the treaty and for which the treaty is in force;

(h) "Third State" means a State not a party to the treaty;

(i) "International organization" means an intergovernmental organization.

2. The provisions of paragraph 1 regarding the use of terms in the present Convention are without prejudice to the use of those terms or to the meanings which may be given to them in the internal law of any State.

Article 3. International Agreements not Within the Scope of the Present Convention

The fact that the present Convention does not apply to international agreements concluded between States and other subjects of international law or between such other subjects of international law, or to international agreements not in written form, shall not affect:

(a) The legal force of such agreements;

(b) The application to them of any of the rules set forth in the present Convention to which they would be subject under international law independently of the Convention;

(c) The application of the Convention to the relations of States as between themselves under international agreements to which other subjects of international law are also parties.

Article 4. Non-Retroactivity of the Present Convention

Without prejudice to the application of any rules set forth in the present Convention to which treaties would be subject under international law independently of the Convention, the Convention applies only to treaties which are concluded by States after the entry into force of the present Convention with regard to such States.

Article 5. Treaties Constituting International Organizations and Treaties Adopted Within an International Organization

The present Convention applies to any treaty which is the constituent instrument of an international organization and to any treaty adopted within an international organization without prejudice to any relevant rules of the organization.

PART II

CONCLUSION AND ENTRY INTO FORCE OF TREATIES

Section 1. Conclusion of Treaties

Article 6. Capacity of States to Conclude Treaties

Every State possesses capacity to conclude treaties.

Article 7. Full Powers

1. A person is considered as representing a State for the purpose of adopting or authenticating the text of a treaty or for the purpose of expressing the consent of the State to be bound by a treaty if:

   (a) He produces appropriate full powers; or

   (b) It appears from the practice of the States concerned or from other circumstances that their intention was to consider that person as representing the State for such purposes and to dispense with full powers.

2. In virtue of their functions and without having to produce full powers, the following are considered as representing their State:

   (a) Heads of State, Heads of Government and Ministers for Foreign Affairs, for the purpose of performing all acts relating to the conclusion of a treaty;

   (b) Heads of diplomatic missions, for the purpose of adopting the text of a treaty between the accrediting State and the State to which they are accredited;

   (c) Representatives accredited by States to an international conference or to an international organization or one of its organs, for the purpose of adopting the text of a treaty in that conference, organization or organ.

Article 8. Subsequent Confirmation of an Act Performed Without Authorization

An act relating to the conclusion of a treaty performed by a person who cannot be considered under article 7 as authorized to represent a State for that purpose is without legal effect unless afterwards confirmed by that State.

Article 9. Adoption of the Text

1. The adoption of the text of a treaty takes place by the consent of all the States participating in its drawing up except as provided in paragraph 2.

2. The adoption of the text of a treaty at an international conference takes place by the vote of two-thirds of the States present and voting, unless by the same majority they shall decide to apply a different rule.

Article 10. Authentication of the Text

The text of a treaty is established as authentic and definitive:

   (a) By such procedure as may be provided for in the text or agreed upon by the States participating in its drawing up; or

(b) Failing such procedure, by the signature, signature *ad referendum* or initialling by the representatives of those States of the text of the treaty or of the Final Act of a conference incorporating the text.

Article 11. Means of Expressing Consent to be Bound by a Treaty

The consent of a State to be bound by a treaty may be expressed by signature, exchange of instruments constituting a treaty, ratification, acceptance, approval or accession, or by any other means if so agreed.

Article 12. Consent to be Bound by a Treaty Expressed by Signature

1. The consent of a State to be bound by a treaty is expressed by the signature of its representative when:

   (a) The treaty provides that signature shall have that effect;

   (b) It is otherwise established that the negotiating States were agreed that signature should have that effect; or

   (c) The intention of the State to give that effect to the signature appears from the full powers of its representative or was expressed during the negotiation.

3. For the purposes of paragraph 1:

   (a) The initialling of a text constitutes a signature of the treaty when it is established that the negotiating States so agreed;

   (b) The signature *ad referendum* of a treaty by a representative, if confirmed by his State, constitutes a full signature of the treaty.

Article 13. Consent to be Bound by a Treaty Expressed by an Exchange of Instruments Constituting a Treaty

The consent of States to be bound by a treaty constituted by instruments exchanged between them is expressed by that exchange when:

(a) The instruments provide that their exchange shall have that effect; or

(b) It is otherwise established that those States were agreed that the exchange of instruments should have that effect.

Article 14. Consent to be Bound by a Treaty Expressed by Ratification, Acceptance or Approval

1. The consent of a State to be bound by a treaty is expressed by ratification when:

   (a) The treaty provides for such consent to be expressed by means of ratification;

   (b) It is otherwise established that the negotiating States were agreed that ratification should be required;

   (c) The representative of the State has signed the treaty subject to ratification; or

   (d) The intention of the State to sign the treaty subject to ratification appears from the full powers of its representative or was expressed during the negotiation.

2. The consent of a State to be bound by a treaty is expressed by acceptance or approval under conditions similar to those which apply to ratification.

Article 15. Consent to be Bound by a Treaty Expressed by Accession

The consent of a State to be bound by a treaty is expressed by accession when:

(a) The treaty provides that such consent may be expressed by that State by means of accession;

(b) It is otherwise established that the negotiating States were agreed that such consent may be expressed by that State by means of accession; or

(c) All the parties have subsequently agreed that such consent may be expressed by that State by means of accession.

Article 16. Exchange or Deposit of Instruments of Ratification, Acceptance, Approval or Accession

Unless the treaty otherwise provides, instruments of ratification, acceptance, approval or accession establish the consent of a State to be bound by a treaty upon:

(a) Their exchange between the contracting States;

(b) Their deposit with the depositary; or

(c) Their notification to the contracting States or to the depositary, if so agreed.

Article 17. Consent to be Bound by Part of a Treaty and Choice of Differing Provisions

1. Without prejudice to articles 19 to 23, the consent of a State to be bound by part of a treaty is effective only if the treaty so permits or the other contracting States so agree.

2. The consent of a State to be bound by a treaty which permits a choice between differing provisions is effective only if it is made clear to which of the provisions the consent relates.

Article 18. Obligation not to Defeat the Object and Purpose of a Treaty Prior to Its Entry into Force

A State is obliged to refrain from acts which would defeat the object and purpose of a treaty when:

(a) It has signed the treaty or has exchanged instruments constituting the treaty subject to ratification, acceptance or approval, until it shall have made its intention clear not to become a party to the treaty; or

(b) It has expressed its consent to be bound by the treaty, pending the entry into force of the treaty and provided that such entry into force is not unduly delayed.

Section 2. Reservations

Article 19. Formulation of Reservations

A State may, when signing, ratifying, accepting, approving or acceding to a treaty, formulate a reservation unless:

(a) The reservation is prohibited by the treaty;

(b) The treaty provides that only specified reservations, which do not include the reservation in question, may be made; or

(c) In cases not falling under sub-paragraphs (a) and (b), the reservation is incompatible with the object and purpose of the treaty.

Article 20. Acceptance of and Objection to Reservations

1. A reservation expressly authorized by a treaty does not require any subsequent acceptance by the other contracting States unless the treaty so provides.

2. When it appears from the limited number of the negotiating States and the object and purpose of a treaty that the application of the treaty in its entirety between all the parties is an essential condition of the consent of each one to be bound by the treaty, a reservation requires acceptance by all the parties.

3. When a treaty is a constituent instrument of an international organization and unless it otherwise provides, a reservation requires the acceptance of the competent organ of that organization.

4. In cases not falling under the preceding paragraphs and unless the treaty otherwise provides:

   (a) Acceptance by another contracting State of a reservation constitutes the reserving State a party to the treaty in relation to that other State if or when the treaty is in force for those States;

(b) An objection by another contracting State to a reservation does not preclude the entry into force of the treaty as between the objecting and reserving States unless a contrary intention is definitely expressed by the objecting State;

(c) An act expressing a State's consent to be bound by the treaty and containing a reservation is effective as soon as at least one other contracting State has accepted the reservation.

5. For the purposes of paragraphs 2 and 4 and unless the treaty otherwise provides, a reservation is considered to have been accepted by a State if it shall have raised no objection to the reservation by the end of a period of twelve months after it was notified of the reservation or by the date on which it expressed its consent to be bound by the treaty, whichever is later.

Article 21. Legal Effects of Reservations and of Objections to Reservations

1. A reservation established with regard to another party in accordance with articles 19, 20 and 23:

   (a) Modifies for the reserving State in its relations with that other party the provisions of the treaty to which the reservation relates to the extent of the reservation; and

   (b) Modifies those provisions to the same extent for that other party in its relations with the reserving State.

2. The reservation does not modify the provisions of the treaty for the other parties to the treaty *inter se*.

3. When a State objecting to a reservation has not opposed the entry into force of the treaty between itself and the reserving State, the provisions to which the reservation relates do not apply as between the two States to the extent of the reservation.

Article 22. Withdrawal of Reservations and of Objections to Reservations

1. Unless the treaty otherwise provides, a reservation may be withdrawn at any time and the consent of a State which has accepted the reservation is not required for its withdrawal.

2. Unless the treaty otherwise provides, an objection to a reservation may be withdrawn at any time.

3. Unless the treaty otherwise provides, or it is otherwise agreed:

    (a) The withdrawal of a reservation becomes operative in relation to another contracting State only when notice of it has been received by that State;

    (b) The withdrawal of an objection to a reservation becomes operative only when notice of it has been received by the State which formulated the reservation.

Article 23. Procedure Regarding Reservations

1. A reservation, an express acceptance of a reservation and an objection to a reservation must be formulated in writing and communicated to the contracting States and other States entitled to become parties to the treaty.

2. If formulated when signing the treaty subject to ratification, acceptance or approval, a reservation must be formally confirmed by the reserving State when expressing its consent to be bound by the treaty. In such a case the reservation shall be considered as having been made on the date of its confirmation.

3. An express acceptance of, or an objection to, a reservation made previously to confirmation of the reservation does not itself require confirmation.

4. The withdrawal of a reservation or of an objection to a reservation must be formulated in writing.

Section 3. Entry into Force and Provisional Application of Treaties

Article 24. Entry into Force

1. A treaty enters into force in such manner and upon such date as it may provide or as the negotiating States may agree.

2. Failing any such provision or agreement, a treaty enters into force as soon as consent to be bound by the treaty has been established for all the negotiating States.

3. When the consent of a State to be bound by a treaty is established on a date after the treaty has come into force, the treaty enters into force for that State on that date, unless the treaty otherwise provides.

4. The provisions of a treaty regulating the authentication of its text, the establishment of the consent of States to be bound by the treaty, the manner or date of its entry into force, reservations, the functions of the depositary and other matters arising necessarily before the entry into force of the treaty apply from the time of the adoption of its text.

Article 25. Provisional Application

1. A treaty or a part of a treaty is applied provisionally pending its entry into force if:

   (a) The treaty itself so provides; or

   (b) The negotiating States have in some other manner so agreed.

2. Unless the treaty otherwise provides or the negotiating States have otherwise agreed, the provisional application of a treaty or a part of a treaty with respect to a State shall be terminated if that State notifies the other States between which the treaty is being applied provisionally of its intention not to become a party to the treaty.

PART III

OBSERVANCE, APPLICATION AND INTERPRETATION OF TREATIES

Section 1. Observance of Treaties

Article 26. *Pacta Sunt Servanda*

Every treaty in force is binding upon the parties to it and must be performed by them in good faith.

Article 27. Internal Law and Observance of Treaties

A party may not invoke the provisions of its internal law as justification for its failure to perform a treaty. This rule is without prejudice to article 46.

Section 2. Application of Treaties

Article 28. Non-Retroactivity of Treaties

Unless a different intention appears from the treaty or is otherwise established, its provisions do not bind a party in relation to any act or fact which took place or any situation which ceased to exist before the date of the entry into force of the treaty with respect to that party.

Article 29. Territorial Scope of Treaties

Unless a different intention appears from the treaty or is otherwise established, a treaty is binding upon each party in respect of its entire territory.

Article 30. Application of Successive Treaties Relating to the Same Subject-Matter

1. Subject to Article 103 of the Charter of the United Nations, the rights and obligations of States parties to successive treaties relating to the same subject-matter shall be determined in accordance with the following paragraphs.

2. When a treaty specifies that it is subject to, or that it is not to be considered as incompatible with, an earlier or later treaty, the provisions of that other treaty prevail.

3. When all the parties to the earlier treaty are parties also to the later treaty but the earlier treaty is not terminated or suspended in operation under article 59, the earlier treaty applies only to the extent that its provisions are compatible with those of the latter treaty.

4. When the parties to the later treaty do not include all the parties to the earlier one:

   (a) As between States parties to both treaties the same rule applies as in paragraph 3;

   (b) As between a State party to both treaties and a State party to only one of the treaties, the treaty to which both States are parties governs their mutual rights and obligations.

5. Paragraph 4 is without prejudice to article 41, or to any question of the termination or suspension of the operation of a treaty under article 60 or to any question of responsibility which may arise for a State from the conclusion or application of a treaty the provisions of which are incompatible with its obligations towards another State under another treaty.

Section 3. Interpretation of Treaties

Article 31. General Rule of Interpretation

1. A treaty shall be interpreted in good faith in accordance with the ordinary meaning to be given to the terms of the treaty in their context and in the light of its object and purpose.

2. The context for the purpose of the interpretation of a treaty shall comprise, in addition to the text, including its preamble and annexes:

   (a) Any agreement relating to the treaty which was made between all the parties in connection with the conclusion of the treaty;

   (b) Any instrument which was made by one or more parties in connection with the conclusion of the treaty and accepted by the other parties as an instrument related to the treaty.

3. There shall be taken into account, together with the context:

   (a) Any subsequent agreement between the parties regarding the interpretation of the treaty or the application of its provisions;

   (b) Any subsequent practice in the application of the treaty which establishes the agreement of the parties regarding its interpretation;

   (c) Any relevant rules of international law applicable in the relations between the parties.

4. A special meaning shall be given to a term if it is established that the parties so intended.

Article 32. Supplementary Means of Interpretation

Recourse may be had to supplementary means of interpretation, including the preparatory work of the treaty and the circumstances of its conclusion, in order to confirm the meaning resulting from the application of article 31, or to determine the meaning when the interpretation according to article 31:

(a) Leaves the meaning ambiguous or obscure; or

(b) Leads to a result which is manifestly absurd or unreasonable.

Article 33. Interpretation of Treaties Authenticated in Two or More Languages

1. When a treaty has been authenticated in two or more languages, the text is equally authoritative in each language, unless the treaty provides or the parties agree that, in case of divergence, a particular text shall prevail.

2. A version of the treaty in a language other than one of those in which the text was authenticated shall be considered an authentic text only if the treaty so provides or the parties so agree.

3. The terms of the treaty are presumed to have the same meaning in each authentic text.

4. Except where a particular text prevails in accordance with paragraph 1, when a comparison of the authentic texts discloses a difference of meaning which the application of articles 31 and 32 does not remove, the meaning which best reconciles the texts, having regard to the object and purpose of the treaty, shall be adopted.

Section 4. Treaties and Third States

Article 34. General Rule Regarding Third States

A treaty does not create either obligations or rights for a third State without its consent.

Article 35. Treaties Providing for Obligations for Third States

An obligation arises for a third State from a provision of a treaty if the parties to the treaty intend the provision to be the means of establishing the obligation and the third State expressly accepts that obligation in writing.

Article 36. Treaties Providing for Rights for Third States

1. A right arises for a third State from a provision of a treaty if the parties to the treaty intend the provision to accord that right either to the third State, or to a group of States to which it belongs, or to all States, and the third State assents thereto. Its assent shall be presumed so long as the contrary is not indicated, unless the treaty otherwise provides.

2. A State exercising a right in accordance with paragraph 1 shall comply with the conditions for its exercise provided for in the treaty or established in conformity with the treaty.

Article 37. Revocation or Modification of Obligations or Rights of Third States

1. When an obligation has arisen for a third State in conformity with article 35, the obligation may be revoked or modified only with the consent of the parties to the treaty and of the third State, unless it is established that they had otherwise agreed.

2. When a right has arisen for a third State in conformity with article 36, the right may not be revoked or modified by the parties if it is estab-

lished that the right was intended not to be revocable or subject to modification without the consent of the third State.

Article 38. Rules in a Treaty Becoming Binding on Third States through International Custom

Nothing in articles 34 to 37 precludes a rule set forth in a treaty from becoming binding upon a third State as a customary rule of international law, recognized as such.

PART IV

AMENDMENT AND MODIFICATION OF TREATIES

Article 39. General Rule Regarding the Amendment of Treaties

A treaty may be amended by agreement between the parties. The rules laid down in Part II apply to such an agreement except in so far as the treaty may otherwise provide.

Article 40. Amendment of Multilateral Treaties

1. Unless the treaty otherwise provides, the amendment of multilateral treaties shall be governed by the following paragraphs.

2. Any proposal to amend a multilateral treaty as between all the parties must be notified to all the contracting States, each one of which shall have the right to take part in:

   (a) The decision as to the action to be taken in regard to such proposal;

   (b) The negotiation and conclusion of any agreement for the amendment of the treaty.

3. Every State entitled to become a party to the treaty shall also be entitled to become a party to the treaty as amended.

4. The amending agreement does not bind any State already a party to the treaty which does not become a party to the amending agreement; article 30, paragraph 4(b), applies in relation to such State.

5. Any State which becomes a party to the treaty after the entry into force of the amending agreement shall, failing an expression of a different intention by that State:

   (a) Be considered as a party to the treaty as amended; and

   (b) Be considered as a party to the unamended treaty in relation to any party to the treaty not bound by the amending agreement.

Article 41. Agreements to Modify Multilateral Treaties Between Certain of the Parties Only

1. Two or more of the parties to a multilateral treaty may conclude an agreement to modify the treaty as between themselves alone if:

   (a) The possibility of such a modification is provided for by the treaty; or

   (b) The modification in question is not prohibited by the treaty and:

      (i) Does not affect the enjoyment by the other parties of their rights under the treaty or the performance of their obligations;

      (ii) Does not relate to a provision, derogation from which is incompatible with the effective execution of the object and purpose of the treaty as a whole.

2. Unless in a case falling under paragraph 1(a) the treaty otherwise provides, the parties in question shall notify the other parties of their intention to conclude the agreement and of the modification to the treaty for which it provides.

PART V

INVALIDITY, TERMINATION AND SUSPENSION OF THE OPERATION OF TREATIES

Section 1. General Provisions

Article 42. Validity and Continuance in Force of Treaties

1. The validity of a treaty or of the consent of a State to be bound by a treaty may be impeached only through the application of the present Convention.

2. The termination of a treaty, its denunciation or the withdrawal of a party, may take place only as a result of the application of the provisions of the treaty or of the present Convention. The same rule applies to suspension of the operation of a treaty.

Article 43. Obligations Imposed by International Law Independently of a Treaty

The invalidity, termination or denunciation of a treaty, the withdrawal of a party from it, or the suspension of its operation, as a result of the application of the present Convention or of the provisions of the treaty, shall not in any way impair the duty of any State to fulfil any obligation embodied in the treaty to which it would be subject under international law independently of the treaty.

Article 44. Separability of Treaty Provisions

1. A right of a party, provided for in a treaty or arising under article 56, to denounce, withdraw from or suspend the operation of the treaty may be exercised only with respect to the whole treaty unless the treaty otherwise provides or the parties otherwise agree.

2. A ground for invalidating, terminating, withdrawing from or suspending the operation of a treaty recognized in the present Convention may be invoked only with respect to the whole treaty except as provided in the following paragraphs or in article 60.

3. If the ground relates solely to particular clauses, it may be invoked only with respect to those clauses where:

(a) The said clauses are separable from the remainder of the treaty with regard to their application;

(b) It appears from the treaty or is otherwise established that acceptance of those clauses was not an essential basis of the consent of the other party or parties to be bound by the treaty as a whole; and

(c) Continued performance of the remainder of the treaty would not be unjust.

4. In cases falling under articles 49 and 50 the State entitled to invoke the fraud or corruption may do so with respect either to the whole treaty or, subject to paragraph 3, to the particular clauses alone.

5. In cases falling under articles 51, 52 and 53, no separation of the provisions of the treaty is permitted.

Article 45. Loss of a Right to Invoke a Ground for Invalidating, Terminating, Withdrawing from or Suspending the Operation of a Treaty

A State may no longer invoke a ground for invalidating, terminating, withdrawing from or suspending the operation of a treaty under articles 46 to 50 or articles 60 and 62 if, after becoming aware of the facts:

(a) It shall have expressly agreed that the treaty is valid or remains in force or continues in operation, as the case may be; or

(b) It must by reason of its conduct be considered as having acquiesced in the validity of the treaty or in its maintenance in force or in operation, as the case may be.

Section 2. Invalidity of Treaties

Article 46. Provisions of Internal Law Regarding Competence to Conclude Treaties

1. A State may not invoke the fact that its consent to be bound by a treaty has been expressed in violation of a provision of its internal law regarding competence to conclude treaties as invalidating its consent unless

that violation was manifest and concerned a rule of its internal law of fundamental importance.

2. A violation is manifest if it would be objectively evident to any State conducting itself in the matter in accordance with normal practice and in good faith.

Article 47. Specific Restrictions on Authority to Express the Consent of a State

If the authority of a representative to express the consent of a State to be bound by a particular treaty has been made subject to a specific restriction, his omission to observe that restriction may not be invoked as invalidating the consent expressed by him unless the restriction was notified to the other negotiating States prior to his expressing such consent.

Article 48. Error

1. A State may invoke an error in a treaty as invalidating its consent to be bound by the treaty if the error relates to a fact or situation which was assumed by that State to exist at the time when the treaty was concluded and formed an essential basis of its consent to be bound by the treaty.

2. Paragraph 1 shall not apply if the State in question contributed by its own conduct to the error or if the circumstances were such as to put that State on notice of a possible error.

3. An error relating only to the wording of the text of a treaty does not affect its validity; article 79 then applies.

Article 49. Fraud

If a State has been induced to conclude a treaty by the fraudulent conduct of another negotiating State, the State may invoke the fraud as invalidating its consent to be bound by the treaty.

Article 50. Corruption of a Representative of a State

If the expression of a State's consent to be bound by a treaty has been procured through the corruption of its representative directly or indirectly by another negotiating State, the State may invoke such corruption as invalidating its consent to be bound by the treaty.

Article 51. Coercion of a Representative of a State

The expression of a State's consent to be bound by a treaty which has been procured by the coercion of its representative through acts or threats directed against him shall be without any legal effect.

Article 52. Coercion of a State by the Threat or Use of Force

A treaty is void if its conclusion has been procured by the threat or use of force in violation of the principles of international law embodied in the Charter of the United Nations.

Article 53. Treaties Conflicting with a Peremptory Norm of General International Law (*Jus Cogens*)

A treaty is void if, at the time of its conclusion, it conflicts with a peremptory norm of general international law. For the purposes of the present Convention, a peremptory norm of general international law is a norm accepted and recognized by the international community of States as a whole as a norm from which no derogation is permitted and which can be modified only by a subsequent norm of general international law having the same character.

Section 3. Termination and Suspension of the Operation of Treaties

Article 54. Termination of or Withdrawal from a Treaty Under Its Provisions or by Consent of the Parties

The termination of a treaty or the withdrawal of a party may take place:

(a) In conformity with the provisions of the treaty; or

(b) At any time by consent of all the parties after consultation with the other contracting States.

Article 55. Reduction of the Parties to a Multilateral Treaty Below the Number Necessary for Its Entry into Force

Unless the treaty otherwise provides, a multilateral treaty does not terminate by reason only of the fact that the number of the parties falls below the number necessary for its entry into force.

Article 56. Denunciation of or Withdrawal from a Treaty Containing no Provision Regarding Termination, Denunciation or Withdrawal

1. A treaty which contains no provision regarding its termination and which does not provide for denunciation or withdrawal is not subject to denunciation or withdrawal unless:

    (a) It is established that the parties intended to admit the possibility of denunciation or withdrawal; or

    (b) A right of denunciation or withdrawal may be implied by the nature of the treaty.

2. A party shall give not less than twelve months' notice of its intention to denounce or withdraw from a treaty under paragraph 1.

Article 57. Suspension of the Operation of a Treaty Under Its Provisions or by Consent of the Parties

The operation of a treaty in regard to all the parties or to a particular party may be suspended:

(a) In conformity with the provisions of the treaty; or

(b) At any time by consent of all the parties after consultation with the other contracting States.

Article 58. Suspension of the Operation of a Multilateral Treaty by Agreement Between Certain of the Parties Only

1. Two or more parties to a multilateral treaty may conclude an agreement to suspend the operation of provisions of the treaty, temporarily and as between themselves alone, if:

(a) The possibility of such a suspension is provided for by the treaty; or

(b) The suspension in question is not prohibited by the treaty and:

(i) Does not affect the enjoyment by the other parties of their rights under the treaty or the performance of their obligations;

(ii) Is not incompatible with the object and purpose of the treaty.

2. Unless in a case falling under paragraph 1(a) the treaty otherwise provides, the parties in question shall notify the other parties of their intention to conclude the agreement and of those provisions of the treaty the operation of which they intend to suspend.

Article 59. Termination or Suspension of the Operation of a Treaty Implied by Conclusion of a Later Treaty

1. A treaty shall be considered as terminated if all the parties to it conclude a later treaty relating to the same subject-matter and:

(a) It appears from the later treaty or is otherwise established that the parties intended that the matter should be governed by that treaty; or

(b) The provisions of the later treaty are so far incompatible with those of the earlier one that the two treaties are not capable of being applied at the same time.

2. The earlier treaty shall be considered as only suspended in operation if it appears from the later treaty or is otherwise established that such was the intention of the parties.

Article 60. Termination or Suspension of the Operation of a Treaty as a Consequence of Its Breach

1. A material breach of a bilateral treaty by one of the parties entitles the other to invoke the breach as a ground for terminating the treaty or suspending its operation in whole or in part.

2. A material breach of a multilateral treaty by one of the parties entitles:

   (a) The other parties by unanimous agreement to suspend the operation of the treaty in whole or in part or to terminate it either:

      (i) In the relations between themselves and the defaulting State, or

      (ii) As between all the parties;

   (b) A party specially affected by the breach to invoke it as a ground for suspending the operation of the treaty in whole or in part in the relations between itself and the defaulting State;

   (c) Any party other than the defaulting State to invoke the breach as a ground for suspending the operation of the treaty in whole or in part with respect to itself if the treaty is of such a character that a material breach of its provisions by one party radically changes the position of every party with respect to the further performance of its obligations under the treaty.

3. A material breach of a treaty, for the purposes of this article, consists in:

   (a) A repudiation of the treaty not sanctioned by the present Convention; or

   (b) The violation of a provision essential to the accomplishment of the object or purpose of the treaty.

4. The foregoing paragraphs are without prejudice to any provision in the treaty applicable in the event of a breach.

5. Paragraphs 1 to 3 do not apply to provisions relating to the protection of the human person contained in treaties of a humanitarian character, in particular to provisions prohibiting any form of reprisals against persons protected by such treaties.

Article 61. Supervening Impossibility of Performance

1. A party may invoke the impossibility of performing a treaty as a ground for terminating or withdrawing from it if the impossibility results from the permanent disappearance or destruction of an object indispensable for the execution of the treaty. If the impossibility is temporary, it may be invoked only as a ground for suspending the operation of the treaty.

2. Impossibility of performance may not be invoked by a party as a ground for terminating, withdrawing from or suspending the operation of a treaty if the impossibility is the result of a breach by that party either of an obligation under the treaty or of any other international obligation owed to any other party to the treaty.

Article 62. Fundamental Change of Circumstances

1. A fundamental change of circumstances which has occurred with regard to those existing at the time of the conclusion of a treaty, and which was not foreseen by the parties, may not be invoked as a ground for terminating or withdrawing from the treaty unless:

   (a) The existence of those circumstances constituted an essential basis of the consent of the parties to be bound by the treaty; and

   (b) The effect of the change is radically to transform the extent of obligations still to be performed under the treaty.

2. A fundamental change of circumstances may not be invoked as a ground for terminating or withdrawing from a treaty:

   (a) If the treaty establishes a boundary; or

   (b) If the fundamental change is the result of a breach by the party invoking it either of an obligation under the treaty or of any other international obligation owed to any other party to the treaty.

3. If, under the foregoing paragraphs, a party may invoke a fundamental change of circumstances as a ground for terminating or withdrawing

from a treaty it may also invoke the change as a ground for suspending the operation of the treaty.

Article 63. Severance of Diplomatic or Consular Relations

The severance of diplomatic or consular relations between parties to a treaty does not affect the legal relations established between them by the treaty except in so far as the existence of diplomatic or consular relations is indispensable for the application of the treaty.

Article 64. Emergence of a New Peremptory Norm of General International Law (*Jus Cogens*)

If a new peremptory norm of general international law emerges, any existing treaty which is in conflict with that norm becomes void and terminates.

Section 4. Procedure

Article 65. Procedure to be Followed with Respect to Invalidity, Termination, Withdrawal from or Suspension of the Operation of a Treaty

1. A party which, under the provisions of the present Convention, invokes either a defect in its consent to be bound by a treaty or a ground for impeaching the validity of a treaty, terminating it, withdrawing from it or suspending its operation, must notify the other parties of its claim. The notification shall indicate the measure proposed to be taken with respect to the treaty and the reasons therefor.

2. If, after the expiry of a period which, except in cases of special urgency, shall not be less than three months after the receipt of the notification, no party has raised any objection, the party making the notification may carry out in the manner provided in article 67 the measure which it has proposed.

3. If, however, objection has been raised by any other party, the parties shall seek a solution through the means indicated in article 33 of the Charter of the United Nations.

4. Nothing in the foregoing paragraphs shall affect the rights or obligations of the parties under any provisions in force binding the parties with regard to the settlement of disputes.

5. Without prejudice to article 45, the fact that a State has not previously made the notification prescribed in paragraph 1 shall not prevent it from making such notification in answer to another party claiming performance of the treaty or alleging its violation.

Article 66. Procedures for Judicial Settlement, Arbitration and Conciliation

If, under paragraph 3 of article 65, no solution has been reached within a period of 12 months following the date on which the objection was raised, the following procedures shall be followed:

(a) Any one of the parties to a dispute concerning the application or the interpretation of articles 53 or 64 may, by a written application, submit it to the International Court of Justice for a decision unless the parties by common consent agree to submit the dispute to arbitration;

(b) Any one of the parties to a dispute concerning the application or the interpretation of any of the other articles in Part V of the present Convention may set in motion the procedure specified in the Annex to the Convention by submitting a request to that effect to the Secretary-General of the United Nations.

Article 67. Instruments for Declaring Invalid, Terminating, Withdrawing from or Suspending the Operation of a Treaty

1. The notification provided for under article 65 paragraph 1 must be made in writing.

2. Any act declaring invalid, terminating, withdrawing from or suspending the operation of a treaty pursuant to the provisions of the treaty or of paragraphs 2 or 3 of article 65 shall be carried out through an instrument communicated to the other parties. If the instrument is not signed by the Head of State, Head of Government or Minister for Foreign Affairs, the representative of the State communicating it may be called upon to produce full powers.

Article 68. Revocation of Notifications and Instruments Provided for in Articles 65 and 67

A notification or instrument provided for in articles 65 or 67 may be revoked at any time before it takes effect.

Section 5. Consequences of the Invalidity, Termination or Suspension of the Operation of a Treaty

Article 69. Consequences of the Invalidity of a Treaty

1. A treaty the invalidity of which is established under the present Convention is void. The provisions of a void treaty have no legal force.

2. If acts have nevertheless been performed in reliance on such a treaty:

   (a) Each party may require any other party to establish as far as possible in their mutual relations the position that would have existed if the acts had not been performed;

   (b) Acts performed in good faith before the invalidity was invoked are not rendered unlawful by reason only of the invalidity of the treaty.

3. In cases falling under articles 49, 50, 51 or 52, paragraph 2 does not apply with respect to the party to which the fraud, the act of corruption or the coercion is imputable.

4. In the case of the invalidity of a particular State's consent to be bound by a multilateral treaty, the foregoing rules apply in the relations between that State and the parties to the treaty.

Article 70. Consequences of the Termination of a Treaty

1. Unless the treaty otherwise provides or the parties otherwise agree, the termination of a treaty under its provisions or in accordance with the present Convention:

   (a) Releases the parties from any obligation further to perform the treaty;

   (b) Does not affect any right, obligation or legal situation of the parties created through the execution of the treaty prior to its termination.

2. If a State denounces or withdraws from a multilateral treaty, paragraph 1 applies in the relations between that State and each of the other par-

ties to the treaty from the date when such denunciation or withdrawal takes effect.

Article 71. Consequences of the Invalidity of a Treaty Which Conflict with a Peremptory Norm of General International Law

1. In the case of a treaty which is void under article 53 the parties shall:

   (a) Eliminate as far as possible the consequences of any act performed in reliance on any provision which conflicts with the peremptory norm of general international law; and

   (b) Bring their mutual relations into conformity with the peremptory norm of general international law.

2. In the case of a treaty which becomes void and terminates under article 64, the termination of the treaty:

   (a) Releases the parties from any obligation further to perform the treaty;

   (b) Does not affect any right, obligation or legal situation of the parties created through the execution of the treaty prior to its termination; provided that those rights, obligations or situations may thereafter be maintained only to the extent that their maintenance is not in itself in conflict with the new peremptory norm of general international law.

Article 72. Consequences of the Suspension of the Operation of a Treaty

1. Unless the treaty otherwise provides or the parties otherwise agree, the suspension of the operation of a treaty under its provisions or in accordance with the present Convention:

   (a) Releases the parties between which the operation of the treaty is suspended from the obligation to perform the treaty in their mutual relations during the period of the suspension;

   (b) Does not otherwise affect the legal relations between the parties established by the treaty.

2. During the period of the suspension the parties shall refrain from acts tending to obstruct the resumption of the operation of the treaty.

PART VI

MISCELLANEOUS PROVISIONS

Article 73. Cases of State Succession, State Responsibility and Outbreak of Hostilities

The provisions of the present Convention shall not prejudge any question that may arise in regard to a treaty from a succession of States or from the international responsibility of a State or from the outbreak of hostilities between States.

Article 74. Diplomatic and Consular Relations and the Conclusion of Treaties

The severance or absence of diplomatic or consular relations between two or more States does not prevent the conclusion of treaties between those States. The conclusion of a treaty does not in itself affect the situation in regard to diplomatic or consular relations.

Article 75. Case of an Aggressor State

The provisions of the present Convention are without prejudice to any obligation in relation to a treaty which may arise for an aggressor State in consequence of measures taken in conformity with the Charter of the United Nations with reference to that State's aggression.

PART VII

DEPOSITARIES, NOTIFICATIONS, CORRECTIONS AND REGISTRATION

Article 76. Depositaries of Treaties

1. The designation of the depositary of a treaty may be made by the negotiating States, either in the treaty itself or in some other manner. The depositary may be one or more States, an international organization or the chief administrative officer of the organization.

2. The functions of the depositary of a treaty are international in character and the depositary is under an obligation to act impartially in their performance. In particular, the fact that a treaty has not entered into force between certain of the parties or that a difference has appeared between a State and a depositary with regard to the performance of the latter's functions shall not affect that obligation.

Article 77. Functions of Depositaries

1. The functions of a depositary, unless otherwise provided in the treaty or agreed by the contracting States, comprise in particular:

   (a) Keeping custody of the original text of the treaty and of any full powers delivered to the depositary;

   (b) Preparing certified copies of the original text and preparing any further text of the treaty in such additional languages as may be required by the treaty and transmitting them to the parties and to the States entitled to become parties to the treaty;

   (c) Receiving any signatures to the treaty and receiving and keeping custody of any instruments, notifications and communications relating to it;

   (d) Examining whether the signature or any instrument, notification or communication relating to the treaty is in due and proper form and, if need be, bringing the matter to the attention of the State in question;

   (e) Informing the parties and the States entitled to become parties to the treaty of acts, notifications and communications relating to the treaty;

   (f) Informing the States entitled to become parties to the treaty when the number of signatures or of instruments of ratification, acceptance, approval or accession required for the entry into force of the treaty has been received or deposited;

   (g) Registering the treaty with the Secretariat of the United Nations;

(h) Performing the functions specified in other provisions of the present Convention.

2. In the event of any difference appearing between a State and the depositary as to the performance of the latter's functions, the depositary shall bring the question to the attention of the signatory States and the contracting States or, where appropriate, of the competent organ of the international organization concerned.

Article 78. Notifications and Communications

Except as the treaty or the present Convention otherwise provide, any notification or communication to be made by any State under the present Convention shall:

(a) If there is no depositary, be transmitted direct to the States for which it is intended, or if there is a depositary, to the latter;

(b) Be considered as having been made by the State in question only upon its receipt by the State to which it was transmitted or, as the case may be, upon its receipt by the depositary;

(c) If transmitted to a depositary, be considered as received by the State for which it was intended only when the latter State has been informed by the depositary in accordance with article 77, paragraph 1 (e).

Article 79. Correction of Errors in Texts or in Certified Copies of Treaties

1. Where, after the authentication of the text of a treaty, the signatory States and the contracting States are agreed that it contains an error, the error shall, unless they decide upon some other means of correction, be corrected:

(a) By having the appropriate correction made in the text and causing the correction to be initialled by duly authorized representatives;

(b) By executing or exchanging an instrument or instruments setting out the correction which it has been agreed to make; or

(c) By executing a corrected text of the whole treaty by the same procedure as in the case of the original text.

2. Where the treaty is one for which there is a depositary, the latter shall notify the signatory States and the contracting States of the error and of the proposal to correct it and shall specify an appropriate time-limit within which objection to the proposed correction may be raised. If, on the expiry of the time-limit:

(a) No objection has been raised, the depositary shall make and initial the correction in the text and shall execute a *procés-verbal* of the rectification of the text and communicate a copy of it to the parties and to the States entitled to become parties to the treaty;

(b) An objection has been raised, the depositary shall communicate the objection to the signatory States and to the contracting States.

3. The rules in paragraphs 1 and 2 apply also where the text has been authenticated in two or more languages and it appears that there is a lack of concordance which the signatory States and the contracting States agree should be corrected.

4. The corrected text replaces the defective text *ab initio*, unless the signatory States and the contracting States otherwise decide.

5. The correction of the text of a treaty that has been registered shall be notified to the Secretariat of the United Nations.

6. Where an error is discovered in a certified copy of a treaty, the depositary shall execute a *procés-verbal* specifying the rectification and communicate a copy of it to the signatory States and to the contracting States.

Article 80. Registration and Publication of Treaties

1. Treaties shall, after their entry into force, be transmitted to the Secretariat of the United Nations for registration or filing and recording, as the case may be, and for publication.

2. The designation of a depositary shall constitute authorization for it to perform the acts specified in the preceding paragraph.

PART VIII

FINAL PROVISIONS

Article 81. Signature

The present Convention shall be open for signature by all States Members of the United Nations or of any of the specialized agencies or of the International Atomic Energy Agency or parties to the Statute of the International Court of Justice, and by any other State invited by the General Assembly of the United Nations to become a party to the Convention, as follows: until 30 November 1969, at the Federal Ministry for Foreign Affairs of the Republic of Austria, and subsequently, until 30 April 1970, at United Nations Headquarters, New York.

Article 82. Ratification

The present Convention is subject to ratification. The instruments of ratification shall be deposited with the Secretary-General of the United Nations.

Article 83. Accession

The present Convention shall remain open for accession by any State belonging to any of the categories mentioned in article 81. The instruments of accession shall be deposited with the Secretary-General of the United Nations.

Article 84. Entry into Force

1. The present Convention shall enter into force on the thirtieth day following the date of deposit of the thirty-fifth instrument of ratification or accession.

2. For each State ratifying or acceding to the Convention after the deposit of the thirty-fifth instrument of ratification or accession, the Convention shall enter into force on the thirtieth day after deposit by such State of its instrument of ratification or accession.

Article 85. Authentic Texts

The original of the present Convention, of which the Chinese, English, French, Russian and Spanish texts are equally authentic, shall be deposited with the Secretary-General of the United Nations.

In witness whereof the undersigned Plenipotentiaries, being duly authorized thereto by their respective Governments, have signed the present Convention.

Done at Vienna, this twenty-third day of May, one thousand nine hundred and sixty-nine.

ANNEX

1. A list of conciliators consisting of qualified jurists shall be drawn up and maintained by the Secretary-General of the United Nations. To this end, every State which is a Member of the United Nations or a party to the present Convention shall be invited to nominate two conciliators, and the names of the persons so nominated shall constitute the list. The term of a conciliator, including that of any conciliator nominated to fill a casual vacancy, shall be five years and may be renewed. A conciliator whose term expires shall continue to fulfil any function for which he shall have been chosen under the following paragraph.

2. When a request has been made to the Secretary-General under article 66, the Secretary-General shall bring the dispute before a conciliation commission constituted as follows:

The State or States constituting one of the parties to the dispute shall appoint:

(a) One conciliator of the nationality of that State or of one of those States, who may or may not be chosen from the list referred to in paragraph 1; and

(b) One conciliator not of the nationality of that State or of any of those States, who shall be chosen from the list.

The State or States constituting the other party to the dispute shall appoint two conciliators in the same way. The four conciliators chosen by the parties shall be appointed within sixty days following the date on which the Secretary-General receives the request.

The four conciliators shall, within sixty days following the date of the last of their own appointments, appoint a fifth conciliator chosen from the list, who shall be chairman.

If the appointment of the chairman or of any of the other conciliators has not been made within the period prescribed above for such appointment, it shall be made by the Secretary-General within sixty days following the expiry of that period. The appointment of the chairman may be made by the Secretary-General either from the list or from the membership of the International Law Commission. Any of the periods within which appointments must be made may be extended by agreement between the parties to the dispute.

Any vacancy shall be filled in the manner prescribed for the initial appointment.

3. The Conciliation Commission shall decide its own procedure. The Commission, with the consent of the parties to the dispute, may invite any party to the treaty to submit to it its views orally or in writing. Decisions and recommendations of the Commission shall be made by a majority vote of the five members.

4. The Commission may draw the attention of the parties to the dispute to any measures which might facilitate an amicable settlement.

5. The Commission shall hear the parties, examine the claims and objections, and make proposals to the parties with a view to reaching an amicable settlement of the dispute.

6. The Commission shall report within twelve months of its constitution. Its report shall be deposited with the Secretary-General and transmitted to the parties to the dispute. The report of the Commission, including any conclusions stated therein regarding the facts or questions of law, shall not be binding upon the parties and it shall have no other character than that of recommendations submitted for the consideration of the parties in order to facilitate an amicable settlement of the dispute.

7. The Secretary-General shall provide the Commission with such assistance and facilities as it may require. The expenses of the Commission shall be borne by the United Nations.

UNIT B	BACKGROUND DOCUMENTS FOR CHAPTER 7
	Document 1: Shearer & Starke Reading

I. A. Shearer, *Starke's International Law*

Pages 31-37 (Butterworths, Boston; 11th Edition 1994). Reprinted by permission of Oxford University Press.

Until recent times, international law consisted for the most part of customary rules. These rules had generally evolved after a long historical process culminating in their recognition by the international community. The preponderance of traditional customary rules was diminished as a result of the large number of "law-making" treaties concluded since the middle of the last century, and must progressively decline in measure as the work of the International Law Commission in codifying and restating customary rules produces results in treaties such as the Vienna Conventions of 18 April 1961, of 24 April 1963, and of 22 May 1969, on Diplomatic Relations, Consular Relations, and the Law of Treaties respectively. Yet according to views recently expressed by some writers, international custom may still have a significant role to play as a dynamic source of fresh rules of international law where the international community undergoes change in new areas untouched by treaties, judicial decisions or the writings of jurists.

The terms "custom" and "usage" are often used interchangeably. Strictly speaking, there is a clear technical distinction between the two. Usage represents the initial stage of custom. Custom begins where usage becomes general. Usage is an international habit of action that has not yet received full legal attestation. Usages may be conflicting, custom must be unified and self-consistent. *Viner's Abridgement,* referring to custom in English law, has the matter in a nutshell.

> A custom, in the intendment of law, is such a usage as hath obtained the force of a law.

A customary element has, as we have seen, been a feature of the rules of international law from antiquity to modern times. In ancient Greece, the rules of war and peace sprang from the common usages observed by the Greek City States. These customary rules crystallised by a process of generalisation and unification of the various usages separately observed by each city republic. A similar process was observable among the small Italian states of the Middle Ages. When in the sixteenth and seventeenth centuries Europe became a complex of highly nationalistic, independent territorial states, the process was translated to a higher and more extensive plane. From the usages developed in the intercourse of modern European states there emerged the earliest rules of international law.

Customary rules crystallise from usages or practices which have evolved in approximately three sets of circumstances:

(a) Diplomatic relations between states.

Acts or declarations by representatives of states, opinions of legal advisers to state governments, bilateral treaties, and press releases or official statements by governments may all constitute evidence of usages followed by states. In this regard, both conduct and statements (written and oral) are on the same footing.

(b) Practice of international organs.

The practice of international organs, again whether by conduct or declarations, may lead to the development of customary rules of international law concerning their status, or their powers and responsibilities. Thus in its Advisory Opinion holding that the International Labour Organisation had power to regulate internationally the conditions of labour of persons employed in agriculture, the Permanent Court of International Justice founded its views to a certain extent on the practice of the Organisation. In a noted Advisory Opinion, the International Court of Justice based its opinion that the United Nations had international legal personality partly on the practice of the United Nations in concluding conventions.

(c) State laws, decisions of state courts, and state military or administrative practices.

A concurrence, although not a mere parallelism, of state laws or of judicial decisions of state courts or of state practices may indicate so wide an adoption of similar rules as to suggest the general recognition of a broad principle of law. This is particularly well illustrated by a decision of the United States Supreme Court, *The Scotia.* The facts were as follows: In 1863 the British Government adopted a series of regulations for preventing collisions at sea. In 1864 the

American Congress adopted practically the same regulations, as did within a short time after, the governments of nearly all the maritime countries. Under these circumstances the *Scotia* (British) collided in mid-ocean with the *Berkshire* (American), which was not carrying the lights required by the new regulations. As a result, the *Berkshire* sank. The question was whether the respective rights and duties of the two vessels were determined by the general maritime law before the British regulations of 1863. It was held that these rights and duties must be determined by the new customary rules of international law that had evolved through the widespread adoption of the British regulations, and that therefore the fault lay with the *Berkshire:*

> This is not giving to the Statutes of any nation extra-territorial effect. It is not treating them as general maritime laws, but it is recognition of the historical fact that, by common consent of mankind, these rules have been acquiesced in as of general obligation. Of that fact we think we may take judicial notice. Foreign municipal laws must indeed be proved as facts, but it is not so with the law of nations.

For evidence of state practices, it may be necessary to refer to official books or documents, such as military, naval, and air force manuals, or the internal regulations of each state's diplomatic and consular services. Comparison of these may indicate the existence of a practice uniformly followed by all states.

A general, although not inflexible, working guide is that before a usage may be considered as amounting to a customary rule of international law, two tests must be satisfied. These tests relate to: (i) the material, and (ii) the psychological aspects involved in the formation of the customary rule.

As regards the material aspect, there must in general be a recurrence or repetition of the acts which give birth to the customary rule. A German court held in the case of *Lübeck v. Mecklenburg-Schwerin* that a single act of a state agency or authority could not create any rights of custom in favour of another state which had benefited by the act; conduct to be creative of customary law must be regular and repeated. Material departures from a practice may negative the existence of a customary rule, but minor deviations may not necessarily have this negative consequence. Apart from recurrence, the antiquity of the acts may be also a pertinent consideration. Yet even a short time may be enough where the state practice has been extensive and for all practical purposes uniform (e.g., as with evolution of the principle that a coastal state has the rights of exploitation, etc., with respect to its continental shelf . . .).

The psychological aspect is better known as the *opinio juris sive necessitatis*, or as one authority has termed it "the mutual conviction that the recurrence . . . is the result of a compulsory rule." This needs further explanation. Recurrence of the usage or practice tends to develop an expectation that, in similar future situations, the same conduct or the abstention there from will be repeated. When this expectation evolves further into a general acknowledgment by states that the conduct or the abstention therefrom is a matter both of right and of obligation, the transition from usage to custom may be regarded as consummated. In this process, there is involved, to some extent, an element of acceptance or assent on the part of states generally. This conviction, this opinio juris, is a convenient if not invariable test that a usage or practice has crystallised into custom; there is, for example, an absence of opinio juris when states conform to a usage for motives of comity or courtesy only. At the same time, the opinio juris is not an essential element of custom, but if it is present, it is helpful as distinguishing custom from a course of action followed as a matter of arbitrary choice or for other reasons.

It would follow from the judgments of the Permanent Court of International Justice in the *Lotus Case* that the opinio juris is a matter of inference from all the circumstances, not merely the detailed acts which constitute the material element of the alleged customary rule. One test for the existence of opinio juris is that set out in *West Rand Central Gold Mining Co. v. R.* There the Court laid down that it must be proved by satisfactory evidence that the alleged rule "is of such a nature, and has been so widely and generally accepted, that it can hardly be supposed that any civilised State would repudiate it." This amounts to a test of "general recognition" by the international society of states.

Such test of "general recognition" underlies the provision in the Statute of the International Court of Justice, under which the Court is directed to apply international custom "as evidence of a general practice accepted as law," and is to be found also in Article 53 of the Vienna Convention of 1969 on the Law of Treaties providing that a norm of jus cogens must be one "accepted and recognised by the international community of States *as a whole*."

The International Court of Justice has held, however, in the *Right of Passage over Indian Territory Case* (Portugal-India), that a *particular* practice between two states only, which is accepted by them as law, may give rise to a binding customary rule between the two.

* * *

Both national and international courts play an important role in the application of custom. Often it is claimed by one of the parties before the court that a certain rule of customary international law exists. The court must then investigate whether or not the rule invoked before it is a validly established rule of international custom, and in the course of this inquiry it examines all possible materials, such as treaties, the practice of states, diplomatic correspondence, decisions of state courts, and juristic writings. In certain cases, the court's function may be more than purely declaratory; while not actually creating new customary rules, the court may feel constrained to carry to a final stage the process of evolution of usages so generally recognised as to suggest that by an inevitable course of development they will crystallise into custom. To use Justice Cardozo's words, by its *imprimatur* the Court will attest the "jural quality" of the custom.

Two instructive cases illustrating the judicial methods in the application of custom are *The Paquete Habana,* a decision of the United States Supreme Court, and the *Lotus Case,* a decision of the Permanent Court of International Justice. In the former case, the Supreme Court, after a detailed investigation of the materials mentioned above, namely state laws and practices, treaties, writings of publicists evidencing usage, and decisions of courts, found that they uniformly proved the existence of a valid customary rule giving immunity to small fishing vessels, honestly pursuing their calling, from belligerent capture in time of war; in the latter case, the Permanent Court, following the same method, decided that there was no customary rule conferring exclusive penal jurisdiction in maritime collision cases (on the high seas) on the country of the ship's flag, as regards all incidents on the ship, because, of the relevant materials considered, state laws were not consistent, decisions of state courts conflicted, no uniform trend could be deduced from treaties, and publicists were divided in their views. Although the same method of detailed consideration of all materials was followed in both cases, weightier proof of the customary rule was required by the Permanent Court than by the Supreme Court, and owing to the absence of such proof the Permanent Court decided against the existence of the rule.

Multilateral law-making conventions may also be the means through which rules of customary international law crystallise and thus become binding even on states not bound contractually by the convention in question. For this very reason a conclusion that a convention, or other international instrument, has passed into customary international law is not lightly to be drawn. The conditions under which a principle or rule may thus be transformed in character from a purely conventional norm binding only the parties, to a generally binding norm were declared by the International Court of Justice in the *North Sea Continental Shelf Cases* as follows:

(i) the provision concerned should, at all events potentially, be of a fundamentally norm-creating character such as could be regarded as forming the basis of a general rule of law;

(ii) there should be widespread and representative participation in the convention, including that of states whose interests are especially affected;

(iii) within the period since the adoption of the convention, short or long as that may be, state practice, including that of states especially affected, should be both extensive and virtually uniform in

> the sense of the provision invoked, and demonstrate also a general recognition that a rule of law or legal obligation is involved (*opinio juris sive necessitatis*).

* * *

The difficulties involved in extracting a customary rule or principle of international law from the mass of heterogeneous documentation of state practice, state judicial decisions, diplomatic history, etc., are not to be minimised, as the two cases just mentioned, amply illustrate. Not only, also, is the documentation itself frequently defective or incomplete, but the practice of some states is documented less adequately than that of other states. Moreover, the experience of the International Law Commission, and of the conferences called from 1958 onwards to consider the Commission's drafts, revealing as it did so much disagreement in areas where there were customary rules assumed to be generally recognised, should induce the utmost caution in drawing inferences as to the existence of such general recognition.

UNIT B	BACKGROUND DOCUMENTS FOR CHAPTER 7
	Document 2: Malcolm Shaw Reading

Malcolm N. Shaw, *International Law*

Pages 68-88 (Cambridge University Press, New York; 5th Edition 2003).

Introduction

In any primitive society certain rules of behaviour emerge and prescribe what is permitted and what is not. Such rules develop almost subconsciously within the group and are maintained by the members of the group by social pressures and with the aid of various other more tangible implements. They are not, at least in the early stages, written down or codified, and survive ultimately because of what can be called an aura of historical legitimacy. As the community develops it will modernise its code of behaviour by the creation of legal machinery, such as courts and legislature. Custom, for this is how the original process can be described, remains and may also continue to evolve. It is regarded as an authentic expression of the needs and values of the community at any given time.

Custom within contemporary legal systems, particularly in the developed world, is relatively cumbersome and unimportant and often of only nostalgic value. In international law on the other hand it is a dynamic source of law in the light of the nature of the international system, and its lack of centralised government organs.

The existence of customary rules can be deduced from the practice and behaviour of states and this is where the problems begin. How can one tell when a particular line of action adopted by a state reflects a legal rule or is merely prompted by, for example, courtesy? Indeed, how can one discover what precisely a state is doing or why, since there is no living "state" but rather thousands of officials in scores of departments exercising governmental functions? Other issues concern the speed of creation of new rules and the effect of protests.

There are disagreements as to the value of a customary system in international law. Some writers deny that custom can be significant today as a source of law, noting that it is too clumsy and slow-moving to accommodate the evolution of international law any more, while others declare that it is a dynamic process of law creation and more important than treaties since it is of universal application. Another view recognises that custom is of value since it is activated by spontaneous behaviour and thus mirrors the contemporary concerns of society. However, since international law now has to contend with a massive increase in the pace and variety of state activities as well as having to come to terms with many different cultural and political traditions, the role of custom is perceived to be much diminished.

There are elements of truth in each of these approaches. Amidst a wide variety of conflicting behaviour, it is not easy to isolate the emergence of a new rule of customary law and there are immense problems involved in collating all the necessary information. It is not always the best instrument available for the regulation of complex issues that arise in world affairs, but in particular situations it may meet the contingencies of modern life. As will be seen, it is possible to point to something called "instant" customary law in certain circumstances that can prescribe valid rules without having to undergo a long period of gestation, and custom can and often does dovetail neatly within the complicated mechanisms now operating for the identification and progressive development of the principles of international law.

More than that, custom does mirror the characteristics of the decentralised international system. It is democratic in that all states may share in the formulation of new rules, though the precept that some are more equal than others in this process is not without its grain of truth. If the international community is unhappy with a particular law it can be changed relatively quickly without the necessity of convening and successfully completing a world conference. It reflects the consensus approach to decision-making with the ability of the majority to create new law binding upon all, while the very participation of states encourages their compliance with customary rules. Its imprecision means flexibility as well as ambiguity. Indeed, the creation of the concept of the exclusive economic zone in the law of the sea may be cited as an example of this process. . . . The essence of custom according to Article 38 is that it should constitute "evidence of a general practice accepted as law." Thus, it is possible to detect two basic elements in the make-up of a custom. These are the material facts, that is, the actual behaviour of states, and the psychological or subjective belief that such behaviour is "law."

[I]t is understandable why the first requirement is mentioned, since customary law is founded upon the performance of state activities and the convergence of practices, in other words, what states actually do. It is the psychological factor (*opinion juris*) that needs some explanation. If one left the definition of custom as state practice then one would be faced with the problem of how to separate international law from principles of morality or social usage. This is because states do not restrict their behaviour to what is legally required. They may pursue a line of conduct purely through a feeling of goodwill and in the hope of reciprocal benefits. States do not have to allow tourists in or launch satellites. There is no law imposing upon them the strict duty to distribute economic aid to developing nations. The bare fact that such things are done does not mean that they have to be done.

The issue therefore is how to distinguish behaviour undertaken because of a law from behaviour undertaken because of a whole series of other reasons ranging from goodwill to pique, and from ideological support to political bribery. And if customary law is restricted to the overt acts of states, one cannot solve this problem.

Accordingly, the second element in the definition of custom has been elaborated. This is the psychological factor, the belief by a state that behaved in a certain way that it was under a legal obligation to act that way. It is known in legal terminology as *opinio juris sive necessitatis* and was first formulated by the French writer François Gény as an attempt to differentiate legal custom from mere social usage.

However, the relative importance of the two factors, the overt action and the subjective conviction, is disputed by various writers. Positivists, with their emphasis upon state sovereignty, stress the paramount importance of the psychological element. States are only bound by what they have consented to, so therefore the material element is minimised to the greater value of *opinio juris*. If states believe that a course of action is legal and perform it, even if only once, then it is to be inferred that they have tacitly consented to the rule involved. Following on from this line of analysis, various positivist thinkers have tended to minimise many of the requirements of the overt manifestation, for example, with regard to repetition and duration. Other writers have taken precisely the opposite line and maintain that *opinio juris* is impossible to prove and therefore of no tremendous consequence. Kelsen, for one, has written that it is the courts that have the discretion to decide whether any set of usages is such as to create a custom and that the subjective perception of the particular state or states is not called upon to give the final verdict as to its legality or not.

The material fact

The actual practice engaged in by states constitutes the initial factor to be brought into account. There are a number of points to be considered concerning the nature of a particular practice by states, including its duration, consistency, repetition and generality. As far as the duration is concerned, most countries specify a recognised time-scale for the acceptance of a practice as a customary rule within their municipal systems. This can vary from "time immemorial" in the English Common Law dating back to 1189, to figures from thirty or forty years on the Continent.

In international law there is no rigid time element and it will depend upon the circumstances of the case and the nature of the usage in question. In certain fields, such as air and space law, the rules have developed quickly; in others, the process is much slower. Duration is thus not the most important of the components of state practice. The essence of custom is to be sought elsewhere.

The basic rule as regards continuity and repetition was laid down in the *Asylum* case decided by the International Court of Justice (ICJ) in 1950. The Court declared that a customary rule must be "in accordance with a constant and uniform usage practised by the States in question." The case concerned Haya de la Torre, a Peruvian, who was sought by his government after an unsuccessful revolt. He was granted asylum by Colombia in its embassy in Lima, but Peru refused to issue a safe conduct to permit Torre to leave the country. Colombia brought the matter before the International Court of Justice and requested a decision recognising that it (Colombia) was competent to define Torre's offence, as to whether it was criminal as Peru maintained, or political, in which case asylum and a safe conduct could be allowed.

The Court, in characterising the nature of a customary rule, held that it had to constitute the expression of a right appertaining to one state (Colombia) and a duty incumbent upon another (Peru). However, the Court felt that in the *Asylum* litigation, state practices had been so uncertain and contradictory as not to amount to a "constant and uniform usage" regarding the unilateral qualification of the offence in question. The issue involved here dealt with a regional custom pertaining only to Latin America and it may be argued that the same approach need not necessarily be followed where a general custom is alleged and that in the latter instance a lower standard of proof would be upheld.

The ICJ emphasised its view that some degree of uniformity amongst state practices was essential before a custom could come into existence in the *Anglo-Norwegian Fisheries* case. The United Kingdom, in its arguments against the Norwegian method of measuring the breadth of the territorial sea, referred to an alleged rule of custom whereby a straight line may be drawn across bays of less than 10 miles from one projection to the other, which could then be regarded as the baseline for the measurement of the territorial sea. The Court dismissed this by pointing out that the actual practice of states did not justify the creation of any such custom. In other words, there had been insufficient uniformity of behaviour.

In the *North Sea Continental Shelf* cases, which involved a dispute between Germany on the one hand and Holland and Denmark on the other over the delimitation of the continental shelf, the ICJ remarked that state practice had to be "both extensive and virtually uniform in the sense of the provision invoked." This was held to be indispensable to the formation of a new rule of customary international law. However, the Court emphasised in the *Nicaragua* v. *United*

States case that it was not necessary that the practice in question had to be "in absolutely rigorous conformity" with the purported customary rule. The Court continued:

> In order to deduce the existence of customary rules, the Court deems it sufficient that the conduct of states should, in general, be consistent with such rules, and that instances of state conduct inconsistent with a given rule should generally have been treated as breaches of that rule, not as indications of the recognition of a new rule.

The threshold that needs to be attained before a legally binding custom can be created will depend both upon the nature of the alleged rule and the opposition it arouses. This partly relates to the problem of ambiguity where it is not possible to point to the alleged custom with any degree of clarity, as in the *Asylum* case where a variety of conflicting and contradictory evidence had been brought forward.

On the other hand, an unsubstantiated claim by a state cannot be accepted because it would amount to unilateral law-making and compromise a reasonably impartial system of international law. If a proposition meets with a great deal of opposition then it would be an undesirable fiction to ignore this and talk of an established rule. Another relevant factor is the strength of the prior rule which is purportedly overthrown. For example, the customary law relating to a state's sovereignty over its airspace developed very quickly in the years immediately before and during the First World War. Similarly, the principle of non-sovereignty over the space route followed by artificial satellites came into being soon after the launching of the first Sputniks. Bin Cheng has argued that in such circumstances repetition is not at all necessary provided the *opinio juris* could be clearly established. Thus, "instant" customary law is possible.

This contention that single acts may create custom has been criticised, particularly in view of the difficulties of proving customary rules any other way but through a series of usages. Nevertheless, the conclusion must be that it is the international context which plays the vital part in the creation of custom. In a society constantly faced with new situations because of the dynamics of progress, there is a clear need for a reasonably speedy method of responding to such changes by a system of prompt rule formation. In new areas of law, customs can be quickly established by state practices by virtue of the newness of the situations involved, the lack of contrary rules to be surmounted and the overwhelming necessity to preserve a sense of regulation in international relations.

One particular analogy that has been used to illustrate the general nature of customary law was considered by de Visscher. He likened the growth of custom to the gradual formation of a road across vacant land. After an initial uncertainty as to direction, the majority of users begin to follow the same line which becomes a single path. Not long elapses before that path is transformed into a road accepted as the only regular way, even though it is not possible to state at which precise moment this latter change occurs. And so it is with the formation of a custom. De Visscher develops this idea by reflecting that just as some make heavier footprints than others due to their greater weight, the more influential states of the world mark the way with more vigour and tend to become the guarantors and defenders of the way forward.

The reasons why a particular state acts in a certain way are varied but are closely allied to how it perceives its interests. This in turn depends upon the power and role of the state and its international standing. Accordingly, custom should to some extent mirror the perceptions of the majority of states, since it is based upon usages which are practised by nations as they express their power and their hopes and fears. But it is inescapable that some states are more influential and powerful than others and that their activities should be regarded as of greater significance. This is reflected in international law so that custom may be created by a few states, provided those states are intimately connected with the issue at hand, whether because of their wealth and power or because of their special relationship with the subject-matter of the practice, as for example maritime nations and sea law. Law cannot be divorced from politics or power and this is one instance of that proposition.

The influence of the United Kingdom, for example, on the development of the law of the sea and prize law in the nineteenth century when it was at the height of its power, was predominant. A number of propositions later accepted as part of international customary law appeared this way. Among many instances of this, one can point to navigation procedures. Similarly, the impact of the Soviet Union (now Russia) and the United States on space law has been paramount.

One can conclude by stating that for a custom to be accepted and recognised it must have the concurrence of the major powers in that particular field. A regulation regarding the breadth of the territorial sea is unlikely to be treated as law if the great maritime nations do not agree to or acquiesce in it, no matter how many land-locked states demand it. Other countries may propose ideas and institute pressure, but without the concurrence of those most interested, it cannot amount to a rule of customary law. This follows from the nature of the international system where all may participate but the views of those with greater power carry greater weight.

Accordingly, the duration and generality of a practice may take second place to the relative importance of the states precipitating the formation of a new customary rule in any given field. Universality is not required, but some correlation with power is. Some degree of continuity must be maintained but this again depends upon the context of operation and the nature of the usage.

Those elements reflect the external manifestations of a practice and establish that it is in existence and exhibited as such. That does not mean that it is law and this factor will be considered in the next subsection. But it does mean that all states who take the trouble can discover its existence. This factor of conspicuousness emphasises both the importance of the context within which the usage operates and the more significant elements of the overt act which affirms the existence of a custom.

The question is raised at this stage of how significant a failure to act is. Just how important is it when a state, or, more particularly, a major state, does not participate in a practice? Can it be construed as acquiescence in the performance of the usage? Or, on the other hand, does it denote indifference implying the inability of the practice to become a custom until a decision one way or the other has been made? Failures to act are in themselves just as much evidence of a state's attitudes as are actions. They similarly reflect the way in which a nation approaches its environment. Britain consistently fails to attack France, while Chad consistently fails to send a man to the moon. But does this mean that Britain recognises a rule not to attack its neighbour and that Chad accepts a custom not to launch rockets to the moon? Of course, the answer is in the first instance yes, and in the second example no. Thus, a failure to act can arise from either a legal obligation not to act, or an incapacity or unwillingness in the particular circumstances to act. Indeed, it has been maintained that the continued habit of not taking actions in certain situations may lead to the formation of a legal rule.

The danger of saying that a failure to act over a long period creates a negative custom, that is, a rule actually not to do it, can be shown by remarking the absurdity of the proposition that a continual failure to act until the late 1950s is evidence of a legal rule not to send artificial satellites or rockets into space. On the other hand, where a particular rule of behaviour is established it can be argued that abstention from protest by states may amount to agreement with that rule.

In the particular circumstances of the *Lotus* case the Permanent Court of International Justice, the predecessor of the International Court of Justice, laid down a high standard by declaring that abstention could only give rise to the recognition of a custom if it was based on a conscious duty to abstain. In other words, states had actually to be aware that they were not acting a particular way because they were under a definite obligation not to act that way. The decision has been criticised and would appear to cover categories of non-acts based on legal obligations, but not to refer to instances where, by simply not acting as against a particular rule in existence, states are tacitly accepting the legality and relevance of that rule.

It should be mentioned, however, that acquiescence must be based upon full knowledge of the rule invoked. Where a failure to take a course of action is in some way connected or influenced or accompanied by a lack of knowledge of all the relevant circumstances, then it cannot be interpreted as acquiescence.

What is state practice?

Some of the ingredients of state activities have been surveyed and attempts made to place them in some kind of relevant context. But what is state practice? Does it cover every kind of behaviour initiated by the state, or is it limited to actual, positive actions? To put it more simply, does it include such things as speeches, informal documents and governmental statements or is it restricted to what states actually do?

It is how states behave in practice that forms the basis of customary law, but evidence of what a state does can be obtained from numerous sources. A state is not a living entity, but consists of governmental departments and thousands of officials, and state activity is spread throughout a whole range of national organs. There are the state's legal officers, legislative institutions, courts, diplomatic agents and political leaders. Each of these engages in activity which relates to the international field and therefore one has to examine all such material sources and more in order to discover evidence of what states do.

The obvious way to find out how countries are behaving is to read the newspapers, consult historical records, listen to what governmental authorities are saying and peruse the many official publications. There are also memoirs of various past leaders, official manuals on legal questions, diplomatic interchanges and the opinions of national legal advisors. All these methods are valuable in seeking to determine actual state practice.

In addition, one may note resolutions in the General Assembly, comments made by governments on drafts produced by the International Law Commission, decisions of the international judicial institutions, decisions of national courts, treaties and the general practice of international organisations.

International organisations in fact may be instrumental in the creation of customary law. For example, the Advisory Opinion of the International Court of Justice declaring that the United Nations possessed international personality was partly based on the actual behavior of the UN. The International Law Commission has pointed out that "records of the cumulative practice of international organisations may be regarded as evidence of customary international law with reference to states' relations to the organizations."

States' municipal laws may in certain circumstances form the basis of customary rules. In the *Scotia* case decided by the US Supreme Court in 1871, a British ship had sunk an American vessel on the high seas. The Court held that British navigational procedures established by an Act of Parliament formed the basis of the relevant international custom since other states had legislated in virtually identical terms. Accordingly, the American vessel, in not displaying the correct lights, was at fault. The view has also been expressed that mere claims as distinct from actual physical acts cannot constitute state practice. This is based on the precept that "until it [a state] takes enforcement action, the claim has little value as a prediction of what the state will actually do." But as has been demonstrated this is decidedly a minority view. Claims and conventions of states in various contexts have been adduced as evidence of state practice and it is logical that this should be so, though the weight to be attached to such claims, may, of course, vary according to the circumstances. This approach is clearly the correct one since the process of claims and counterclaims is one recognised method by which states communicate to each other their perceptions of the status of international rules and norms. In this sense they operate in the same way as physical acts. Whether *in abstracto* or with regard to a particular situation, they constitute the raw material out of which may be fashioned rules of international law. It is suggested that the formulation that "state practice covers any act or statements by a state from which views about customary law may be inferred," is substantially correct. However, it should be noted that not all elements of practice are equal in their weight and the value to be given to state conduct will depend upon its nature and provenance.

Opinio juris

Once one has established the existence of a specified usage, it becomes necessary to consider how the state views its own behaviour. Is it to be regarded as a moral or political or legal act or statement? The *opinio juris*, or belief that a state activity is legally obligatory, is the factor which turns the usage into a custom and renders it part of the rules of international law. To put it slightly differently, states will behave a certain way because they are convinced it is binding upon them to do so.

The Permanent Court of International Justice expressed this point of view when it dealt with the *Lotus* case. The issue at hand concerned a collision on the high seas (where international law applies) between the *Lotus,* a French ship, and the *Boz-Kourt,* a Turkish ship. Several people aboard the latter ship were drowned and Turkey alleged negligence by the French officer of the watch. When the *Lotus* reached Istanbul, the French officer was arrested on a charge of manslaughter and the case turned on whether Turkey had jurisdiction to try him. Among the various arguments adduced, the French maintained that there existed a rule of customary law to the effect that the flag state of the accused (France) had exclusive jurisdiction in such cases and that accordingly the national state of the victim (Turkey) was barred from trying him. To justify this, France referred to the absence of previous criminal prosecutions by such states in similar situations and from this deduced tacit consent in the practice which therefore became a legal custom.

The Court rejected this and declared that even if such a practice of abstention from instituting criminal proceedings could be proved in fact, it would not amount to a custom. It held that "only if such abstention were based on their [the states] being conscious of a duty to abstain would it be possible to speak of an international custom." Thus the essential ingredient of obligation was lacking and the practice remained a practice, nothing more.

A similar approach occurred in the *North Sea Continental Shelf* cases. In the general process of delimiting the continental shelf of the North Sea in pursuance of oil and gas exploration, lines were drawn dividing the whole area into national spheres. However, West Germany could not agree with either Holland or Denmark over the respective boundary lines and the matter came before the International Court of Justice.

Article 6 of the Geneva Convention on the Continental Shelf of 1958 provided that where agreement could not be reached, and unless special circumstances justified a different approach, the boundary line was to be determined in accordance with the principle of equidistance from the nearest points of the baselines from which the breadth of the territorial sea of each state is measured. This would mean a series of lines drawn at the point where Germany met Holland on the one side and Denmark on the other and projected outwards into the North Sea. However, because Germany's coastline is concave, such equidistant lines would converge and enclose a relatively small triangle of the North Sea. The Federal Republic had signed but not ratified the 1958 Geneva Convention and was therefore not bound by its terms. The question thus was whether a case could be made out that the "equidistance-special circumstances principle" had been absorbed into customary law and was accordingly binding upon Germany.

The Court concluded in the negative and held that the provision in the Geneva Convention did not reflect an already existing custom. It was emphasised that when the International Law Commission had considered this point in the draft treaty which formed the basis of discussion at Geneva, the principle of equidistance had been proposed with considerable hesitation, somewhat on an experimental basis and not at all as an emerging rule of customary international law. The issue then turned on whether practice subsequent to the Convention had created a customary rule. The Court answered in the negative and declared that although time was not of itself a decisive factor (only three years had elapsed before the proceedings were brought):

> an indispensable requirement would be that within the period in question, short though it might be, state practice, including that of states whose interests are specially affected, should have been both extensive and virtually uniform in the sense of the provision invoked, and should moreover have occurred in such a way as to show a general recognition that a rule of law or legal obligation is involved.

This approach was maintained by the Court in the *Nicaragua* case and express reference made to the *North Sea Continental Shelf* cases. The Court noted that:

> for a new customary rule to be formed, not only must the acts concerned 'amount to a settled practice,' but they must be accompanied by the *opinio juris sive necessitatis.* Either the States taking such action or other States in a position to react to it, must have behaved so that their conduct is 'evidence of a belief that this practice is rendered obligatory by the existence of a rule of law requiring it. The need for such a belief, i.e. the existence of a subjective element, is implicit in the very notion of the *opinio juris sive necessitatis.*'

It is thus clear that the Court has adopted and maintained a high threshold with regard to the overt proving of the subjective constituent of customary law formation.

The great problem connected with the *opinio juris* is that if it calls for behaviour in accordance with law, how can new customary rules be created since that obviously requires action different from or contrary to what until then is regarded as law? If a country claims a 3 mile territorial sea in the belief that this is legal, how can the rule be changed in customary law to allow claims of, for example, 12 miles since that cannot also be in accordance with prevailing law? Obviously if one takes a restricted view of the psychological aspects, then logically the law will become stultified and this demonstrably has not happened.

Thus, one has to treat the matter in terms of a process whereby states behave in a certain way in the belief that such behaviour is law or is becoming law. It will then depend upon how other states react as to whether this process of legislation is accepted or rejected. It follows that rigid definitions as to legality have to be modified to see whether the legitimating stamp of state activity can be provided or not. If a state proclaims a 12 mile limit to its territorial sea in the belief that although the 3 mile limit has been accepted law, the circumstances are so altering that a 12 mile limit might now be treated as becoming law, it is vindicated if other states follow suit and a new rule of customary law is established. If other states reject the proposition, then the projected rule withers away and the original rule stands, reinforced by state practice and common acceptance. As the Court itself noted in the *Nicaragua* case, "[r]eliance by a State on a novel right or an unprecedented exception to the principle might, if shared in principle by other States, tend towards a modification of customary international law." The difficulty in this kind of approach is that it is sometimes hard to pinpoint exactly when one rule supersedes another, but that is a complication inherent in the nature of custom. Change is rarely smooth but rather spasmodic.

This means taking a more flexible view of the *opinio juris* and tying it more firmly with the overt manifestations of a custom into the context of national and international behaviour. This should be done to accommodate the idea of an action which, while contrary to law, contains the germ of a new law and relates to the difficulty of actually proving that a state, in behaving a certain way, does so in the belief that it is in accordance with the law. An extreme expression of this approach is to infer or deduce the *opinio juris* from the material acts. Judge

Tanaka, in his Dissenting Opinion in the *North Sea Continental Shelf* cases, remarked that there was:

> no other way than to ascertain the existence of *opinio juris* from the fact of the external existence of a certain custom and its necessity felt in the international community, rather than to seek evidence as to the subjective motives for each example of State practice.

However, states must be made aware that when one state takes a course of action, it does so because it regards it as within the confines of international law, and not as, for example, purely a political or moral gesture. There has to be an aspect of legality about the behaviour and the acting state will have to confirm that this is so, so that the international community can easily distinguish legal from non-legal practices. This is essential to the development and presentation of a legal framework amongst the states.

Protest, acquiescence and change in customary law

Customary law is thus established by virtue of a pattern of claim, absence of protest by states particularly interested in the matter at hand and acquiescence by other states. Together with related notions such as recognition, admissions and estoppel, such conduct or abstinence from conduct forms part of a complex framework within which legal principles are created and deemed applicable to states.

The Chamber of the International Court in the *Gulf of Maine* case defined acquiescence as "equivalent to tacit recognition manifested by unilateral conduct which the other party may interpret as consent" and as founded upon the principles of good faith and equity. Generally, where states are seen to acquiesce in the behaviour of other states without protesting against them, the assumption must be that such behaviour is accepted as legitimate.

Some writers have maintained that acquiescence can amount to consent to a customary rule and that the absence of protest implies agreement. In other words where a state or states take action which they declare to be legal, the silence of other states can be used as an expression of *opinio juris* or concurrence in the new legal rule. This means that actual protests are called for to break the legitimising process.

In the *Lotus* case, the Court held that "only if such abstention were based on their [the states] being conscious of having a duty to abstain would it be possible to speak of an international custom." Thus, one cannot infer a rule prohibiting certain action merely because states do not indulge in that activity. But the question of not reacting when a state behaves in a certain way is a slightly different one. It would seem that where a new rule is created in new fields of international law, for example space law, acquiescence by other states is to be regarded as reinforcing the rule whether it stems from actual agreement or lack of interest, depending always upon the particular circumstances of the case. Acquiescence in a new rule which deviates from an established custom is more problematic.

The decision in the *Anglo-Norwegian Fisheries* case may appear to suggest that where a state acts contrary to an established customary rule and other states acquiesce in this, then that state is to be treated as not bound by the original rule. The Court noted that "in any event the . . . rule would appear to be inapplicable as against Norway inasmuch as she had always opposed any attempt to apply it to the Norwegian coast." In other words, a state opposing the existence of a custom from its inception would not be bound by it, but the problem of one or more states seeking to dissent from recognised customs by adverse behaviour coupled with the acquiescence or non-reaction of other states remains unsettled.

States fail to protest for very many reasons. A state might not wish to give offence gratuitously or it might wish to reinforce political ties or other diplomatic and political considerations may be relevant. It could be that to protest over every single act with which a state does not agree would be an excessive requirement. It is, therefore, unrealistic to expect every state to react to every single act of every other state. If one accepted that a failure to protest validated a derogation from an established custom in every case then scores of special relationships would emerge between different states depending upon acquiescence and protest. In many cases a protest might be purely formal or part of diplomatic manoeuvring designed to exert pressure in a totally different field and thus not intended to alter legal relationships.

Where a new rule which contradicts a prior rule is maintained by a large number of states, the protests of a few states would not overrule it, and the abstention from reaction by other countries would merely reinforce it. Constant protest on the part of a particular state when reinforced by the acquiescence of other states might create a recognised exception to the rule, but it will depend to a great extent on the facts of the situation and the views of the international community. Behaviour contrary to a custom contains within itself the seeds of a new rule and if it is endorsed by other nations, the previous law will disappear and be replaced, or alternatively there could be a period of time during which the two customs co-exist until one of them is generally accepted, as was the position for many years with regard to the limits of the territorial sea. It follows from the above, therefore, that customary rules are binding upon all states except for such states as have dissented from the start of that custom. This raises the question of new states and custom, for the logic of the traditional approach would be for such states to be bound by all existing customs as at the date of independence. The opposite view, based upon the consent theory of law, would permit such states to choose which customs to adhere to at that stage, irrespective of the attitude of other states. However, since such an approach could prove highly disruptive, the proviso is often made that by entering into relations without reservation with other states, new states signify their acceptance of the totality of international law.

Regional and local custom

It is possible for rules to develop which will bind only a set group of states, such as those in Latin America, or indeed just two states. Such an approach may be seen as part of the need for "respect for regional legal traditions."

In the *Asylum* case, the International Court of Justice discussed the Colombian claim of a regional or local custom peculiar to the Latin American states, which would validate its position over the granting of asylum. The Court declared that the "party which relies on a custom of this kind must prove that this custom is established in such a manner that it has become binding on the other party." It found that such a custom could not be proved because of uncertain and contradictory evidence.

In such cases, the standard of proof required, especially as regards the obligation accepted by the party against whom the local custom is maintained, is higher than in cases where an ordinary or general custom is alleged.

In the *Right of Passage over Indian Territory* case, Portugal claimed that there existed a right of passage over Indian territory as between the Portuguese enclaves, and this was upheld by the International Court of Justice over India's objections that no local custom could be established between only two states. The Court declared that it was satisfied that there had in the past existed a constant and uniform practice allowing free passage and that the "practice was accepted as law by the parties and has given rise to a right and a correlative obligation."

Such local customs therefore depend upon a particular activity by one state being accepted by the other state (or states) as an expression of a legal obligation or right. While in the case of a general customary rule the process of consensus is at work so that a majority or a substantial minority of interested states can be sufficient to create a new custom, a local custom needs the positive acceptance of both (or all) parties to the rule. This is because local customs are an exception to the general nature of customary law, which involves a fairly flexible approach to law-making by all states, and instead constitutes a reminder of the former theory of consent whereby states are bound only by what they assent to. Exceptions may prove the rule, but they need greater proof than the rule to establish themselves.

UNIT B	BACKGROUND DOCUMENTS FOR CHAPTER 7
	Document 3: Ian Brownlie Reading

Ian Brownlie, *Principles of Public International Law*

Pages 4-11 (Oxford University Press, New York; 5th Edition 1998).
Reprinted by permission of Oxford University Press.

Definition. Article 38 refers to "international custom, as evidence of a general practice accepted as law," and Brierly remarks that "what is sought for is a general recognition among States of a certain practice as obligatory." Although occasionally the terms are used interchangeably, "custom" and "usage" are terms of art and have different meanings. A usage is a general practice which does not reflect a legal obligation, and examples are ceremonial salutes at sea and the practice of exempting diplomatic vehicles from parking prohibitions.

Evidence. The material sources of custom are very numerous and include the following: diplomatic correspondence, policy statements, press releases, the opinions of official legal advisers, official manuals on legal questions, e.g. manuals of military law, executive decisions and practices, orders to naval forces etc., comments by governments on drafts produced by the International Law Commission, state legislation, international and national judicial decisions, recitals in treaties and other international instruments, a pattern of treaties in the same form, the practice of international organs, and resolutions relating to legal questions in the United Nations General Assembly. Obviously the value of these sources varies and much depends on the circumstances.

The elements of custom

(a) Duration. Provided the consistency and generality of a practice are proved, no particular duration is required: the passage of time will of course be a part of the evidence of generality and consistency. A long (and, much less, an immemorial) practice is not necessary, and rules relating to airspace and the

continental shelf have emerged from fairly quick maturing of practice. The International Court does not emphasize the time element as such in its practice.

(b) Uniformity, consistency of the practice. This is very much a matter of appreciation and a tribunal will have considerable freedom of determination in many cases. Complete uniformity is not required, but substantial uniformity is, and thus in the *Fisheries* case the Court refused to accept the existence of a ten-mile rule for bays.

The leading pronouncements by the Court appear in the judgment in the *Asylum* case:

> The party which relies on a custom . . . must prove that this custom is established in such a manner that it has become binding on the other party . . . that the rule invoked . . . is in accordance with a constant and uniform usage practised by the States in question, and that this usage is the expression of a right appertaining to the State granting asylum and a duty incumbent on the territorial State. This follows from Article 38 of the Statute of the Court, which refers to international custom 'as evidence of a general practice accepted as law.'
>
> The facts brought to the knowledge of the Court disclose so much uncertainty and contradiction, so much fluctuation and discrepancy in the exercise of diplomatic asylum and in the official views expressed on different occasions; there has been so much inconsistency in the rapid succession of conventions on asylum, ratified by some States and rejected by others, and the practice has been so much influenced by considerations of political expediency in the various cases, that it is not possible to discern in all this any constant and uniform usage, accepted as law. . . .

(c) Generality of the practice. This is an aspect which complements that of consistency. Certainly universality is not required, but the real problem is to determine the value of abstention from protest by a substantial number of states in face of a practice followed by some others. Silence may denote either tacit agreement or a simple lack of interest in the issue. It may be that the Court in the *Lotus* case misjudged the consequences of absence of protest and also the significance of fairly general abstention from prosecutions by states other than the flag state. In the *Fisheries Jurisdiction* case (*United Kingdom* v. *Iceland*) the International Court referred to the extension of a fishery zone up to a twelve-mile limit "which appears now to be generally accepted" and to "an increasing and widespread acceptance of the concept of preferential rights for coastal states" in a situation of special dependence on coastal fisheries.

(d) Opinio juris et necessitatis. The Statute of the International Court refers to "a general practice *accepted as law.*" Brierly speaks of recognition by states of a certain practice "as obligatory," and Hudson requires a "conception that the practice is required by, or consistent with, prevailing international law." Some writers do not consider this psychological element to be a requirement for the

formation of custom, but it is in fact a necessary ingredient. The sense of legal obligation, as opposed to motives of courtesy, fairness, or morality, is real enough, and the practice of states recognizes a distinction between obligation and usage. The essential problem is surely one of proof, and especially the incidence of the burden of proof.

In terms of the practice of the International Court of Justice—which provides a general guide to the nature of the problem—there are two methods of approach. In many cases the Court is willing to assume the existence of an *opinio juris* on the bases of evidence of a general practice, or a consensus in the literature, or the previous determinations of the Court or other international tribunals. However, in a significant minority of cases the Court has adopted a more rigorous approach and has called for more positive evidence of the recognition of the validity of the rules in question in the practice of states. The choice of approach appears to depend upon the nature of the issues (that is, the state of the law may be a primary point in contention), and the discretion of the Court.

Three cases have involved the more exacting second method of approach, of which the first was the *Lotus,* in which the Permanent Court said:

> Even if the rarity of the judicial decisions to be found among the reported cases were sufficient to prove in point of fact the circumstances alleged by the Agent for the French Government, it would merely show that States had often, in practice, abstained from instituting criminal proceedings, and not that they recognized themselves as being obliged to do so; for only if such abstention were based on their being conscious of a duty to abstain would it be possible to speak of an international custom. The alleged fact does not allow one to infer that States have been conscious of having such a duty; on the other hand . . . there are other circumstances calculated to show that the contrary is true.

Presumably the same principles should apply to both positive conduct and abstention, yet in the *Lotus* the Court was not ready to accept continuous conduct as prima facie evidence of a legal duty and required a high standard of proof of the issue of *opinio juris.*

In the *North Sea Continental Shelf Cases* the International Court was also strict in requiring proof of the *opinio juris.* The Court did not presume the existence of *opinio juris* either in the context of the argument that the equidistance-special circumstances basis of delimiting the continental shelf had become a part of general or customary law at the date of the Geneva Convention of 1958, or in relation to the proposition that the *subsequent* practice of states based upon the Convention had produced a customary rule. However, it is incorrect to regard the precise findings as in all respects incompatible with the view that the existence of a general practice raises a presumption of *opinio juris.* In regard to the position *before* the Convention concerning the equidistance principle, there was little "practice" apart from the records of the International Law Commission, which revealed the experimental aspect of the principle prior to 1958. In considering the argument that practice *based upon* the Convention had produced a customary rule the Court made it clear that its unfavourable reception to the argument rested primarily upon two factors: (*a*) the peculiar form of the equidistance principle in Article 6 of the Convention was such that the rules were not of a norm creating character; (*b*) the Convention had only been in force for less than three years when the proceedings were brought and consequently:

> Although the passage of only a short period of time is not necessarily, or of itself, a bar to the formation of a new rule of customary international law on the basis of what was originally a purely conventional rule, an indispensable requirement would be that within the period in question, short though it might be, State practice, including that of States whose interests are specially affected, should have been both extensive and virtually uniform in the sense of the provision invoked;—and should moreover have occurred in such a way as to show a general recognition that a rule of law or legal obligation is involved.

Nevertheless, the general tenor of the Judgment is hostile to the presumption as to *opinio juris* and the Court quoted the passage from the *Lotus* case set out above.

A broadly similar approach was adopted by the Judgment of the Court in the *Case of Nicaragua* v. *United States* (Merits), and the Court expressly referred to the *North Sea Cases:*

> In considering the instances of the conduct above described, the Court has to emphasize that, as was observed in the *North Sea Continental Shelf* cases, for a new customary rule to be formed, not only must the acts concerned 'amount to a settled practice,' but they must be accompanied by the *opinio juris sive necessitatis.* Either the States taking such action or other States in a position to react to it, must have behaved so that their conduct is 'evidence of a belief that this practice is rendered obligatory by the existence of a rule of law requiring it. The need for such a belief, i.e., the existence of a subjective element, is implicit in the very notion of the *opinio juris sive necessitatis.*'

Bilateral relations and local customs. In the case concerning *U.S. Nationals in Morocco* the Court quoted the first of the passages from the *Asylum* case quoted earlier and continued: "In the present case there has not been sufficient evidence to enable the Court to reach a conclusion that a right to exercise consular jurisdiction founded upon custom or usage has been established *in such a manner that it has become binding on Morocco.*"

In this case the Court may seem to have confused the question of law-making and the question of opposability, i.e. the specific relations of the United States and Morocco. The fact is that general formulae concerning custom do not necessarily help in penetrating the complexities of the particular case. The case concerning a *Right of Passage over Indian Territory* raised an issue of bilateral relations, the existence of a local custom in favour of Portugal in respect of territorial enclaves inland from the port of Daman (Damão). In this type of case the general law is to be varied and the proponent of the special right has to give affirmative proof of a sense of obligation on the part of the territorial sovereign: *opinio juris* is here not to be presumed on the basis of continuous practice and the notion of *opinio juris* merges into the principle of acquiescence.

The persistent objector. The way in which, as a matter of practice, custom resolves itself into a question of special relations is illustrated further by the rule that a state may contract out of a custom in the process of formation. Evidence of objection must be clear and there is probably a presumption of acceptance which is to be rebutted. Whatever the theoretical underpinnings of the principle, it is well recognized by international tribunals, and in the practice of states. Given the majoritarian tendency of international relations the principle is likely to have increased prominence.

The subsequent objector. In the *Fisheries* case part of the Norwegian argument was that certain rules were not rules of general international law, and, even if they were, they did not bind Norway, which had "consistently and unequivocally manifested a refusal to accept them." The United Kingdom admitted the general principle of the Norwegian argument here while denying that, as a matter of fact, Norway had consistently and unequivocally manifested a refusal to accept the rules. Thus the United Kingdom regarded the question as one of persistent objection. The Court did not deal with the issue in this way, however, and the *ratio* in this respect was that Norway had departed from the alleged rules, if they existed, *and other states had acquiesced* in this practice. But the Court is not too explicit about the role of acquiescence in validating a subsequent contracting out of rules. Here one has to face the problem of change in a customary regime. Presumably, if a substantial number of states assert a new rule, the momentum of increased defection, complemented by acquiescence, may result in a new rule, as in the case of the law on the continental shelf. If the process is slow and neither the new rule nor the old have a majority of adherents then the consequence is a network of special relations based on opposability, acquiescence, and historic title.

Proof of custom. In principle a court is presumed to know the law and may apply a custom even if it has not been expressly pleaded. In practice the proponent of a custom has a burden of proof the nature of which will vary according to the subject-matter and the form of the pleadings. Thus in the *Lotus* case the Court spoke of the plaintiff's burden in respect of a general custom. Where a local or regional custom is alleged, the proponent "must prove that this custom is established in such a manner that it has become binding on the other Party."

UNIT B

BACKGROUND DOCUMENTS FOR CHAPTER 8

Document 1: New York Convention

CONVENTION ON THE RECOGNITION AND ENFORCEMENT OF FOREIGN ARBITRAL AWARDS

June 10, 1958, 330 U.N.T.S. 3 (June 27, 1959).

Article I

1. This Convention shall apply to the recognition and enforcement of arbitral awards made in the territory of a State other than the State where the recognition and enforcement of such awards are sought, and arising out of differences between persons, whether physical or legal. It shall also apply to arbitral awards not considered as domestic awards in the State where their recognition and enforcement are sought.

2. The term "arbitral awards" shall include not only awards made by arbitrators appointed for each case but also those made by permanent arbitral bodies to which the parties have submitted.

3. When signing, ratifying or acceding to this Convention, or notifying extension under Article X hereof, any State may on the basis of reciprocity declare that it will apply the Convention to the recognition and enforcement of awards made only in the territory of another Contracting State. It may also declare that it will apply the Convention only to differences arising out of legal relationships, whether contractual or not, which are considered as commercial under the national law of the State making such declaration.

Article II

1. Each Contracting State shall recognize an agreement in writing under which the parties undertake to submit to arbitration all or any differences which have arisen or which may arise between them in respect of a defined legal relationship, whether contractual or not, concerning a subject matter capable of settlement by arbitration.

2. The term "agreement in writing" shall include an arbitral clause in a contract or an arbitration agreement, signed by the parties or contained in an exchange of letters or telegrams.

3. The court of a Contracting State, when seized of an action in a matter in respect of which the parties have made an agreement within the meaning of this Article, shall, at the request of one of the parties, refer the parties to arbitration, unless it finds that the said agreement is null and void, inoperative or incapable of being performed.

Article III

Each Contracting State shall recognize arbitral awards as binding and enforce them in accordance with the rules of procedure of the territory where the award is relied upon, under the conditions laid down in the following Articles. There shall not be imposed substantially more onerous conditions or higher fees or charges on the recognition or enforcement of arbitral awards to which this Convention applies than are imposed on the recognition or enforcement of domestic arbitral awards.

Article IV

1. To obtain the recognition and enforcement mentioned in the preceding Article, the party applying for recognition and enforcement shall, at the time of the application, supply:

    (a) The duly authenticated original award or a duly certified copy thereof;

    (b) The original agreement referred to in Article II or a duly certified copy thereof.

2. If said award or agreement is not made in an official language of the country in which the award is relied upon, the party applying for recognition and enforcement of the award shall produce a translation of these

documents into such language. The translation shall be certified by an official or sworn translator or by a diplomatic or consular agent.

Article V

1. Recognition and enforcement of the award may be refused, at the request of the party against whom it is invoked, only if that party furnishes to the competent authority where the recognition and enforcement is sought, proof that:

    (a) The parties to the agreement referred to in Article II were, under the law applicable to them, under some incapacity, or the said agreement is not valid under the law to which the parties have subjected it or, failing any indication thereon, under the law of the country where the award was made; or

    (b) The party against whom the award is invoked was not given proper notice of the appointment of the arbitrator or of the arbitration proceedings or was otherwise unable to present his case; or

    (c) The award deals with a difference not contemplated by or not falling within the terms of the submission to arbitration, or it contains decisions on matters beyond the scope of the submission to arbitration, provided that, if the decisions on matters submitted to arbitration can be separated from those not so submitted, that part of the award which contains decisions on matters submitted to arbitration may be recognized and enforced; or

    (d) The composition of the arbitral authority or the arbitral procedure was not in accordance with the agreement of the parties, or, failing such agreement, was not in accordance with the law of the country where the arbitration took place; or

    (e) The award has not yet become binding on the parties, or has been set aside or suspended by a competent authority of the country in which, or under the law of which, that award was made.

2. Recognition and enforcement of an arbitral award may also be refused if the competent authority in the country where recognition and enforcement is sought finds that:

(a) The subject matter of the difference is not capable of settlement by arbitration under the law of the country; or

(b) The recognition and enforcement of the award would be contrary to the public policy of that country.

Article VI

If an application for the setting aside or suspension of the award has been made to a competent authority referred to in Article V (1) (e), the authority before which the award is sought to be relied upon may, if it considers it proper, adjourn the decision on the enforcement of the award and may also, on the application of the party claiming enforcement of the award, order the other party to give suitable security.

Article VII

1. The provisions of the present Convention shall not affect the validity of multilateral or bilateral agreements concerning the recognition and enforcement of arbitral awards entered into by the Contracting States nor deprive any interested party of any right he may have to avail himself of an arbitral award in the manner and to the extent allowed by the law or the treaties of the country where such award is sought to be relied upon.

2. The Geneva Protocol on Arbitration Clauses of 1923 and the Geneva Convention on the Execution of Foreign Arbitral Awards of 1927 shall cease to have effect between Contracting States on their becoming bound and to the extent that they become bound, by this Convention.

Article VIII

1. This Convention shall be open until 31 December 1958 for signature on behalf of any Member of the United Nations and also on behalf of any other State which is or hereafter becomes a member of any specialized agency of the United Nations, or which is or hereafter becomes a party to the Statute of the International Court of Justice, or any other State to which an invitation has been addressed by the General Assembly of the United Nations.

2. This Convention shall be ratified and the instrument of ratification shall be deposited with the Secretary-General of the United Nations.

Article IX

1. This Convention shall be open for accession to all States referred to in Article VIII.

2. Accession shall be effected by the deposit of an instrument of accession with the Secretary-General of the United Nations.

Article X

1. Any State may, at the time of signature, ratification or accession, declare that this Convention shall extend to all or any of the territories for the international relations of which it is responsible. Such a declaration shall take effect when the Convention enters into force for the State concerned.

2. At any time thereafter any such extension shall be made by notification addressed to the Secretary-General of the United Nations and shall take effect as from the ninetieth day after the day of receipt by the Secretary-General of the United Nations of this notification, or as from the date of entry into force of the Convention for the State concerned, whichever is later.

3. With respect to those territories to which this Convention is not extended at the time of signature, ratification or accession, each State concerned shall consider the possibility of taking the necessary steps in order to extend the application of this Convention to such territories, subject, where necessary for constitutional reasons, to the consent of the Governments of such territories.

Article XI

In the case of a federal or non-unitary State, the following provisions shall apply:

(a) With respect to those Articles of this Convention that come within the legislative jurisdiction of the federal authority, the obligations of the federal Government shall to this extent be the same as those of Contracting States which are not federal States;

(b) With respect to those Articles of this Convention that come within the legislative jurisdiction of constituent states or provinces which are not, under the constitutional system of the federation, bound to take legislative action, the federal Government shall bring such Articles with a favourable recommendation to the notice of the appropriate authorities of constituent states or provinces at the earliest possible moment;

(c) A federal State Party to this Convention shall, at the request of any other Contracting State transmitted through the Secretary-General of the United Nations, supply a statement of the law and practice of the federation and its constituent units in regard to any particular provision of this Convention, showing the extent to which effect has been given to that provision by legislative or other action.

Article XII

1. This Convention shall come into force on the ninetieth day following the date of deposit of the third instrument of ratification or accession.

2. For each State ratifying or acceding to this Convention after the deposit of the third instrument of ratification or accession, this Convention shall enter into force on the ninetieth day after deposit by such State of its instrument of ratification or accession.

Article XIII

1. Any Contracting State may denounce this Convention by written notification to the Secretary-General of the United Nations. Denunciation shall take effect one year after the date of receipt of the notification by the Secretary-General.

2. Any State which has made a declaration or notification under Article X may, at any time thereafter, by notification to the Secretary-General of the United Nations, declare that this Convention shall cease to extend to the territory concerned one year after the date of the receipt of the notification by the Secretary-General.

3. This Convention shall continue to be applicable to arbitral awards in respect of which recognition and enforcement proceedings have been instituted before the denunciation takes effect.

Article XIV

A Contracting State shall not be entitled to avail itself of the present Convention against other Contracting States except to the extent that it is itself bound to apply the Convention.

Article XV

The Secretary-General of the United Nations shall notify the States contemplated in Article VIII of the following:

(a) Signatures and ratifications in accordance with Article VIII;

(b) Accessions in accordance with Article IX;

(c) Declarations and notifications under Articles I, X, XI;

(d) The date upon which this Convention enters into force in accordance with Article XII;

(e) Denunciations and notifications in accordance with Article XIII.

Article XVI

1. This Convention, of which the Chinese, English, French, Russian, and Spanish texts shall be equally authentic, shall be deposited in the archives of the United Nations.

2. The Secretary-General of the United Nations shall transmit a certified copy of this Convention to the States contemplated in Article VIII.

UNIT B

BACKGROUND DOCUMENTS FOR CHAPTER 8

Document 2: ICC Arbitration Rules

RULES OF ARBITRATION OF THE INTERNATIONAL CHAMBER OF COMMERCE

In force as from January 1, 1998, as corrected.

INTRODUCTORY PROVISIONS

Article 1. International Court of Arbitration

1. The International Court of Arbitration (the "Court") of the International Chamber of Commerce (the "ICC") is the arbitration body attached to the ICC. . . . Members of the Court are appointed by the World Council of the ICC. The function of the Court is to provide for the settlement by arbitration of business disputes of an international character in accordance with the Rules of Arbitration of the International Chamber of Commerce (the "Rules"). If so empowered by an arbitration agreement, the Court shall also provide for the settlement by arbitration in accordance with these Rules of business disputes not of an international character.

2. The Court does not itself settle disputes. It has the function of ensuring the application of these Rules. It draws up its own Internal Rules. . . .

3. The Chairman of the Court, or, in the Chairman's absence or otherwise at his request, one of its Vice-Chairmen shall have the power to take urgent decisions on behalf of the Court, provided that any such decision is reported to the Court at its next session.

4. As provided for in its Internal Rules, the Court may delegate to one or more committees composed of its members the power to take certain decisions, provided that any such decision is reported to the Court at its next session.

5. The Secretariat of the Court (the "Secretariat") under the direction of its Secretary General (the "Secretary General") shall have its seat at the headquarters of the ICC.

Article 2. Definitions

In these Rules:

(i) "Arbitral Tribunal" includes one or more arbitrators.

(ii) "Claimant" includes one or more claimants and "Respondent" includes one or more respondents.

(iii) "Award" includes, *inter alia*, an interim, partial or final Award.

Article 3. Written Notifications or Communications; Time Limits

1. All pleadings and other written communications submitted by any party, as well as all documents annexed thereto, shall be supplied in a number of copies sufficient to provide one copy for each party, plus one for each arbitrator, and one for the Secretariat. A copy of any communication from the Arbitral Tribunal to the parties shall be sent to the Secretariat.

2. All notifications or communications from the Secretariat and the Arbitral Tribunal shall be made to the last address of the party or its representative for whom the same are intended, as notified either by the party in question or by the other party. Such notification or communication may be made by delivery against receipt, registered post, courier, facsimile transmission, telex, telegram or any other means of telecommunication that provides a record of the sending thereof.

3. A notification or communication shall be deemed to have been made on the day it was received by the party itself or by its representative, or would have been received if made in accordance with the preceding paragraph.

4. Periods of time specified in or fixed under the present Rules, shall start to run on the day following the date a notification or communication is deemed to have been made in accordance with the preceding paragraph. When the day next following such date is an official holiday, or a non-business day in the country where the notification or communication is deemed to have been made, the period of time shall commence on the first following business day. Official holidays and non-business days are included in the calculation of the period of time. If the last day of the relevant period of time granted is an official holiday or a non-business day in the country where the notification or communication is deemed to have been made, the period of time shall expire at the end of the first following business day.

COMMENCING THE ARBITRATION

Article 4. Request for Arbitration

1. A party wishing to have recourse to arbitration under these Rules shall submit its Request for Arbitration (the "Request") to the Secretariat, which shall notify the Claimant and Respondent of the receipt of the Request and the date of such receipt.

2. The date on which the Request is received by the Secretariat shall, for all purposes, be deemed to be the date of the commencement of the arbitral proceedings.

3. The Request shall, *inter alia*, contain the following information:

   (a) The name in full, description and address of each of the parties;

   (b) A description of the nature and circumstances of the dispute giving rise to the claim(s);

   (c) A statement of the relief sought, including, to the extent possible, an indication of any amount(s) claimed;

   (d) The relevant agreements and, in particular, the arbitration agreement;

(e) All relevant particulars concerning the number of arbitrators and their choice in accordance with the provisions of Articles 8, 9 and 10, and any nomination of an arbitrator required thereby; and

(f) Any comments as to the place of arbitration, the applicable rules of law and the language of the arbitration.

4. Together with the Request, the Claimant shall submit the number of copies thereof required by Article 3(1) and shall make the [required] advance payment on administrative expenses. . . . In the event that the Claimant fails to comply with either of these requirements, the Secretariat may fix a time limit within which the Claimant must comply, failing which the file shall be closed without prejudice to the right of the Claimant to submit the same claims at a later date in another Request.

5. The Secretariat shall send a copy of the Request and the documents annexed thereto to the Respondent for its Answer to the Request once the Secretariat has sufficient copies of the Request and the required advance payment.

6. When a party submits a Request in connection with a legal relationship in respect of which arbitration proceedings between the same parties are already pending under these Rules, the Court may, at the request of a party, decide to include the claims contained in the Request in the pending proceedings provided that the Terms of Reference have not been signed or approved by the Court. Once the Terms of Reference have been signed or approved by the Court, claims may only be included in the pending proceedings subject to the provisions of Article 19.

Article 5. Answer to the Request; Counterclaims

1. Within 30 days from the receipt of the Request from the Secretariat, the Respondent shall file an Answer (the "Answer") which shall, *inter alia*, contain the following information:

   (a) Its name in full, description and address;

   (b) Its comments as to the nature and circumstances of the dispute giving rise to the claim(s);

(c) Its response to the relief sought;

(d) Any comments concerning the number of arbitrators and their choice in light of the Claimant's proposals and in accordance with the provisions of Articles 8, 9 and 10, and any nomination of an arbitrator required thereby; and

(e) Any comments as to the place of arbitration, the applicable rules of law and the language of the arbitration.

2. The Secretariat may grant the Respondent an extension of the time for filing the Answer, provided the application for such an extension contains the Respondent's comments concerning the number of arbitrators and their choice and, where required by Articles 8, 9 and 10, the nomination of an arbitrator. If the Respondent fails to do so, the Court shall proceed in accordance with these Rules.

3. The Answer shall be supplied to the Secretariat in the number of copies specified by Article 3(1).

4. A copy of the Answer and the documents annexed thereto shall be communicated by the Secretariat to the Claimant.

5. Any counterclaim(s) made by the Respondent shall be filed with its Answer and shall provide:

(a) A description of the nature and circumstances of the dispute giving rise to the counterclaim(s); and

(b) A statement of the relief sought, including, to the extent possible, an indication of any amount(s) counterclaimed.

6. The Claimant shall file a Reply to any counterclaim within 30 days from the date of receipt of the counterclaim(s) communicated by the Secretariat. The Secretariat may grant the Claimant an extension of time for filing the Reply.

Article 6. Effect of the Arbitration Agreement

1. Where the parties have agreed to submit to arbitration under the Rules, they shall be deemed to have submitted *ipso facto* to the Rules in effect

on the date of commencement of the arbitration proceedings, unless they have agreed to submit to the Rules in effect on the date of their arbitration agreement.

2. If the Respondent does not file an Answer, as provided by Article 5, or if any party raises one or more pleas concerning the existence, validity or scope of the arbitration agreement, the Court may decide, without prejudice to the admissibility or merits of the plea or pleas, that the arbitration shall proceed if it is *prima facie* satisfied that an arbitration agreement under the Rules may exist. In such a case, any decision as to the jurisdiction of the Arbitral Tribunal shall be taken by the Arbitral Tribunal itself. If the Court is not so satisfied, the parties shall be notified that the arbitration cannot proceed. In such a case, any party retains the right to ask any court having jurisdiction whether or not there is a binding arbitration agreement.

3. If any of the parties refuses or fails to take part in the arbitration or any stage thereof, the arbitration shall proceed notwithstanding such refusal or failure.

4. Unless otherwise agreed, the Arbitral Tribunal shall not cease to have jurisdiction by reason of any claim that the contract is null and void or allegation that it is non-existent, provided that the Arbitral Tribunal upholds the validity of the arbitration agreement. The Arbitral Tribunal shall continue to have jurisdiction to determine the respective rights of the parties and to adjudicate their claims and pleas even though the contract itself may be non-existent or null and void.

THE ARBITRAL TRIBUNAL

Article 7. General Provisions

1. Every arbitrator must be and remain independent of the parties involved in the arbitration.

2. Before appointment or confirmation, a prospective arbitrator shall sign a statement of independence and disclose in writing to the Secretariat any facts or circumstances which might be of such a nature as to call into question the arbitrator's independence in the eyes of the parties. The Secretariat shall provide such information to the parties in writing and fix a time limit for any comments from them.

3. An arbitrator shall immediately disclose in writing to the Secretariat and to the parties any facts or circumstances of a similar nature which may arise during the arbitration.

4. The decisions of the Court as to the appointment, confirmation, challenge or replacement of an arbitrator shall be final and the reasons for such decisions shall not be communicated.

5. By accepting to serve, every arbitrator undertakes to carry out his responsibilities in accordance with these Rules.

6. Insofar as the parties have not provided otherwise, the Arbitral Tribunal shall be constituted in accordance with the provisions of Articles 8, 9 and 10.

Article 8. Number of Arbitrators

1. The disputes shall be decided by a sole arbitrator or by three arbitrators.

2. Where the parties have not agreed upon the number of arbitrators, the Court shall appoint a sole arbitrator, save where it appears to the Court that the dispute is such as to warrant the appointment of three arbitrators. In such case, the Claimant shall nominate an arbitrator within a period of 15 days from the receipt of the notification of the decision of the Court, and the Respondent shall nominate an arbitrator within a period of 15 days from the receipt of the notification of the nomination made by the Claimant.

3. Where the parties have agreed that the dispute shall be settled by a sole arbitrator, they may, by agreement, nominate the sole arbitrator for confirmation. If the parties fail to nominate a sole arbitrator within 30 days from the date when the Claimant's Request for Arbitration has been received by the other party, or within such additional time as may be allowed by the Secretariat, the sole arbitrator shall be appointed by the Court.

4. Where the dispute is to be referred to three arbitrators, each party shall nominate in the Request and the Answer, respectively, one arbitrator for confirmation. If a party fails to nominate an arbitrator, the appointment shall be made by the Court. The third arbitrator, who will act as chairman of the Arbitral Tribunal, shall be appointed by the Court, unless the parties have agreed upon another procedure for such ap-

pointment, in which case the nomination will be subject to confirmation pursuant to Article 9. Should such procedure not result in a nomination within the time limit fixed by the parties or the Court, the third arbitrator shall be appointed by the Court.

Article 9. Appointment and Confirmation of the Arbitrators

1. In confirming or appointing arbitrators, the Court shall consider the prospective arbitrator's nationality, residence and other relationships with the countries of which the parties or the other arbitrators are nationals and the prospective arbitrator's availability and ability to conduct the arbitration in accordance with these Rules. The same shall apply where the Secretary General confirms arbitrators pursuant to Article 9(2).

2. The Secretary General may confirm as co-arbitrators, sole arbitrators and chairmen of Arbitral Tribunals persons nominated by the parties or pursuant to their particular agreements, provided they have filed a statement of independence without qualification or a qualified statement of independence has not given rise to objections. Such confirmation shall be reported to the Court at its next session. If the Secretary General considers that a co-arbitrator, sole arbitrator or chairman of an Arbitral Tribunal should not be confirmed, the matter shall be submitted to the Court.

3. Where the Court is to appoint a sole arbitrator or the chairman of an Arbitral Tribunal, it shall make the appointment upon a proposal of a National Committee of the ICC that it considers to be appropriate. If the Court does not accept the proposal made, or if the National Committee fails to make the proposal requested within the time limit fixed by the Court, the Court may repeat its request or may request a proposal from another National Committee that it considers to be appropriate.

4. Where the Court considers that the circumstances so demand, it may choose the sole arbitrator or the chairman of the Arbitral Tribunal from a country where there is no National Committee, provided that neither of the parties objects within the time limit fixed by the Court.

5. The sole arbitrator or the chairman of the Arbitral Tribunal shall be of a nationality other than those of the parties. However, in suitable circumstances and provided that neither of the parties objects within the time

limit fixed by the Court, the sole arbitrator or the chairman of the Arbitral Tribunal may be chosen from a country of which any of the parties is a national.

6. Where the Court is to appoint an arbitrator on behalf of a party which has failed to nominate one, it shall make the appointment upon a proposal of the National Committee of the country of which that party is a national. If the Court does not accept the proposal made, or if the National Committee fails to make the proposal requested within the time limit fixed by the Court, or if the country of which the said party is a national has no National Committee, the Court shall be at liberty to choose any person whom it regards as suitable. The Secretariat shall inform the National Committee, if one exists, of the country of which such person is a national.

Article 10. Multiple Parties

1. Where there are multiple parties, whether as Claimant or as Respondent, and where the dispute is to be referred to three arbitrators, the multiple Claimants, jointly, and the multiple Respondents, jointly, shall nominate an arbitrator for confirmation pursuant to Article 9.

2. In the absence of such a joint nomination and where all parties are unable to agree to a method for the constitution of the Arbitral Tribunal, the Court may appoint each member of the Arbitral Tribunal and shall designate one of them to act as chairman. In such case, the Court shall be at liberty to choose any person it regards as suitable to act as arbitrator, applying Article 9 when it considers this appropriate.

Article 11. Challenge of Arbitrators

1. A challenge of an arbitrator, whether for an alleged lack of independence or otherwise, shall be made by the submission to the Secretariat of a written statement specifying the facts and circumstances on which the challenge is based.

2. For a challenge to be admissible, it must be sent by a party either within 30 days from receipt by that party of the notification of the appointment or confirmation of the arbitrator, or within 30 days from the date when the party making the challenge was informed of the facts and circumstances on which the challenge is based if such date is subsequent to the receipt of such notification.

3. The Court shall decide on the admissibility, and, at the same time, if necessary, on the merits of a challenge after the Secretariat has afforded an opportunity for the arbitrator concerned, the other party or parties and any other members of the Arbitral Tribunal to comment in writing within a suitable period of time. Such comments shall be communicated to the parties and to the arbitrators.

Article 12. Replacement of Arbitrators

1. An arbitrator shall be replaced upon his death, upon the acceptance by the Court of the arbitrator's resignation, upon acceptance by the Court of a challenge or, upon the request of all the parties.

2. An arbitrator shall also be replaced on the Court's own initiative when it decides that he is prevented *de jure* or *de facto* from fulfilling his functions, or that he is not fulfilling his functions in accordance with the Rules or within the prescribed time limits.

3. When, on the basis of information that has come to its attention, the Court considers applying Article 12(2), it shall decide on the matter after the arbitrator concerned, the parties and any other members of the Arbitral Tribunal have had an opportunity to comment in writing within a suitable period of time. Such comments shall be communicated to the parties and to the arbitrators.

4. When an arbitrator is to be replaced, the Court has discretion to decide whether or not to follow the original nominating process. Once reconstituted, and after having invited the parties to comment, the Arbitral Tribunal shall determine if and to what extent prior proceedings shall be repeated before the reconstituted Arbitral Tribunal.

5. Subsequent to the closing of the proceedings, instead of replacing an arbitrator who has died or been removed by the Court pursuant to Articles 12(1) and 12(2), the Court may decide, when it considers it appropriate, that the remaining arbitrators shall continue the arbitration. In making such determination, the Court shall take into account the views of the remaining arbitrators and of the parties and such other matters that it considers appropriate in the circumstances.

THE ARBITRAL PROCEEDINGS

Article 13. Transmission of the File to the Arbitral Tribunal

The Secretariat shall transmit the file to the Arbitral Tribunal as soon as it has been constituted, provided the advance on costs requested by the Secretariat at this stage has been paid.

Article 14. Place of the Arbitration

1. The place of the arbitration shall be fixed by the Court unless agreed upon by the parties.

2. The Arbitral Tribunal may, after consultation with the parties, conduct hearings and meetings at any location it considers appropriate unless otherwise agreed by the parties.

3. The Arbitral Tribunal may deliberate at any location it considers appropriate.

Article 15. Rules Governing the Proceedings

1. The proceedings before the Arbitral Tribunal shall be governed by these Rules, and, where these Rules are silent by any rules which the parties or, failing them, the Arbitral Tribunal may settle on, whether or not reference is thereby made to the rules of procedure of a national law to be applied to the arbitration.

2. In all cases, the Arbitral Tribunal shall act fairly and impartially and ensure that each party has a reasonable opportunity to present its case.

Article 16. Language of the Arbitration

In the absence of an agreement by the parties, the Arbitral Tribunal shall determine the language or languages of the arbitration, due regard being given to all relevant circumstances, including the language of the contract.

Article 17. Applicable Rules of Law

1. The parties shall be free to agree upon the rules of law to be applied by the Arbitral Tribunal to the merits of the dispute. In the absence of any

such agreement, the Arbitral Tribunal shall apply the rules of law which it determines to be appropriate.

2. In all cases the Arbitral Tribunal shall take account of the provisions of the contract and the relevant trade usages.

3. The Arbitral Tribunal shall assume the powers of an *amiable compositeur* or decide *ex aequo et bono* only if the parties have agreed to give it such powers.

Article 18. Terms of Reference; Procedural Timetable

1. As soon as it has received the file from the Secretariat, the Arbitral Tribunal shall draw up, on the basis of documents or in the presence of the parties and in the light of their most recent submissions, a document defining its Terms of Reference. This document shall include the following particulars:

   (a) The full names and descriptions of the parties;

   (b) The addresses of the parties to which notifications and communications arising in the course of the arbitration may be made;

   (c) A summary of the parties' respective claims and of the relief sought by each party, with an indication to the extent possible of the amounts claimed or counterclaimed;

   (d) Unless the Arbitral Tribunal considers it inappropriate, a list of issues to be determined;

   (e) The full names, descriptions and addresses of the arbitrators;

   (f) The place of the arbitration; and

   (g) Particulars of the applicable procedural rules and, if such is the case, reference to the power conferred upon the Arbitral Tribunal to act as *amiable compositeur* or to decide *ex aequo et bono*.

2. The Terms of Reference shall be signed by the parties and the Arbitral Tribunal. Within two months of the date on which the file has been transmitted to it, the Arbitral Tribunal shall transmit to the Court the Terms of Reference signed by it and by the parties. The Court may extend this time limit pursuant to a reasoned request from the Arbitral Tribunal or on its own initiative if it decides it is necessary to do so.

3. If any of the parties refuses to take part in the drawing up of the Terms of Reference or to sign the same, they shall be submitted to the Court for approval. When the Terms of Reference have been signed in accordance with Article 18(2) or approved by the Court, the arbitration shall proceed.

4. When drawing up the Terms of Reference, or as soon as possible thereafter, the Arbitral Tribunal, after having consulted the parties, shall establish in a separate document a provisional timetable that it intends to follow for the conduct of the arbitration and shall communicate it to the Court and the parties. Any subsequent modifications of the provisional timetable shall be communicated to the Court and the parties.

Article 19. New Claims

After the Terms of Reference have been signed or approved by the Court, no party shall make new claims or counterclaims which fall outside the limits of the Terms of Reference unless it has been authorized to do so by the Arbitral Tribunal, which shall consider the nature of such new claims or counterclaims, the stage of the arbitration and other relevant circumstances.

Article 20. Establishing the Facts of the Case

1. The Arbitral Tribunal shall proceed within as short a time as possible to establish the facts of the case by all appropriate means.

2. After studying the written submissions of the parties and all documents relied upon, the Arbitral Tribunal shall hear the parties together in person if any of them so requests or, failing such a request, it may of its own motion decide to hear them.

3. The Arbitral Tribunal may decide to hear witnesses, experts appointed by the parties or any other person, in the presence of the parties, or in their absence provided they have been duly summoned.

4. The Arbitral Tribunal, after having consulted the parties, may appoint one or more experts, define their terms of reference and receive their reports. At the request of a party, the parties shall be given the opportunity to question at a hearing any such expert appointed by the Tribunal.

5. At any time during the proceedings, the Arbitral Tribunal may summon any party to provide additional evidence.

6. The Arbitral Tribunal may decide the case solely on the documents submitted by the parties unless any of the parties requests a hearing.

7. The Arbitral Tribunal may take measures for protecting trade secrets and confidential information.

Article 21. Hearings

1. When a hearing is to be held, the Arbitral Tribunal, giving reasonable notice, shall summon the parties to appear before it on the day and at the place fixed by it.

2. If any of the parties, although duly summoned, fails to appear without valid excuse, the Arbitral Tribunal shall have the power to proceed with the hearing.

3. The Arbitral Tribunal shall be in full charge of the hearings, at which all the parties shall be entitled to be present. Save with the approval of the Arbitral Tribunal and the parties, persons not involved in the proceedings shall not be admitted.

4. The parties may appear in person or through duly authorized representatives. In addition, they may be assisted by advisers.

Article 22. Closing of the Proceedings

1. When it is satisfied that the parties have had a reasonable opportunity to present their cases, the Arbitral Tribunal shall declare the proceedings closed. Thereafter, no further submission or argument may be made, or evidence produced, unless requested or authorized by the Arbitral Tribunal.

2. When the Arbitral Tribunal has declared the proceedings closed, it shall indicate to the Secretariat an approximate date by which the draft Award will be submitted to the Court for approval pursuant to Article 27. Any postponement of that date shall be communicated to the Secretariat by the Arbitral Tribunal.

Article 23. Conservatory and Interim Measures

1. Unless the parties have otherwise agreed, as soon as the file has been transmitted to it, the Arbitral Tribunal may, at the request of a party, order any interim or conservatory measure it deems appropriate. The Arbitral Tribunal may make the granting of any such measure subject to appropriate security being furnished by the requesting party. Any such measure shall take the form of an order, giving reasons, or of an Award, as the Arbitral Tribunal considers appropriate.

2. Before the file is transmitted to the Arbitral Tribunal, and in appropriate circumstances even thereafter, the parties may apply to any competent judicial authority for interim or conservatory measures. The application of a party to a judicial authority for such measures or for the implementation of any such measures ordered by an Arbitral Tribunal shall not be deemed to be an infringement or a waiver of the arbitration agreement and shall not affect the relevant powers reserved to the Arbitral Tribunal. Any such application and any measures taken by the judicial authority must be notified without delay to the Secretariat. The Secretariat shall inform the Arbitral Tribunal thereof.

AWARDS

Article 24. Time Limit for the Award

1. The time limit within which the Arbitral Tribunal must render its final Award is six months. Such time limit shall start to run from the date of the last signature by the Arbitral Tribunal or of the parties of the Terms of Reference, or, in the case of application of Article 18(3), the date of the notification to the Arbitral Tribunal by the Secretariat of the approval of the Terms of Reference by the Court.

2. The Court may extend this time limit pursuant to a reasoned request from the Arbitral Tribunal or on its own initiative if it decides it is necessary to do so.

Article 25. Making of the Award

1. When the Arbitral Tribunal is composed of more than one arbitrator, an Award is given by a majority decision. If there be no majority, the Award shall be made by the chairman of the Arbitral Tribunal alone.

2. The Award shall state the reasons upon which it is based.

3. The Award shall be deemed to be made at the place of the arbitration and on the date stated therein.

Article 26. Award by Consent

If the parties reach a settlement after the file has been transmitted to the Arbitral Tribunal in accordance with Article 13, the settlement shall be recorded in the form of an Award made by consent of the parties if so requested by the parties and if the Arbitral Tribunal agrees to do so.

Article 27. Scrutiny of the Award by the Court

Before signing any Award, the Arbitral Tribunal shall submit it in draft form to the Court. The Court may lay down modifications as to the form of the Award and, without affecting the Arbitral Tribunal's liberty of decision, may also draw its attention to points of substance. No Award shall be rendered by the Arbitral Tribunal until it has been approved by the Court as to its form.

Article 28. Notification, Deposit and Enforceability of the Award

1. Once an Award has been made, the Secretariat shall notify to the parties the text signed by the Arbitral Tribunal, provided always that the costs of the arbitration have been fully paid to the ICC by the parties or by one of them.

2. Additional copies certified true by the Secretary General shall be made available on request and at any time to the parties, but to no one else.

3. By virtue of the notification made in accordance with Paragraph 1 of this Article, the parties waive any other form of notification or deposit on the part of the Arbitral Tribunal.

4. An original of each Award made in accordance with the present Rules shall be deposited with the Secretariat.

5. The Arbitral Tribunal and the Secretariat shall assist the parties in complying with whatever further formalities may be necessary.

6. Every Award shall be binding on the parties. By submitting the dispute to arbitration under these Rules, the parties undertake to carry out any Award without delay and shall be deemed to have waived their right to any form of recourse insofar as such waiver can validly be made.

Article 29. Correction and Interpretation of the Award

1. On its own initiative, the Arbitral Tribunal may correct a clerical, computational or typographical error, or any errors of similar nature contained in an Award, provided such correction is submitted for approval to the Court within 30 days of the date of such Award.

2. Any application of a party for the correction of an error of the kind referred to in Article 29(1), or for the interpretation of an Award, must be made to the Secretariat within 30 days of the receipt of the Award by such party, in a number of copies as stated in Article 3(1). After transmittal of the application to the Arbitral Tribunal, the latter shall grant the other party a short time limit, normally not exceeding 30 days, from the receipt of the application by that party to submit any comments thereon. If the Arbitral Tribunal decides to correct or interpret the Award, it shall submit its decision in draft form to the Court not later than 30 days following the expiration of the time limit for the receipt of any comments from the other party or within such other period as the Court may decide.

3. The decision to correct or to interpret the Award shall take the form of an addendum and shall constitute part of the Award. The provisions of Articles 25, 27 and 28 shall apply *mutatis mutandis*.

COSTS

Article 30. Advance to Cover the Costs of the Arbitration

1. After receipt of the Request, the Secretary General may request the Claimant to pay a provisional advance in an amount intended to cover

the costs of arbitration until the Terms of Reference have been drawn up.

2. As soon as practicable, the Court shall fix the advance on costs in an amount likely to cover the fees and expenses of the arbitrators and the ICC administrative costs for the claims and counterclaims which have been referred to it by the parties. This amount may be subject to readjustment at any time during the arbitration. Where, apart from the claims, counterclaims are submitted, the Court may fix separate advances on costs for the claims and the counterclaims.

3. The advance on costs fixed by the Court shall be payable in equal shares by the Claimant and the Respondent. Any provisional advance paid on the basis of Article 30(1) will be considered as a partial payment thereof. However, any party shall be free to pay the whole of the advance on costs in respect of the principal claim or the counterclaim should the other party fail to pay its share. When the Court has set separate advances on costs in accordance with Article 30(2), each of the parties shall pay the advance on costs corresponding to its claims.

4. When a request for an advance on costs has not been complied with, and after consultation with the Arbitral Tribunal, the Secretary General may direct the Arbitral Tribunal to suspend its work and set a time limit, which must be not less than 15 days, on the expiry of which the relevant claims, or counterclaims, shall be considered as withdrawn. Should the party in question wish to object to this measure, it must make a request within the aforementioned period for the matter to be decided by the Court. Such party shall not be prevented, on the ground of such withdrawal, from reintroducing the same claims or counterclaims at a later date in another proceeding.

5. If one of the parties claims a right to a set-off with regard to either claims or counterclaims, such set-off shall be taken into account in determining the advance to cover the costs of arbitration in the same way as a separate claim insofar as it may require the Arbitral Tribunal to consider additional matters.

Article 31. Decision as to the Costs of the Arbitration

1. The costs of the arbitration shall include the fees and expenses of the arbitrators and the ICC administrative expenses fixed by the Court, in accordance with the scale in force at the time of the commencement of

the arbitral proceedings, as well as the fees and expenses of any experts appointed by the Arbitral Tribunal and the reasonable legal and other costs incurred by the parties for the arbitration.

2. The Court may fix the fees of the arbitrators at a figure higher or lower than that which would result from the application of the relevant scale should this be deemed necessary due to the exceptional circumstances of the case. Decisions on costs other than those fixed by the Court may be taken by the Arbitral Tribunal at any time during the proceedings.

3. The final Award shall fix the costs of the arbitration and decide which of the parties shall bear them or in what proportion they shall be borne by the parties.

MISCELLANEOUS

Article 32. Modified Time Limits

1. The parties may agree to shorten the various time limits set out in these Rules. Any such agreement entered into subsequent to the constitution of an Arbitral Tribunal shall become effective only upon the approval of the Arbitral Tribunal.

2. The Court, on its own initiative, may extend any time limit which has been modified pursuant to Article 32(1) if it decides that it is necessary to do so in order that the Arbitral Tribunal or the Court may fulfil their responsibilities in accordance with these Rules.

Article 33. Waiver

A party which proceeds with the arbitration without raising its objection to a failure to comply with any provision of these Rules, or of any other rules applicable to the proceedings, any direction given by the Arbitral Tribunal, or any requirement under the arbitration agreement relating to the constitution of the Arbitral Tribunal, or to the conduct of the proceedings, shall be deemed to have waived its right to object.

Article 34. Exclusion of Liability

Neither the arbitrators, nor the Court and its members, nor the ICC and its employees, nor the ICC National Committees shall be liable to any person for any act or omission in connection with the arbitration.

Article 35. General Rule

In all matters not expressly provided for in these Rules, the Court and the Arbitral Tribunal shall act in the spirit of these Rules and shall make every effort to make sure that the Award is enforceable at law.

UNIT B	BACKGROUND DOCUMENT FOR CHAPTER 9
	Document: Rome Statute

ROME STATUTE OF THE INTERNATIONAL CRIMINAL COURT

June 17, 1998, 2187 U.N.T.S. 3 (July 1, 2002).

PREAMBLE

The States Parties to this Statute,

Conscious that all peoples are united by common bonds, their cultures pieced together in a shared heritage, and concerned that this delicate mosaic may be shattered at any time,

Mindful that during this century millions of children, women and men have been victims of unimaginable atrocities that deeply shock the conscience of humanity,

Recognizing that such grave crimes threaten the peace, security and well-being of the world,

Affirming that the most serious crimes of concern to the international community as a whole must not go unpunished and that their effective prosecution must be ensured by taking measures at the national level and by enhancing international cooperation,

Determined to put an end to impunity for the perpetrators of these crimes and thus to contribute to the prevention of such crimes,

Recalling that it is the duty of every State to exercise its criminal jurisdiction over those responsible for international crimes,

Reaffirming the Purposes and Principles of the Charter of the United Nations, and in particular that all States shall refrain from the threat or use of force against the territorial integrity or political independence of any State, or in any other manner inconsistent with the Purposes of the United Nations,

Emphasizing in this connection that nothing in this Statute shall be taken as authorizing any State Party to intervene in an armed conflict or in the internal affairs of any State,

Determined to these ends and for the sake of present and future generations, to establish an independent permanent International Criminal Court in relationship with the United Nations system, with jurisdiction over the most serious crimes of concern to the international community as a whole,

Emphasizing that the International Criminal Court established under this Statute shall be complementary to national criminal jurisdictions,

Resolved to guarantee lasting respect for and the enforcement of international justice,

Have agreed as follows

PART 1

ESTABLISHMENT OF THE COURT

Article 1. The Court

An International Criminal Court ("the Court") is hereby established. It shall be a permanent institution and shall have the power to exercise its jurisdiction over persons for the most serious crimes of international concern, as referred to in this Statute, and shall be complementary to national criminal jurisdictions. The jurisdiction and functioning of the Court shall be governed by the provisions of this Statute.

Article 2. Relationship of the Court with the United Nations

The Court shall be brought into relationship with the United Nations through an agreement to be approved by the Assembly of States Parties to this Statute and thereafter concluded by the President of the Court on its behalf.

Article 3. Seat of the Court

1. The seat of the Court shall be established at The Hague in the Netherlands ("the host State").

2. The Court shall enter into a headquarters agreement with the host State, to be approved by the Assembly of States Parties and thereafter concluded by the President of the Court on its behalf.

3. The Court may sit elsewhere, whenever it considers it desirable, as provided in this Statute.

Article 4. Legal Status and Powers of the Court

1. The Court shall have international legal personality. It shall also have such legal capacity as may be necessary for the exercise of its functions and the fulfilment of its purposes.

2. The Court may exercise its functions and powers, as provided in this Statute, on the territory of any State Party and, by special agreement, on the territory of any other State.

PART 2

JURISDICTION, ADMISSIBILITY AND APPLICABLE LAW

Article 5. Crimes Within the Jurisdiction of the Court

1. The jurisdiction of the Court shall be limited to the most serious crimes of concern to the international community as a whole. The Court has jurisdiction in accordance with this Statute with respect to the following crimes:

    (a) The crime of genocide;

    (b) Crimes against humanity;

    (c) War crimes;

    (d) The crime of aggression.

2. The Court shall exercise jurisdiction over the crime of aggression once a provision is adopted in accordance with Articles 121 and 123 defining

the crime and setting out the conditions under which the Court shall exercise jurisdiction with respect to this crime. Such a provision shall be consistent with the relevant provisions of the Charter of the United Nations.

Article 6. Genocide

For the purpose of this Statute, "genocide" means any of the following acts committed with intent to destroy, in whole or in part, a national, ethnical, racial or religious group, as such:

(a) Killing members of the group;

(b) Causing serious bodily or mental harm to members of the group;

(c) Deliberately inflicting on the group conditions of life calculated to bring about its physical destruction in whole or in part;

(d) Imposing measures intended to prevent births within the group;

(e) Forcibly transferring children of the group to another group.

Article 7. Crimes Against Humanity

1. For the purpose of this Statute, "crime against humanity" means any of the following acts when committed as part of a widespread or systematic attack directed against any civilian population, with knowledge of the attack:

(a) Murder;

(b) Extermination;

(c) Enslavement;

(d) Deportation or forcible transfer of population;

(e) Imprisonment or other severe deprivation of physical liberty in violation of fundamental rules of international law;

(f) Torture;

(g) Rape, sexual slavery, enforced prostitution, forced pregnancy, enforced sterilization, or any other form of sexual violence of comparable gravity;

(h) Persecution against any identifiable group or collectivity on political, racial, national, ethnic, cultural, religious, gender as defined in paragraph 3, or other grounds that are universally recognized as impermissible under international law, in connection with any act referred to in this paragraph or any crime within the jurisdiction of the Court;

(i) Enforced disappearance of persons;

(j) The crime of apartheid;

(k) Other inhumane acts of a similar character intentionally causing great suffering, or serious injury to body or to mental or physical health.

2. For the purpose of paragraph 1:

(a) "Attack directed against any civilian population" means a course of conduct involving the multiple commission of acts referred to in paragraph 1 against any civilian population, pursuant to or in furtherance of a State or organizational policy to commit such attack;

(b) "Extermination" includes the intentional infliction of conditions of life, *inter alia* the deprivation of access to food and medicine, calculated to bring about the destruction of part of a population;

(c) "Enslavement" means the exercise of any or all of the powers attaching to the right of ownership over a person and includes the exercise of such power in the course of trafficking in persons, in particular women and children;

(d) "Deportation or forcible transfer of population" means forced displacement of the persons concerned by expulsion or other coercive acts from the area in which they are lawfully present, without grounds permitted under international law;

(e) "Torture" means the intentional infliction of severe pain or suffering, whether physical or mental, upon a person in the custody or under the control of the accused; except that torture shall not include pain or suffering arising only from, inherent in or incidental to, lawful sanctions;

(f) "Forced pregnancy" means the unlawful confinement of a woman forcibly made pregnant, with the intent of affecting the ethnic composition of any population or carrying out other grave violations of international law. This definition shall not in any way be interpreted as affecting national laws relating to pregnancy;

(g) "Persecution" means the intentional and severe deprivation of fundamental rights contrary to international law by reason of the identity of the group or collectivity;

(h) "The crime of apartheid" means inhumane acts of a character similar to those referred to in paragraph 1, committed in the context of an institutionalized regime of systematic oppression and domination by one racial group over any other racial group or groups and committed with the intention of maintaining that regime;

(i) "Enforced disappearance of persons" means the arrest, detention or abduction of persons by, or with the authorization, support or acquiescence of, a State or a political organization, followed by a refusal to acknowledge that deprivation of freedom or to give information on the fate or whereabouts of those persons, with the intention of removing them from the protection of the law for a prolonged period of time.

3. For the purpose of this Statute, it is understood that the term "gender" refers to the two sexes, male and female, within the context of society. The term "gender" does not indicate any meaning different from the above.

Article 8. War Crimes

1. The Court shall have jurisdiction in respect of war crimes in particular when committed as part of a plan or policy or as part of a large-scale commission of such crimes.

2. For the purpose of this Statute, "war crimes" means:

(a) Grave breaches of the Geneva Conventions of 12 August 1949, namely, any of the following acts against persons or property protected under the provisions of the relevant Geneva Convention:

(i) Wilful killing;

(ii) Torture or inhuman treatment, including biological experiments;

(iii) Wilfully causing great suffering, or serious injury to body or health;

(iv) Extensive destruction and appropriation of property, not justified by military necessity and carried out unlawfully and wantonly;

(v) Compelling a prisoner of war or other protected person to serve in the forces of a hostile Power;

(vi) Wilfully depriving a prisoner of war or other protected person of the rights of fair and regular trial;

(vii) Unlawful deportation or transfer or unlawful confinement;

(viii) Taking of hostages.

(b) Other serious violations of the laws and customs applicable in international armed conflict, within the established framework of international law, namely, any of the following acts:

(i) Intentionally directing attacks against the civilian population as such or against individual civilians not taking direct part in hostilities;

(ii) Intentionally directing attacks against civilian objects, that is, objects which are not military objectives;

(iii) Intentionally directing attacks against personnel, installations, material, units or vehicles involved in a humanitarian assistance or peacekeeping mission in accordance with the Charter of the United Nations, as long as they are entitled to the protection given to civilians or civilian objects under the international law of armed conflict;

(iv) Intentionally launching an attack in the knowledge that such attack will cause incidental loss of life or injury to civilians or damage to civilian objects or widespread, long-term and severe damage to the natural environment which would be clearly excessive in relation to the concrete and direct overall military advantage anticipated;

(v) Attacking or bombarding, by whatever means, towns, villages, dwellings or buildings which are undefended and which are not military objectives;

(vi) Killing or wounding a combatant who, having laid down his arms or having no longer means of defence, has surrendered at discretion;

(vii) Making improper use of a flag of truce, of the flag or of the military insignia and uniform of the enemy or of the United Nations, as well as of the distinctive emblems of the Geneva Conventions, resulting in death or serious personal injury;

(viii) The transfer, directly or indirectly, by the Occupying Power of parts of its own civilian population into the territory it occupies, or the deportation or transfer of all or parts of the population of the occupied territory within or outside this territory;

(ix) Intentionally directing attacks against buildings dedicated to religion, education, art, science or charitable purposes, historic monuments, hospitals and places where the sick and wounded are collected, provided they are not military objectives;

(x) Subjecting persons who are in the power of an adverse party to physical mutilation or to medical or scientific experiments of any kind which are neither justified by the medical, dental or hospital treatment of the person concerned nor carried out in his or her interest, and which cause death to or seriously endanger the health of such person or persons;

(xi) Killing or wounding treacherously individuals belonging to the hostile nation or army;

(xii) Declaring that no quarter will be given;

(xiii) Destroying or seizing the enemy's property unless such destruction or seizure be imperatively demanded by the necessities of war;

(xiv) Declaring abolished, suspended or inadmissible in a court of law the rights and actions of the nationals of the hostile party;

(xv) Compelling the nationals of the hostile party to take part in the operations of war directed against their own country, even if they were in the belligerent's service before the commencement of the war;

(xvi) Pillaging a town or place, even when taken by assault;

(xvii) Employing poison or poisoned weapons;

(xviii) Employing asphyxiating, poisonous or other gases, and all analogous liquids, materials or devices;

(xix) Employing bullets which expand or flatten easily in the human body, such as bullets with a hard envelope which does not entirely cover the core or is pierced with incisions;

(xx) Employing weapons, projectiles and material and methods of warfare which are of a nature to cause superfluous injury or unnecessary suffering or which are inherently indiscriminate in violation of the international law of armed conflict, provided that such weapons, projectiles and material and methods of warfare are the subject of a comprehensive prohibition and are included in an annex to this Statute, by an amendment in accordance with the relevant provisions set forth in Articles 121 and 123;

(xxi) Committing outrages upon personal dignity, in particular humiliating and degrading treatment;

(xxii) Committing rape, sexual slavery, enforced prostitution, forced pregnancy, as defined in Article 7, paragraph 2 (f), enforced sterilization, or any other form of sexual violence also constituting a grave breach of the Geneva Conventions;

(xxiii) Utilizing the presence of a civilian or other protected person to render certain points, areas or military forces immune from military operations;

(xxiv) Intentionally directing attacks against buildings, material, medical units and transport, and personnel using the distinctive emblems of the Geneva Conventions in conformity with international law;

(xxv) Intentionally using starvation of civilians as a method of warfare by depriving them of objects indispensable to their survival, including wilfully impeding relief supplies as provided for under the Geneva Conventions;

(xxvi) Conscripting or enlisting children under the age of fifteen years into the national armed forces or using them to participate actively in hostilities.

(c) In the case of an armed conflict not of an international character, serious violations of Article 3 common to the four Geneva Conventions of 12 August 1949, namely, any of the following acts committed against persons taking no active part in the hostilities, including members of armed forces who have laid down their arms and those placed *hors de combat* by sickness, wounds, detention or any other cause:

(i) Violence to life and person, in particular murder of all kinds, mutilation, cruel treatment and torture;

(ii) Committing outrages upon personal dignity, in particular humiliating and degrading treatment;

(iii) Taking of hostages;

(iv) The passing of sentences and the carrying out of executions without previous judgement pronounced by a regularly constituted court, affording all judicial guarantees which are generally recognized as indispensable.

(d) Paragraph 2 (c) applies to armed conflicts not of an international character and thus does not apply to situations of internal disturbances and tensions, such as riots, isolated and sporadic acts of violence or other acts of a similar nature.

(e) Other serious violations of the laws and customs applicable in armed conflicts not of an international character, within the established framework of international law, namely, any of the following acts:

(i) Intentionally directing attacks against the civilian population as such or against individual civilians not taking direct part in hostilities;

(ii) Intentionally directing attacks against buildings, material, medical units and transport, and personnel using the distinctive emblems of the Geneva Conventions in conformity with international law;

(iii) Intentionally directing attacks against personnel, installations, material, units or vehicles involved in a humanitarian assistance or peacekeeping mission in accordance with the Charter of the United Nations, as long as they are entitled to the protection given to civilians or civilian objects under the international law of armed conflict;

(iv) Intentionally directing attacks against buildings dedicated to religion, education, art, science or charitable purposes, historic monuments, hospitals and places where the sick and wounded are collected, provided they are not military objectives;

(v) Pillaging a town or place, even when taken by assault;

(vi) Committing rape, sexual slavery, enforced prostitution, forced pregnancy, as defined in Article 7, paragraph 2 (f), enforced sterilization, and any other form of sexual violence also constituting a serious violation of Article 3 common to the four Geneva Conventions;

(vii) Conscripting or enlisting children under the age of fifteen years into armed forces or groups or using them to participate actively in hostilities;

(viii) Ordering the displacement of the civilian population for reasons related to the conflict, unless the security of the civilians involved or imperative military reasons so demand;

(ix) Killing or wounding treacherously a combatant adversary;

(x) Declaring that no quarter will be given;

(xi) Subjecting persons who are in the power of another party to the conflict to physical mutilation or to medical or scientific experiments of any kind which are neither justified by the medical, dental or hospital treatment of the person concerned nor carried out in his or her interest, and which cause death to or seriously endanger the health of such person or persons;

(xii) Destroying or seizing the property of an adversary unless such destruction or seizure be imperatively demanded by the necessities of the conflict;

(f) Paragraph 2 (e) applies to armed conflicts not of an international character and thus does not apply to situations of internal disturbances and tensions, such as riots, isolated and sporadic acts of violence or other acts of a similar nature. It applies to armed conflicts that take place in the territory of a State when there is protracted armed conflict between governmental authorities and organized armed groups or between such groups.

3. Nothing in paragraph 2 (c) and (e) shall affect the responsibility of a Government to maintain or re-establish law and order in the State or to defend the unity and territorial integrity of the State, by all legitimate means.

Article 9. Elements of Crimes

1. Elements of Crimes shall assist the Court in the interpretation and application of Articles 6, 7 and 8. They shall be adopted by a two-thirds majority of the members of the Assembly of States Parties.

2. Amendments to the Elements of Crimes may be proposed by:

   (a) Any State Party;

   (b) The judges acting by an absolute majority;

   (c) The Prosecutor.

   Such amendments shall be adopted by a two-thirds majority of the members of the Assembly of States Parties.

3. The Elements of Crimes and amendments thereto shall be consistent with this Statute.

Article 10

Nothing in this Part shall be interpreted as limiting or prejudicing in any way existing or developing rules of international law for purposes other than this Statute.

Article 11. Jurisdiction *Ratione Temporis*

1. The Court has jurisdiction only with respect to crimes committed after the entry into force of this Statute.

2. If a State becomes a Party to this Statute after its entry into force, the Court may exercise its jurisdiction only with respect to crimes committed after the entry into force of this Statute for that State, unless that State has made a declaration under Article 12, paragraph 3.

Article 12. Preconditions to the Exercise of Jurisdiction

1. A State which becomes a Party to this Statute thereby accepts the jurisdiction of the Court with respect to the crimes referred to in Article 5.

2. In the case of Article 13, paragraph (a) or (c), the Court may exercise its jurisdiction if one or more of the following States are Parties to this Statute or have accepted the jurisdiction of the Court in accordance with paragraph 3:

   (a) The State on the territory of which the conduct in question occurred or, if the crime was committed on board a vessel or aircraft, the State of registration of that vessel or aircraft;

   (b) The State of which the person accused of the crime is a national.

3. If the acceptance of a State which is not a Party to this Statute is required under paragraph 2, that State may, by declaration lodged with the Registrar, accept the exercise of jurisdiction by the Court with respect to the crime in question. The accepting State shall cooperate with the Court without any delay or exception in accordance with Part 9.

Article 13. Exercise of Jurisdiction

The Court may exercise its jurisdiction with respect to a crime referred to in Article 5 in accordance with the provisions of this Statute if:

(a) A situation in which one or more of such crimes appears to have been committed is referred to the Prosecutor by a State Party in accordance with Article 14;

(b) A situation in which one or more of such crimes appears to have been committed is referred to the Prosecutor by the Security Council acting under Chapter VII of the Charter of the United Nations; or

(c) The Prosecutor has initiated an investigation in respect of such a crime in accordance with Article 15.

Article 14. Referral of a Situation by a State Party

1. A State Party may refer to the Prosecutor a situation in which one or more crimes within the jurisdiction of the Court appear to have been committed requesting the Prosecutor to investigate the situation for the purpose of determining whether one or more specific persons should be charged with the commission of such crimes.

2. As far as possible, a referral shall specify the relevant circumstances and be accompanied by such supporting documentation as is available to the State referring the situation.

Article 15. Prosecutor

1. The Prosecutor may initiate investigations *proprio motu* on the basis of information on crimes within the jurisdiction of the Court.

2. The Prosecutor shall analyse the seriousness of the information received. For this purpose, he or she may seek additional information from States, organs of the United Nations, intergovernmental or non-governmental organizations, or other reliable sources that he or she deems appropriate, and may receive written or oral testimony at the seat of the Court.

3. If the Prosecutor concludes that there is a reasonable basis to proceed with an investigation, he or she shall submit to the Pre-Trial Chamber a request for authorization of an investigation, together with any supporting material collected. Victims may make representations to the Pre-Trial Chamber, in accordance with the Rules of Procedure and Evidence.

4. If the Pre-Trial Chamber, upon examination of the request and the supporting material, considers that there is a reasonable basis to proceed with an investigation, and that the case appears to fall within the jurisdiction of the Court, it shall authorize the commencement of the investigation, without prejudice to subsequent determinations by the Court with regard to the jurisdiction and admissibility of a case.

5. The refusal of the Pre-Trial Chamber to authorize the investigation shall not preclude the presentation of a subsequent request by the Prosecutor based on new facts or evidence regarding the same situation.

6. If, after the preliminary examination referred to in paragraphs 1 and 2, the Prosecutor concludes that the information provided does not constitute a reasonable basis for an investigation, he or she shall inform those who provided the information. This shall not preclude the Prosecutor from considering further information submitted to him or her regarding the same situation in the light of new facts or evidence.

Article 16. Deferral of Investigation or Prosecution

No investigation or prosecution may be commenced or proceeded with under this Statute for a period of 12 months after the Security Council, in a resolution adopted under Chapter VII of the Charter of the United Nations, has requested the Court to that effect; that request may be renewed by the Council under the same conditions.

Article 17. Issues of Admissibility

1. Having regard to paragraph 10 of the Preamble and Article 1, the Court shall determine that a case is inadmissible where:

    (a) The case is being investigated or prosecuted by a State which has jurisdiction over it, unless the State is unwilling or unable genuinely to carry out the investigation or prosecution;

    (b) The case has been investigated by a State which has jurisdiction over it and the State has decided not to prosecute the person concerned, unless the decision resulted from the unwillingness or inability of the State genuinely to prosecute;

    (c) The person concerned has already been tried for conduct which is the subject of the complaint, and a trial by the Court is not permitted under Article 20, paragraph 3;

(d) The case is not of sufficient gravity to justify further action by the Court.

2. In order to determine unwillingness in a particular case, the Court shall consider, having regard to the principles of due process recognized by international law, whether one or more of the following exist, as applicable:

(a) The proceedings were or are being undertaken or the national decision was made for the purpose of shielding the person concerned from criminal responsibility for crimes within the jurisdiction of the Court referred to in Article 5;

(b) There has been an unjustified delay in the proceedings which in the circumstances is inconsistent with an intent to bring the person concerned to justice;

(c) The proceedings were not or are not being conducted independently or impartially, and they were or are being conducted in a manner which, in the circumstances, is inconsistent with an intent to bring the person concerned to justice.

3. In order to determine inability in a particular case, the Court shall consider whether, due to a total or substantial collapse or unavailability of its national judicial system, the State is unable to obtain the accused or the necessary evidence and testimony or otherwise unable to carry out its proceedings.

Article 18. Preliminary Rulings Regarding Admissibility

1. When a situation has been referred to the Court pursuant to Article 13 (a) and the Prosecutor has determined that there would be a reasonable basis to commence an investigation, or the Prosecutor initiates an investigation pursuant to Articles 13 (c) and 15, the Prosecutor shall notify all States Parties and those States which, taking into account the information available, would normally exercise jurisdiction over the crimes concerned. The Prosecutor may notify such States on a confidential basis and, where the Prosecutor believes it necessary to protect persons, prevent destruction of evidence or prevent the absconding of persons, may limit the scope of the information provided to States.

2. Within one month of receipt of that notification, a State may inform the Court that it is investigating or has investigated its nationals or others

within its jurisdiction with respect to criminal acts which may constitute crimes referred to in Article 5 and which relate to the information provided in the notification to States. At the request of that State, the Prosecutor shall defer to the State's investigation of those persons unless the Pre-Trial Chamber, on the application of the Prosecutor, decides to authorize the investigation.

3. The Prosecutor's deferral to a State's investigation shall be open to review by the Prosecutor six months after the date of deferral or at any time when there has been a significant change of circumstances based on the State's unwillingness or inability genuinely to carry out the investigation.

4. The State concerned or the Prosecutor may appeal to the Appeals Chamber against a ruling of the Pre-Trial Chamber, in accordance with Article 82. The appeal may be heard on an expedited basis.

5. When the Prosecutor has deferred an investigation in accordance with paragraph 2, the Prosecutor may request that the State concerned periodically inform the Prosecutor of the progress of its investigations and any subsequent prosecutions. States Parties shall respond to such requests without undue delay.

6. Pending a ruling by the Pre-Trial Chamber, or at any time when the Prosecutor has deferred an investigation under this Article, the Prosecutor may, on an exceptional basis, seek authority from the Pre-Trial Chamber to pursue necessary investigative steps for the purpose of preserving evidence where there is a unique opportunity to obtain important evidence or there is a significant risk that such evidence may not be subsequently available.

7. A State which has challenged a ruling of the Pre-Trial Chamber under this Article may challenge the admissibility of a case under Article 19 on the grounds of additional significant facts or significant change of circumstances.

Article 19. Challenges to the Jurisdiction of the Court or the Admissibility of a Case

1. The Court shall satisfy itself that it has jurisdiction in any case brought before it. The Court may, on its own motion, determine the admissibility of a case in accordance with Article 17.

2. Challenges to the admissibility of a case on the grounds referred to in Article 17 or challenges to the jurisdiction of the Court may be made by:

    (a) An accused or a person for whom a warrant of arrest or a summons to appear has been issued under Article 58;

    (b) A State which has jurisdiction over a case, on the ground that it is investigating or prosecuting the case or has investigated or prosecuted; or

    (c) A State from which acceptance of jurisdiction is required under Article 12.

3. The Prosecutor may seek a ruling from the Court regarding a question of jurisdiction or admissibility. In proceedings with respect to jurisdiction or admissibility, those who have referred the situation under Article 13, as well as victims, may also submit observations to the Court.

4. The admissibility of a case or the jurisdiction of the Court may be challenged only once by any person or State referred to in paragraph 2. The challenge shall take place prior to or at the commencement of the trial. In exceptional circumstances, the Court may grant leave for a challenge to be brought more than once or at a time later than the commencement of the trial. Challenges to the admissibility of a case, at the commencement of a trial, or subsequently with the leave of the Court, may be based only on Article 17, paragraph 1 (c).

5. A State referred to in paragraph 2 (b) and (c) shall make a challenge at the earliest opportunity.

6. Prior to the confirmation of the charges, challenges to the admissibility of a case or challenges to the jurisdiction of the Court shall be referred to the Pre-Trial Chamber. After confirmation of the charges, they shall be referred to the Trial Chamber. Decisions with respect to jurisdiction or admissibility may be appealed to the Appeals Chamber in accordance with Article 82.

7. If a challenge is made by a State referred to in paragraph 2 (b) or (c), the Prosecutor shall suspend the investigation until such time as the Court makes a determination in accordance with Article 17.

8. Pending a ruling by the Court, the Prosecutor may seek authority from the Court:

   (a) To pursue necessary investigative steps of the kind referred to in Article 18, paragraph 6;

   (b) To take a statement or testimony from a witness or complete the collection and examination of evidence which had begun prior to the making of the challenge; and

   (c) In cooperation with the relevant States, to prevent the absconding of persons in respect of whom the Prosecutor has already requested a warrant of arrest under Article 58.

9. The making of a challenge shall not affect the validity of any act performed by the Prosecutor or any order or warrant issued by the Court prior to the making of the challenge.

10. If the Court has decided that a case is inadmissible under Article 17, the Prosecutor may submit a request for a review of the decision when he or she is fully satisfied that new facts have arisen which negate the basis on which the case had previously been found inadmissible under Article 17.

11. If the Prosecutor, having regard to the matters referred to in Article 17, defers an investigation, the Prosecutor may request that the relevant State make available to the Prosecutor information on the proceedings. That information shall, at the request of the State concerned, be confidential. If the Prosecutor thereafter decides to proceed with an investigation, he or she shall notify the State to which deferral of the proceedings has taken place.

Article 20. *Ne Bis In Idem*

1. Except as provided in this Statute, no person shall be tried before the Court with respect to conduct which formed the basis of crimes for which the person has been convicted or acquitted by the Court.

2. No person shall be tried by another court for a crime referred to in Article 5 for which that person has already been convicted or acquitted by the Court.

3. No person who has been tried by another court for conduct also proscribed under Article 6, 7 or 8 shall be tried by the Court with respect to the same conduct unless the proceedings in the other court:

   (a) Were for the purpose of shielding the person concerned from criminal responsibility for crimes within the jurisdiction of the Court; or

   (b) Otherwise were not conducted independently or impartially in accordance with the norms of due process recognized by international law and were conducted in a manner which, in the circumstances, was inconsistent with an intent to bring the person concerned to justice.

Article 21. Applicable Law

1. The Court shall apply:

   (a) In the first place, this Statute, Elements of Crimes and its Rules of Procedure and Evidence;

   (b) In the second place, where appropriate, applicable treaties and the principles and rules of international law, including the established principles of the international law of armed conflict;

   (c) Failing that, general principles of law derived by the Court from national laws of legal systems of the world including, as appropriate, the national laws of States that would normally exercise jurisdiction over the crime, provided that those principles are not inconsistent with this Statute and with international law and internationally recognized norms and standards.

2. The Court may apply principles and rules of law as interpreted in its previous decisions.

3. The application and interpretation of law pursuant to this Article must be consistent with internationally recognized human rights, and be without any adverse distinction founded on grounds such as gender as defined in Article 7, paragraph 3, age, race, colour, language, religion or belief, political or other opinion, national, ethnic or social origin, wealth, birth or other status.

PART 3

GENERAL PRINCIPLES OF CRIMINAL LAW

Article 22. *Nullum Crimen Sine Lege*

1. A person shall not be criminally responsible under this Statute unless the conduct in question constitutes, at the time it takes place, a crime within the jurisdiction of the Court.

2. The definition of a crime shall be strictly construed and shall not be extended by analogy. In case of ambiguity, the definition shall be interpreted in favour of the person being investigated, prosecuted or convicted.

3. This Article shall not affect the characterization of any conduct as criminal under international law independently of this Statute.

Article 23. *Nulla Poena Sine Lege*

A person convicted by the Court may be punished only in accordance with this Statute.

Article 24. Non-Retroactivity *Ratione Personae*

1. No person shall be criminally responsible under this Statute for conduct prior to the entry into force of the Statute.

2. In the event of a change in the law applicable to a given case prior to a final judgement, the law more favourable to the person being investigated, prosecuted or convicted shall apply.

Article 25. Individual Criminal Responsibility

1. The Court shall have jurisdiction over natural persons pursuant to this Statute.

2. A person who commits a crime within the jurisdiction of the Court shall be individually responsible and liable for punishment in accordance with this Statute.

3. In accordance with this Statute, a person shall be criminally responsible and liable for punishment for a crime within the jurisdiction of the Court if that person:

   (a) Commits such a crime, whether as an individual, jointly with another or through another person, regardless of whether that other person is criminally responsible;

   (b) Orders, solicits or induces the commission of such a crime which in fact occurs or is attempted;

   (c) For the purpose of facilitating the commission of such a crime, aids, abets or otherwise assists in its commission or its attempted commission, including providing the means for its commission;

   (d) In any other way contributes to the commission or attempted commission of such a crime by a group of persons acting with a common purpose. Such contribution shall be intentional and shall either:

      (i) Be made with the aim of furthering the criminal activity or criminal purpose of the group, where such activity or purpose involves the commission of a crime within the jurisdiction of the Court; or

      (ii) Be made in the knowledge of the intention of the group to commit the crime;

   (e) In respect of the crime of genocide, directly and publicly incites others to commit genocide;

   (f) Attempts to commit such a crime by taking action that commences its execution by means of a substantial step, but the crime does not occur because of circumstances independent of the person's intentions. However, a person who abandons the effort to commit the crime or otherwise prevents the completion of the crime shall not be liable for punishment under this Statute for the attempt to commit that crime if that person completely and voluntarily gave up the criminal purpose.

4. No provision in this Statute relating to individual criminal responsibility shall affect the responsibility of States under international law.

Article 26. Exclusion of Jurisdiction over Persons Under Eighteen

The Court shall have no jurisdiction over any person who was under the age of 18 at the time of the alleged commission of a crime.

Article 27. Irrelevance of Official Capacity

1. This Statute shall apply equally to all persons without any distinction based on official capacity. In particular, official capacity as a Head of State or Government, a member of a Government or parliament, an elected representative or a government official shall in no case exempt a person from criminal responsibility under this Statute, nor shall it, in and of itself, constitute a ground for reduction of sentence.

2. Immunities or special procedural rules which may attach to the official capacity of a person, whether under national or international law, shall not bar the Court from exercising its jurisdiction over such a person.

Article 28. Responsibility of Commanders and other Superiors

In addition to other grounds of criminal responsibility under this Statute for crimes within the jurisdiction of the Court:

(a) A military commander or person effectively acting as a military commander shall be criminally responsible for crimes within the jurisdiction of the Court committed by forces under his or her effective command and control, or effective authority and control as the case may be, as a result of his or her failure to exercise control properly over such forces, where:

(i) That military commander or person either knew or, owing to the circumstances at the time, should have known that the forces were committing or about to commit such crimes; and

(ii) That military commander or person failed to take all necessary and reasonable measures within his or her power to prevent or repress their commission or to submit the matter to the competent authorities for investigation and prosecution.

(b) With respect to superior and subordinate relationships not described in paragraph (a), a superior shall be criminally responsible for crimes within the jurisdiction of the Court committed by subordinates under his or her effective authority and control, as a result of his or her failure to exercise control properly over such subordinates, where:

(i) The superior either knew, or consciously disregarded information which clearly indicated, that the subordinates were committing or about to commit such crimes;

(ii) The crimes concerned activities that were within the effective responsibility and control of the superior; and

(iii) The superior failed to take all necessary and reasonable measures within his or her power to prevent or repress their commission or to submit the matter to the competent authorities for investigation and prosecution.

Article 29. Non-Applicability of Statute of Limitations

The crimes within the jurisdiction of the Court shall not be subject to any statute of limitations.

Article 30. Mental Element

1. Unless otherwise provided, a person shall be criminally responsible and liable for punishment for a crime within the jurisdiction of the Court only if the material elements are committed with intent and knowledge.

2. For the purposes of this Article, a person has intent where:

   (a) In relation to conduct, that person means to engage in the conduct;

   (b) In relation to a consequence, that person means to cause that consequence or is aware that it will occur in the ordinary course of events.

3. For the purposes of this Article, "knowledge" means awareness that a circumstance exists or a consequence will occur in the ordinary course of events. "Know" and "knowingly" shall be construed accordingly.

Article 31. Grounds for Excluding Criminal Responsibility

1. In addition to other grounds for excluding criminal responsibility provided for in this Statute, a person shall not be criminally responsible if, at the time of that person's conduct:

   (a) The person suffers from a mental disease or defect that destroys that person's capacity to appreciate the unlawfulness or nature of his or her conduct, or capacity to control his or her conduct to conform to the requirements of law;

   (b) The person is in a state of intoxication that destroys that person's capacity to appreciate the unlawfulness or nature of his or her conduct, or capacity to control his or her conduct to conform to the requirements of law, unless the person has become voluntarily intoxicated under such circumstances that the person knew, or disregarded the risk, that, as a result of the intoxication, he or she was likely to engage in conduct constituting a crime within the jurisdiction of the Court;

   (c) The person acts reasonably to defend himself or herself or another person or, in the case of war crimes, property which is essential for the survival of the person or another person or property which is essential for accomplishing a military mission, against an imminent and unlawful use of force in a manner proportionate to the degree of danger to the person or the other person or property protected. The fact that the person was involved in a defensive operation conducted by forces shall not in itself constitute a ground for excluding criminal responsibility under this subparagraph;

   (d) The conduct which is alleged to constitute a crime within the jurisdiction of the Court has been caused by duress resulting from a threat of imminent death or of continuing or imminent serious bodily harm against that person or another person, and the person acts necessarily and reasonably to avoid this threat, provided that the person does not intend to cause a greater harm than the one sought to be avoided. Such a threat may either be:

      (i) Made by other persons; or

(ii) Constituted by other circumstances beyond that person's control.

2. The Court shall determine the applicability of the grounds for excluding criminal responsibility provided for in this Statute to the case before it.

3. At trial, the Court may consider a ground for excluding criminal responsibility other than those referred to in paragraph 1 where such a ground is derived from applicable law as set forth in Article 21. The procedures relating to the consideration of such a ground shall be provided for in the Rules of Procedure and Evidence.

Article 32. Mistake of Fact or Mistake of Law

1. A mistake of fact shall be a ground for excluding criminal responsibility only if it negates the mental element required by the crime.

2. A mistake of law as to whether a particular type of conduct is a crime within the jurisdiction of the Court shall not be a ground for excluding criminal responsibility. A mistake of law may, however, be a ground for excluding criminal responsibility if it negates the mental element required by such a crime, or as provided for in Article 33.

Article 33. Superior Orders and Prescription of Law

1. The fact that a crime within the jurisdiction of the Court has been committed by a person pursuant to an order of a Government or of a superior, whether military or civilian, shall not relieve that person of criminal responsibility unless:

   (a) The person was under a legal obligation to obey orders of the Government or the superior in question;

   (b) The person did not know that the order was unlawful; and

   (c) The order was not manifestly unlawful.

2. For the purposes of this Article, orders to commit genocide or crimes against humanity are manifestly unlawful.

PART 4

COMPOSITION AND ADMINISTRATION OF THE COURT

Article 34. Organs of the Court

The Court shall be composed of the following organs:

(a) The Presidency;

(b) An Appeals Division, a Trial Division and a Pre-Trial Division;

(c) The Office of the Prosecutor;

(d) The Registry.

Article 35. Service of Judges

1. All judges shall be elected as full-time members of the Court and shall be available to serve on that basis from the commencement of their terms of office.

2. The judges composing the Presidency shall serve on a full-time basis as soon as they are elected.

3. The Presidency may, on the basis of the workload of the Court and in consultation with its members, decide from time to time to what extent the remaining judges shall be required to serve on a full-time basis. Any such arrangement shall be without prejudice to the provisions of Article 40.

4. The financial arrangements for judges not required to serve on a full-time basis shall be made in accordance with Article 49.

Article 36. Qualifications, Nomination and Election of Judges

1. Subject to the provisions of paragraph 2, there shall be 18 judges of the Court.

2. (a) The Presidency, acting on behalf of the Court, may propose an increase in the number of judges specified in paragraph 1, indicating the reasons why this is considered necessary and ap-

propriate. The Registrar shall promptly circulate any such proposal to all States Parties.

(b) Any such proposal shall then be considered at a meeting of the Assembly of States Parties to be convened in accordance with Article 112. The proposal shall be considered adopted if approved at the meeting by a vote of two thirds of the members of the Assembly of States Parties and shall enter into force at such time as decided by the Assembly of States Parties.

(c) (i) Once a proposal for an increase in the number of judges has been adopted under subparagraph (b), the election of the additional judges shall take place at the next session of the Assembly of States Parties in accordance with paragraphs 3 to 8, and Article 37, paragraph 2;

(ii) Once a proposal for an increase in the number of judges has been adopted and brought into effect under subparagraphs (b) and (c) (i), it shall be open to the Presidency at any time thereafter, if the workload of the Court justifies it, to propose a reduction in the number of judges, provided that the number of judges shall not be reduced below that specified in paragraph 1. The proposal shall be dealt with in accordance with the procedure laid down in subparagraphs (a) and (b). In the event that the proposal is adopted, the number of judges shall be progressively decreased as the terms of office of serving judges expire, until the necessary number has been reached.

3. (a) The judges shall be chosen from among persons of high moral character, impartiality and integrity who possess the qualifications required in their respective States for appointment to the highest judicial offices.

(b) Every candidate for election to the Court shall:

(i) Have established competence in criminal law and procedure, and the necessary relevant experience, whether as judge, prosecutor, advocate or in other similar capacity, in criminal proceedings; or

(ii) Have established competence in relevant areas of international law such as international humanitarian law and the law of human rights, and extensive experience in a professional legal capacity which is of relevance to the judicial work of the Court;

(c) Every candidate for election to the Court shall have an excellent knowledge of and be fluent in at least one of the working languages of the Court.

4. (a) Nominations of candidates for election to the Court may be made by any State Party to this Statute, and shall be made either:

(i) By the procedure for the nomination of candidates for appointment to the highest judicial offices in the State in question; or

(ii) By the procedure provided for the nomination of candidates for the International Court of Justice in the Statute of that Court.

Nominations shall be accompanied by a statement in the necessary detail specifying how the candidate fulfils the requirements of paragraph 3.

(b) Each State Party may put forward one candidate for any given election who need not necessarily be a national of that State Party but shall in any case be a national of a State Party.

(c) The Assembly of States Parties may decide to establish, if appropriate, an Advisory Committee on nominations. In that event, the Committee's composition and mandate shall be established by the Assembly of States Parties.

5. For the purposes of the election, there shall be two lists of candidates:

List A containing the names of candidates with the qualifications specified in paragraph 3 (b) (i); and

List B containing the names of candidates with the qualifications specified in paragraph 3 (b) (ii).

A candidate with sufficient qualifications for both lists may choose on which list to appear. At the first election to the Court, at least nine judges shall be elected from list A and at least five judges from list B. Subsequent elections shall be so organized as to maintain the equivalent proportion on the Court of judges qualified on the two lists.

6. (a) The judges shall be elected by secret ballot at a meeting of the Assembly of States Parties convened for that purpose under Article 112. Subject to paragraph 7, the persons elected to the Court shall be the 18 candidates who obtain the highest number of votes and a two-thirds majority of the States Parties present and voting.

(b) In the event that a sufficient number of judges is not elected on the first ballot, successive ballots shall be held in accordance with the procedures laid down in subparagraph (a) until the remaining places have been filled.

7. No two judges may be nationals of the same State. A person who, for the purposes of membership of the Court, could be regarded as a national of more than one State shall be deemed to be a national of the State in which that person ordinarily exercises civil and political rights.

8. (a) The States Parties shall, in the selection of judges, take into account the need, within the membership of the Court, for:

(i) The representation of the principal legal systems of the world;

(ii) Equitable geographical representation; and

(iii) A fair representation of female and male judges.

(b) States Parties shall also take into account the need to include judges with legal expertise on specific issues, including, but not limited to, violence against women or children.

9. (a) Subject to subparagraph (b), judges shall hold office for a term of nine years and, subject to subparagraph (c) and to Article 37, paragraph 2, shall not be eligible for re-election.

   (b) At the first election, one third of the judges elected shall be selected by lot to serve for a term of three years; one third of the judges elected shall be selected by lot to serve for a term of six years; and the remainder shall serve for a term of nine years.

   (c) A judge who is selected to serve for a term of three years under subparagraph (b) shall be eligible for re-election for a full term.

10. Notwithstanding paragraph 9, a judge assigned to a Trial or Appeals Chamber in accordance with Article 39 shall continue in office to complete any trial or appeal the hearing of which has already commenced before that Chamber.

Article 37. Judicial Vacancies

1. In the event of a vacancy, an election shall be held in accordance with Article 36 to fill the vacancy.

2. A judge elected to fill a vacancy shall serve for the remainder of the predecessor's term and, if that period is three years or less, shall be eligible for re-election for a full term under Article 36.

Article 38. The Presidency

1. The President and the First and Second Vice-Presidents shall be elected by an absolute majority of the judges. They shall each serve for a term of three years or until the end of their respective terms of office as judges, whichever expires earlier. They shall be eligible for re-election once.

2. The First Vice-President shall act in place of the President in the event that the President is unavailable or disqualified. The Second Vice-President shall act in place of the President in the event that both the President and the First Vice-President are unavailable or disqualified.

3. The President, together with the First and Second Vice-Presidents, shall constitute the Presidency, which shall be responsible for:

(a) The proper administration of the Court, with the exception of the Office of the Prosecutor; and

(b) The other functions conferred upon it in accordance with this Statute.

4. In discharging its responsibility under paragraph 3 (a), the Presidency shall coordinate with and seek the concurrence of the Prosecutor on all matters of mutual concern.

Article 39. Chambers

1. As soon as possible after the election of the judges, the Court shall organize itself into the divisions specified in Article 34, paragraph (b). The Appeals Division shall be composed of the President and four other judges, the Trial Division of not less than six judges and the Pre-Trial Division of not less than six judges. The assignment of judges to divisions shall be based on the nature of the functions to be performed by each division and the qualifications and experience of the judges elected to the Court, in such a way that each division shall contain an appropriate combination of expertise in criminal law and procedure and in international law. The Trial and Pre-Trial Divisions shall be composed predominantly of judges with criminal trial experience.

2. (a) The judicial functions of the Court shall be carried out in each division by Chambers.

(b) (i) The Appeals Chamber shall be composed of all the judges of the Appeals Division;

(ii) The functions of the Trial Chamber shall be carried out by three judges of the Trial Division;

(iii) The functions of the Pre-Trial Chamber shall be carried out either by three judges of the Pre-Trial Division or by a single judge of that division in accordance with this Statute and the Rules of Procedure and Evidence;

(c) Nothing in this paragraph shall preclude the simultaneous constitution of more than one Trial Chamber or Pre-Trial Chamber when the efficient management of the Court's workload so requires.

3. (a) Judges assigned to the Trial and Pre-Trial Divisions shall serve in those divisions for a period of three years, and thereafter until the completion of any case the hearing of which has already commenced in the division concerned.

   (b) Judges assigned to the Appeals Division shall serve in that division for their entire term of office.

4. Judges assigned to the Appeals Division shall serve only in that division. Nothing in this Article shall, however, preclude the temporary attachment of judges from the Trial Division to the Pre-Trial Division or vice versa, if the Presidency considers that the efficient management of the Court's workload so requires, provided that under no circumstances shall a judge who has participated in the pre-trial phase of a case be eligible to sit on the Trial Chamber hearing that case.

Article 40. Independence of the Judges

1. The judges shall be independent in the performance of their functions.

2. Judges shall not engage in any activity which is likely to interfere with their judicial functions or to affect confidence in their independence.

3. Judges required to serve on a full-time basis at the seat of the Court shall not engage in any other occupation of a professional nature.

4. Any question regarding the application of paragraphs 2 and 3 shall be decided by an absolute majority of the judges. Where any such question concerns an individual judge, that judge shall not take part in the decision.

Article 41. Excusing and Disqualification of Judges

1. The Presidency may, at the request of a judge, excuse that judge from the exercise of a function under this Statute, in accordance with the Rules of Procedure and Evidence.

2. (a) A judge shall not participate in any case in which his or her impartiality might reasonably be doubted on any ground. A judge shall be disqualified from a case in accordance with this paragraph if, *inter alia*, that judge has previously been involved in any capacity in that case before the Court or in a related criminal case at the national level involving the person

being investigated or prosecuted. A judge shall also be disqualified on such other grounds as may be provided for in the Rules of Procedure and Evidence.

(b) The Prosecutor or the person being investigated or prosecuted may request the disqualification of a judge under this paragraph.

(c) Any question as to the disqualification of a judge shall be decided by an absolute majority of the judges. The challenged judge shall be entitled to present his or her comments on the matter, but shall not take part in the decision.

Article 42. The Office of the Prosecutor

1. The Office of the Prosecutor shall act independently as a separate organ of the Court. It shall be responsible for receiving referrals and any substantiated information on crimes within the jurisdiction of the Court, for examining them and for conducting investigations and prosecutions before the Court. A member of the Office shall not seek or act on instructions from any external source.

2. The Office shall be headed by the Prosecutor. The Prosecutor shall have full authority over the management and administration of the Office, including the staff, facilities and other resources thereof. The Prosecutor shall be assisted by one or more Deputy Prosecutors, who shall be entitled to carry out any of the acts required of the Prosecutor under this Statute. The Prosecutor and the Deputy Prosecutors shall be of different nationalities. They shall serve on a full-time basis.

3. The Prosecutor and the Deputy Prosecutors shall be persons of high moral character, be highly competent in and have extensive practical experience in the prosecution or trial of criminal cases. They shall have an excellent knowledge of and be fluent in at least one of the working languages of the Court.

4. The Prosecutor shall be elected by secret ballot by an absolute majority of the members of the Assembly of States Parties. The Deputy Prosecutors shall be elected in the same way from a list of candidates provided by the Prosecutor. The Prosecutor shall nominate three candidates for each position of Deputy Prosecutor to be filled. Unless a shorter term is decided upon at the time of their election, the Prosecutor and the Dep-

uty Prosecutors shall hold office for a term of nine years and shall not be eligible for re-election.

5. Neither the Prosecutor nor a Deputy Prosecutor shall engage in any activity which is likely to interfere with his or her prosecutorial functions or to affect confidence in his or her independence. They shall not engage in any other occupation of a professional nature.

6. The Presidency may excuse the Prosecutor or a Deputy Prosecutor, at his or her request, from acting in a particular case.

7. Neither the Prosecutor nor a Deputy Prosecutor shall participate in any matter in which their impartiality might reasonably be doubted on any ground. They shall be disqualified from a case in accordance with this paragraph if, *inter alia*, they have previously been involved in any capacity in that case before the Court or in a related criminal case at the national level involving the person being investigated or prosecuted.

8. Any question as to the disqualification of the Prosecutor or a Deputy Prosecutor shall be decided by the Appeals Chamber.

    (a) The person being investigated or prosecuted may at any time request the disqualification of the Prosecutor or a Deputy Prosecutor on the grounds set out in this Article;

    (b) The Prosecutor or the Deputy Prosecutor, as appropriate, shall be entitled to present his or her comments on the matter;

9. The Prosecutor shall appoint advisers with legal expertise on specific issues, including, but not limited to, sexual and gender violence and violence against children.

Article 43. The Registry

1. The Registry shall be responsible for the non-judicial aspects of the administration and servicing of the Court, without prejudice to the functions and powers of the Prosecutor in accordance with Article 42.

2. The Registry shall be headed by the Registrar, who shall be the principal administrative officer of the Court. The Registrar shall exercise his or her functions under the authority of the President of the Court.

3. The Registrar and the Deputy Registrar shall be persons of high moral character, be highly competent and have an excellent knowledge of and be fluent in at least one of the working languages of the Court.

4. The judges shall elect the Registrar by an absolute majority by secret ballot, taking into account any recommendation by the Assembly of States Parties. If the need arises and upon the recommendation of the Registrar, the judges shall elect, in the same manner, a Deputy Registrar.

5. The Registrar shall hold office for a term of five years, shall be eligible for re-election once and shall serve on a full-time basis. The Deputy Registrar shall hold office for a term of five years or such shorter term as may be decided upon by an absolute majority of the judges, and may be elected on the basis that the Deputy Registrar shall be called upon to serve as required.

6. The Registrar shall set up a Victims and Witnesses Unit within the Registry. This Unit shall provide, in consultation with the Office of the Prosecutor, protective measures and security arrangements, ulfillmen and other appropriate assistance for witnesses, victims who appear before the Court, and others who are at risk on account of testimony given by such witnesses. The Unit shall include staff with expertise in trauma, including trauma related to crimes of sexual violence.

Article 44. Staff

1. The Prosecutor and the Registrar shall appoint such qualified staff as may be required to their respective offices. In the case of the Prosecutor, this shall include the appointment of investigators.

2. In the employment of staff, the Prosecutor and the Registrar shall ensure the highest standards of efficiency, competency and integrity, and shall have regard, *mutatis mutandis*, to the criteria set forth in Article 36, paragraph 8.

3. The Registrar, with the agreement of the Presidency and the Prosecutor, shall propose Staff Regulations which include the terms and conditions upon which the staff of the Court shall be appointed, remunerated and dismissed. The Staff Regulations shall be approved by the Assembly of States Parties.

4. The Court may, in exceptional circumstances, employ the expertise of gratis personnel offered by States Parties, intergovernmental organizations or non-governmental organizations to assist with the work of any of the organs of the Court. The Prosecutor may accept any such offer on behalf of the Office of the Prosecutor. Such gratis personnel shall be employed in accordance with guidelines to be established by the Assembly of States Parties.

Article 45. Solemn Undertaking

Before taking up their respective duties under this Statute, the judges, the Prosecutor, the Deputy Prosecutors, the Registrar and the Deputy Registrar shall each make a solemn undertaking in open court to exercise his or her respective functions impartially and conscientiously.

Article 46. Removal from Office

1. A judge, the Prosecutor, a Deputy Prosecutor, the Registrar or the Deputy Registrar shall be removed from office if a decision to this effect is made in accordance with paragraph 2, in cases where that person:

   (a) Is found to have committed serious misconduct or a serious breach of his or her duties under this Statute, as provided for in the Rules of Procedure and Evidence; or

   (b) Is unable to exercise the functions required by this Statute.

2. A decision as to the removal from office of a judge, the Prosecutor or a Deputy Prosecutor under paragraph 1 shall be made by the Assembly of States Parties, by secret ballot:

   (a) In the case of a judge, by a two-thirds majority of the States Parties upon a recommendation adopted by a two-thirds majority of the other judges;

   (b) In the case of the Prosecutor, by an absolute majority of the States Parties;

   (c) In the case of a Deputy Prosecutor, by an absolute majority of the States Parties upon the recommendation of the Prosecutor.

3. A decision as to the removal from office of the Registrar or Deputy Registrar shall be made by an absolute majority of the judges.

4. A judge, Prosecutor, Deputy Prosecutor, Registrar or Deputy Registrar whose conduct or ability to exercise the functions of the office as required by this Statute is challenged under this Article shall have full opportunity to present and receive evidence and to make submissions in accordance with the Rules of Procedure and Evidence. The person in question shall not otherwise participate in the consideration of the matter.

Article 47. Disciplinary Measures

A judge, Prosecutor, Deputy Prosecutor, Registrar or Deputy Registrar who has committed misconduct of a less serious nature than that set out in Article 46, paragraph 1, shall be subject to disciplinary measures, in accordance with the Rules of Procedure and Evidence.

Article 48. Privileges and Immunities

1. The Court shall enjoy in the territory of each State Party such privileges and immunities as are necessary for the ulfillment of its purposes.

2. The judges, the Prosecutor, the Deputy Prosecutors and the Registrar shall, when engaged on or with respect to the business of the Court, enjoy the same privileges and immunities as are accorded to heads of diplomatic missions and shall, after the expiry of their terms of office, continue to be accorded immunity from legal process of every kind in respect of words spoken or written and acts performed by them in their official capacity.

3. The Deputy Registrar, the staff of the Office of the Prosecutor and the staff of the Registry shall enjoy the privileges and immunities and facilities necessary for the performance of their functions, in accordance with the agreement on the privileges and immunities of the Court.

4. Counsel, experts, witnesses or any other person required to be present at the seat of the Court shall be accorded such treatment as is necessary for the proper functioning of the Court, in accordance with the agreement on the privileges and immunities of the Court.

5. The privileges and immunities of:

   (a) A judge or the Prosecutor may be waived by an absolute majority of the judges;

(b) The Registrar may be waived by the Presidency;

(c) The Deputy Prosecutors and staff of the Office of the Prosecutor may be waived by the Prosecutor;

(d) The Deputy Registrar and staff of the Registry may be waived by the Registrar.

Article 49. Salaries, Allowances and Expenses

The judges, the Prosecutor, the Deputy Prosecutors, the Registrar and the Deputy Registrar shall receive such salaries, allowances and expenses as may be decided upon by the Assembly of States Parties. These salaries and allowances shall not be reduced during their terms of office.

Article 50. Official and Working Languages

1. The official languages of the Court shall be Arabic, Chinese, English, French, Russian and Spanish. The judgements of the Court, as well as other decisions resolving fundamental issues before the Court, shall be published in the official languages. The Presidency shall, in accordance with the criteria established by the Rules of Procedure and Evidence, determine which decisions may be considered as resolving fundamental issues for the purposes of this paragraph.

2. The working languages of the Court shall be English and French. The Rules of Procedure and Evidence shall determine the cases in which other official languages may be used as working languages.

3. At the request of any party to a proceeding or a State allowed to intervene in a proceeding, the Court shall authorize a language other than English or French to be used by such a party or State, provided that the Court considers such authorization to be adequately justified.

Article 51. Rules of Procedure and Evidence

1. The Rules of Procedure and Evidence shall enter into force upon adoption by a two-thirds majority of the members of the Assembly of States Parties.

2. Amendments to the Rules of Procedure and Evidence may be proposed by:

(a) Any State Party;

(b) The judges acting by an absolute majority; or

(c) The Prosecutor.

Such amendments shall enter into force upon adoption by a two-thirds majority of the members of the Assembly of States Parties.

3. After the adoption of the Rules of Procedure and Evidence, in urgent cases where the Rules do not provide for a specific situation before the Court, the judges may, by a two-thirds majority, draw up provisional Rules to be applied until adopted, amended or rejected at the next ordinary or special session of the Assembly of States Parties.

4. The Rules of Procedure and Evidence, amendments thereto and any provisional Rule shall be consistent with this Statute. Amendments to the Rules of Procedure and Evidence as well as provisional Rules shall not be applied retroactively to the detriment of the person who is being investigated or prosecuted or who has been convicted.

5. In the event of conflict between the Statute and the Rules of Procedure and Evidence, the Statute shall prevail.

Article 52. Regulations of the Court

1. The judges shall, in accordance with this Statute and the Rules of Procedure and Evidence, adopt, by an absolute majority, the Regulations of the Court necessary for its routine functioning.

2. The Prosecutor and the Registrar shall be consulted in the elaboration of the Regulations and any amendments thereto.

3. The Regulations and any amendments thereto shall take effect upon adoption unless otherwise decided by the judges. Immediately upon adoption, they shall be circulated to States Parties for comments. If within six months there are no objections from a majority of States Parties, they shall remain in force.

* * *

[PARTS 5-13 NOT INCLUDED]

www.ingramcontent.com/pod-product-compliance
Ingram Content Group UK Ltd.
Pitfield, Milton Keynes, MK11 3LW, UK
UKHW041103150926
475561UK00001BA/13

9 780761 833093